BRIGHTER CHILD® BOOK OF MATH
GRADES 3-4
Table of Contents

Send all inquiries to:
School Specialty Publishing
8720 Orion Place
Columbus, OH 43240-2111

ISBN 0-7696-8513-7

1 2 3 4 5 6 QPD 12 11 10 09

Math Manipulatives

Below are suggested materials to support the activities in this book and help you create a stimulating math environment in your home. Most of these can be purchased at a teacher store.

- paper
- two-pocket folders
- Unifix cubes
- pattern blocks
- number line
- hundred chart
- place value mat
- base-ten blocks
- geoboard and rubber bands
- calendar
- analog clock
- digital clock
- "play" clock
- pencils
- resealable plastic bags
- envelopes
- play money (or real)
- money chart
- ice-cream sticks
- buttons
- sea shells
- marbles
- uncooked pasta
- beans
- paper clips
- collections of other small objects
- markers
- crayons
- playground chalk
- double-sided counters
- flash cards
- attribute blocks
- tangrams
- calculator
- game pieces
- dice
- spinners

Place Value

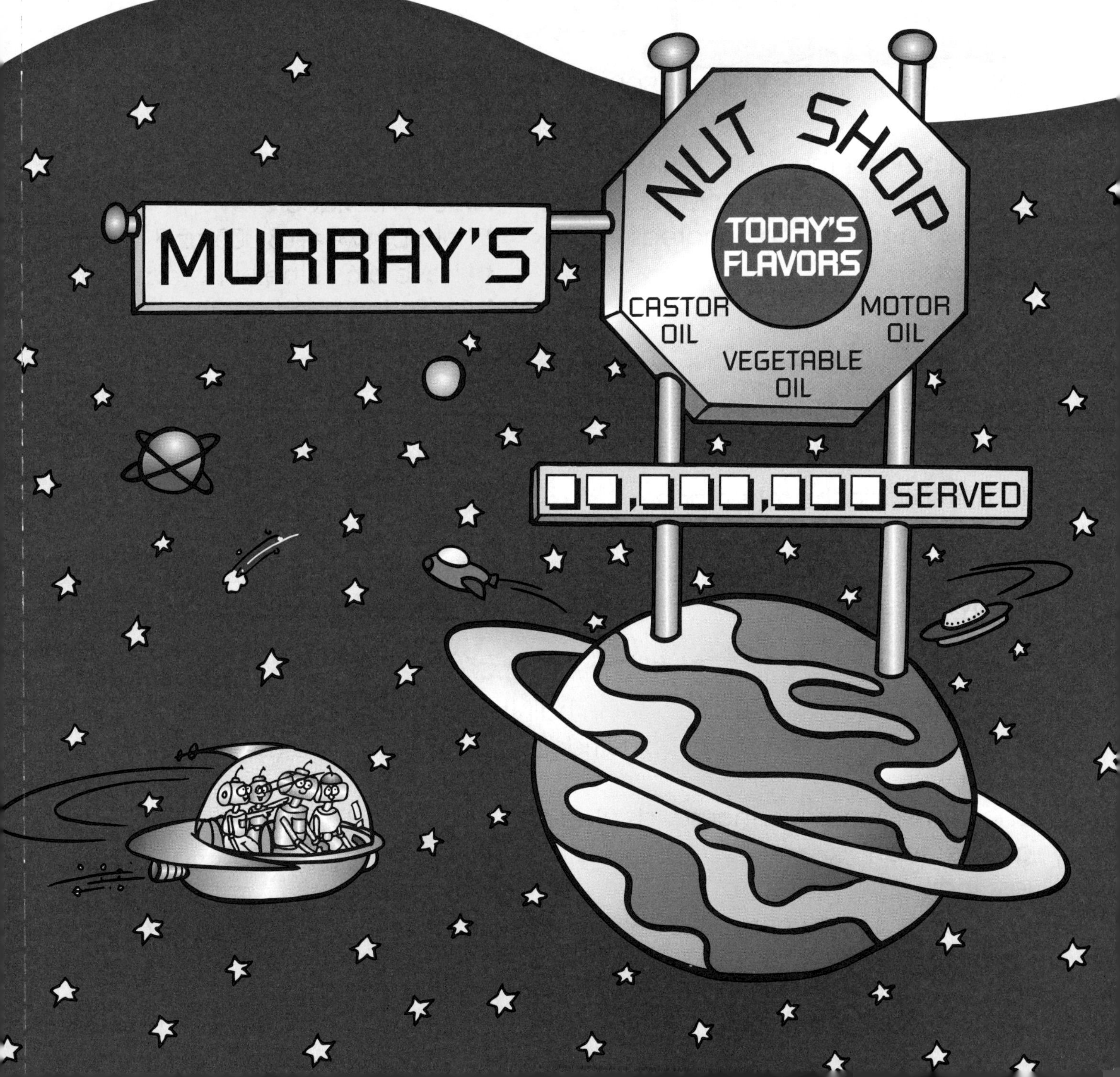

Name ______________________________

Place Value Riddles

Using the clues below, choose the number each riddle describes. As you read, draw an **X** on all the numbers that do not fit the clue. After you have read all the clues for each riddle, there should be only one number left.

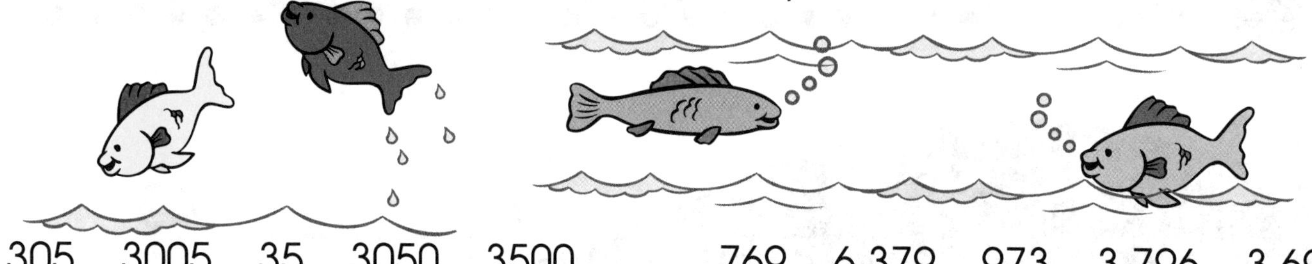

305 3005 35 3050 3500

1. I am greater than 300.
2. I have a 5 in the ones place.
3. I have a zero in the hundreds place.
4. Circle the number.

769 6,379 973 3,796 3,691

1. I have a number greater than 6 in the tens place.
2. I am between 3,000 and 4,000.
3. I have a 6 in the hundreds place.
4. Circle the number.

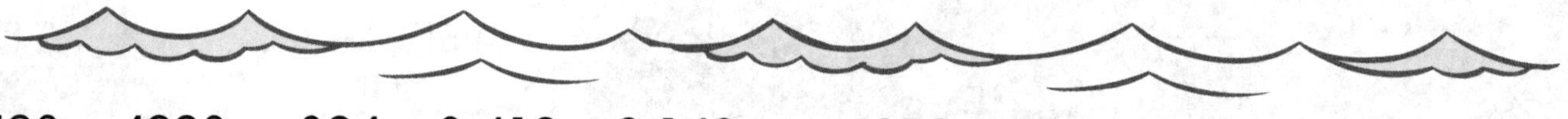

423 4023 324 3,412 2,143

1. I have a 2 in the tens place.
2. I am less than 1,000.
3. I have a 4 in the ones place.
4. Circle the number.

4058 584 845 5048 8540

1. I have a 4 in the tens place.
2. I am greater than 5,000.
3. I have a 0 in the hundreds place.
4. Circle the number.

Now, fold a blank sheet of paper in half three times to create eight boxes. Create eight of these place value riddles. You may want to use words like these when writing your clues:

ones, tens, hundreds, thousands place
greater than
less than
have a ___ somewhere

Name ________________________________

4–3–2–1–Blast Off!

Color these spaces red:

- three thousand five
- 1,000 less than 3,128
- six thousand eight hundred eighty-nine
- 100 more than 618,665
- 10 less than 2,981
- fifty-nine thousand two

Color these spaces blue:

- 10 less than 4,786
- eight thousand six hundred two
- 1,000 less than 638,961
- two thousand four hundred fifty-one
- 100 more than 81,136
- 10,000 less than 48,472

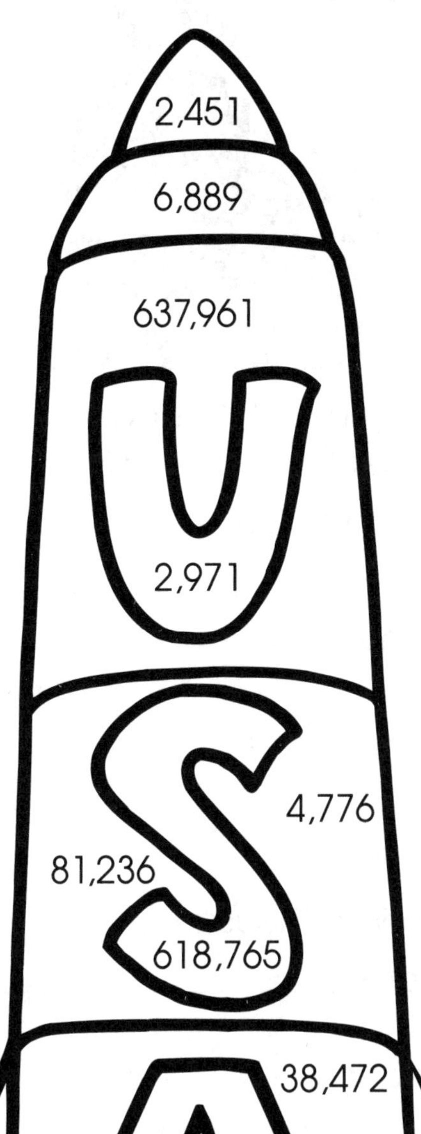

Place Value

1	,	2	3	4	,	5	6	7
millions		hundred thousands	ten thousands	thousands		hundreds	tens	ones

Write each numeral in its correct place.

1. The number 8,672,019 has:

_____ thousands　　_____ ten　　_____ hundred thousands

_____ millions　　_____ ones　　_____ ten thousands

_____ hundreds

2. What number has:

6 ones　　3 millions　　9 tens

7 hundreds　　4 ten thousands　　8 thousands

5 hundred thousands

The number is ____________________ .

3. The number 6,792,510 has:

_____ ten thousands　　_____ millions　　_____ hundreds

_____ ones　　_____ thousands　　_____ ten

_____ hundred thousands

4. What number has:

5 millions　　3 tens　　6 thousands

1 hundred　　8 ten thousands　　4 ones

0 hundred thousands

The number is ____________________ .

Name ____________________

Estimate by Rounding Numbers

Estimate by rounding numbers to different place values. Use these rules.

Example: Round 283 to the nearest hundred.

- Find the digit in the place to be rounded. — (2)83
- Now, look at the digit to its right. — (2)83
- If the digit to the right is less than 5, the digit being rounded remains the same.
- If the digit to the right is 5 or more, the digit being rounded is increased by 1. — (2)83 Rounds to 300
- Digits to the right of the place to be rounded become 0's. Digits to the left remain the same.

Examples: Round 4,385 . . .

to the nearest thousand	to the nearest hundred	to the nearest ten
4,385	4,385	4,385
3 is less than 5.	8 is more than 5.	5 = 5.
The 4 stays the same.	The 3 is rounded up to 4.	The 8 is rounded up to 9.
4,000	4,400	4,390

Complete the table.

NUMBERS TO BE ROUNDED	ROUND TO THE NEAREST THOUSAND	NEAREST HUNDRED	NEAREST TEN
2,725			
10,942			
6,816			
2,309			
7,237			
959			

Name ______________________

The First State

What state is known as the first state? Follow the directions below to find out.

1. If 31,842 rounded to the nearest thousand is 31,000, put an **A** above number 2.
2. If 62 rounded to the nearest ten is 60, put an **E** above number 2 .
3. If 4,234 rounded to the nearest hundred is 4,200, put an **R** above number 7.
4. If 677 rounded to the nearest hundred is 600, put an **L** above number 3.
5. If 344 rounded to the nearest ten is 350, put an **E** above number 5.
6. If 5,599 rounded to the nearest thousand is 6,000, put an **A** above number 4.
7. If 1,549 rounded to the nearest hundred is 1,500, put an **A** above number 6.
8. If 885 rounded to the nearest hundred is 800, put a **W** above number 2.
9. If 521 rounded to the nearest ten is 520, put an **E** above number 8.
10. If 74 rounded to the nearest ten is 80, put an **R** above number 6.
11. If 3,291 rounded to the nearest thousand is 3,000, put an **L** above number 3.
12. If 248 rounded to the nearest hundred is 300, put an **R** above number 4.
13. If 615 rounded to the nearest ten is 620, put a **D** above number 1.
14. If 188 rounded to the nearest ten is 200, put a **W** above number 1.
15. If 6,817 rounded to the nearest thousand is 7,000, put a **W** above number 5.

Peach Blossom
State Flower

Blue Hen Chicken
State Bird

Fort Christina—site of the first state's first permanent settlement. Built by the Swedes and Finns.

____ ____ ____ ____ ____ ____ ____ ____
1 2 3 4 5 6 7 8

Addition

Name ______________________________

Dial-A-Word

Use the phone pad to calculate the "value" of the words.

Example: PHONE = 74663
PHONE = 7 + 4 + 6 + 6 + 3 = 26

(your name) = ______________________________ = __________

CALCULATOR = ______________________________ = __________

DICTIONARY = ______________________________ = __________

PET TRICKS = ______________________________ = __________

BASEBALL GAME = ______________________________ = __________

COMPUTERS = ______________________________ = __________

TENNIS SHOES = ______________________________ = __________

ADDITION = ______________________________ = __________

MENTAL MATH = ______________________________ = __________

1	ABC 2	DEF 3
GHI 4	JKL 5	MNO 6
PQRS 7	TUV 8	WXYZ 9
*	0	#
CLR	SEND	MUTE

Mushrooming Addition

Follow the arrows to **add**.

Example: 52 + 28 = 80
28 + 91 = 119
119 + 80 = ?

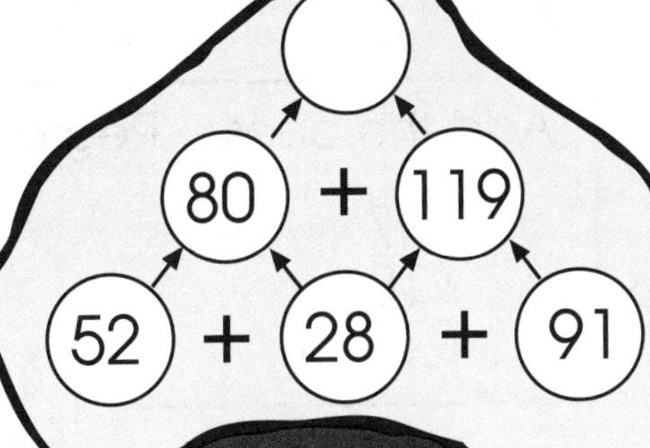

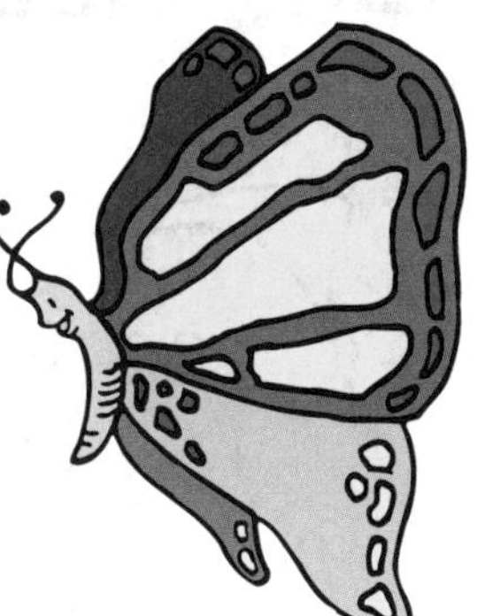

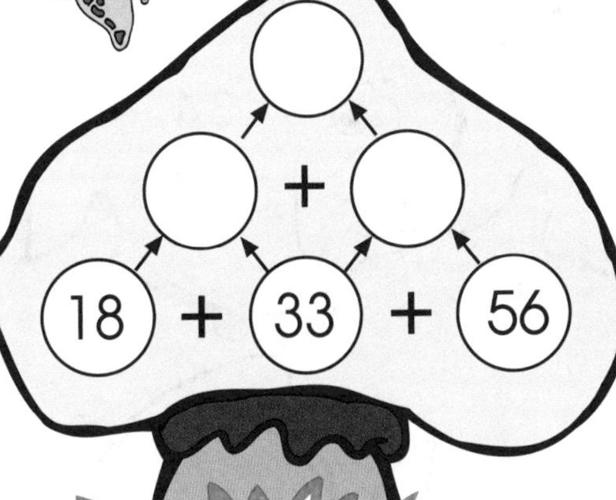

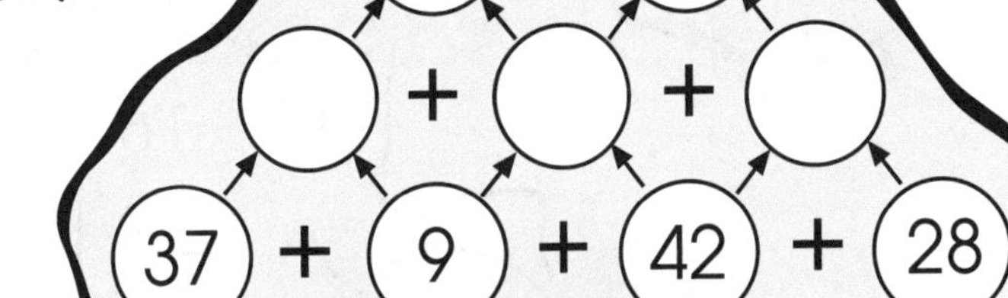

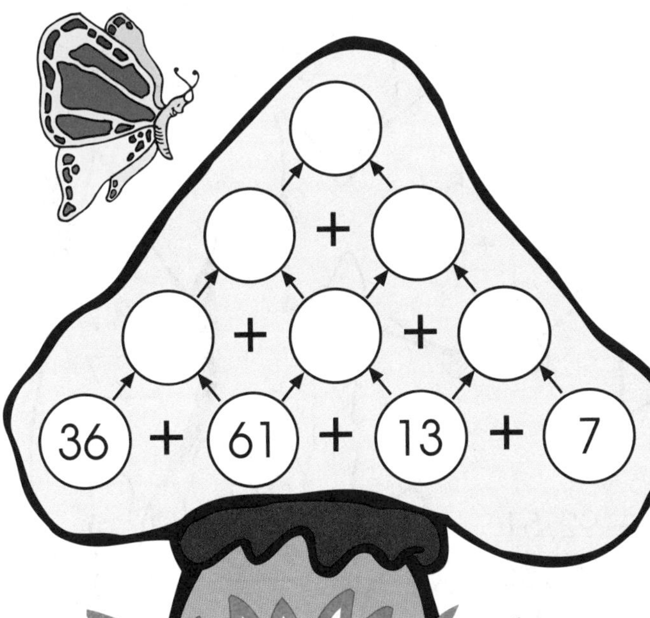

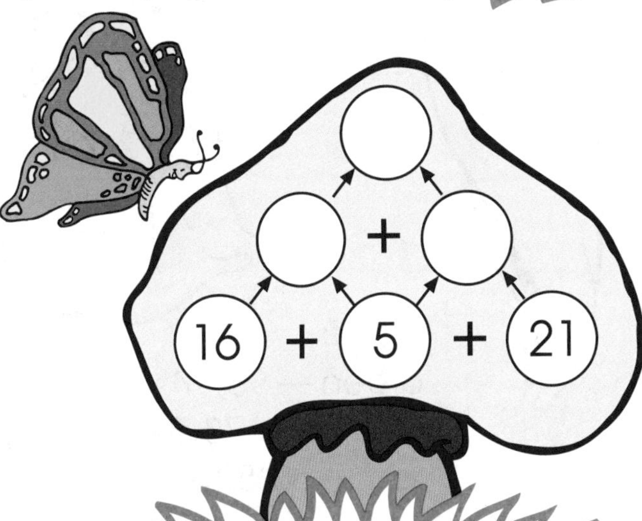

Name ____________________

Fishy Addition

Add the ones.	Regroup, if needed.	Add the tens.
47 +18	1 47 +18 5	1 47 +18 65

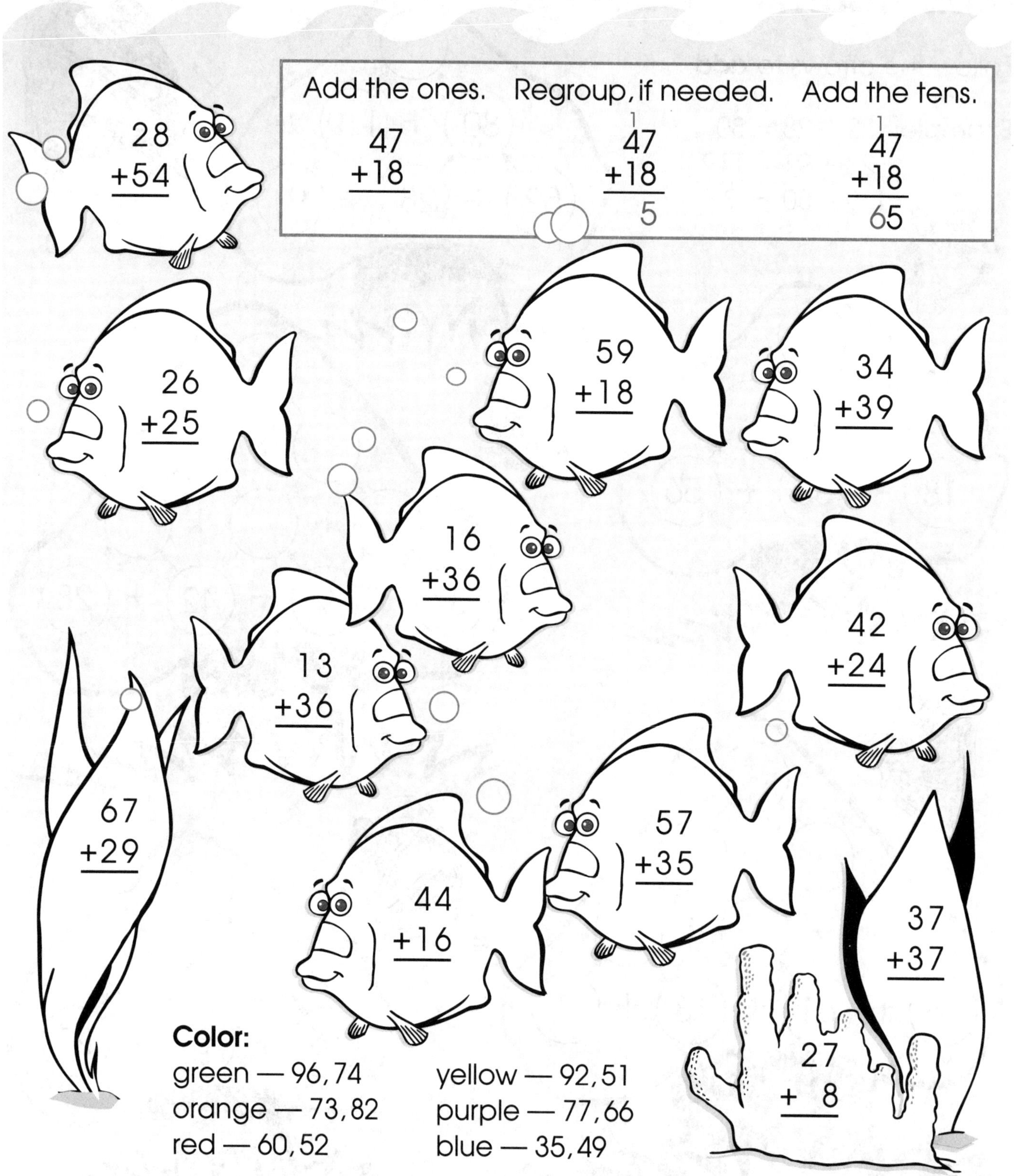

28 +54

26 +25

59 +18

34 +39

16 +36

13 +36

42 +24

67 +29

57 +35

44 +16

37 +37

27 + 8

Color:

green — 96, 74
orange — 73, 82
red — 60, 52
yellow — 92, 51
purple — 77, 66
blue — 35, 49

Name ____________________

Addition Ace

Add. Color the ribbon according to the code below.

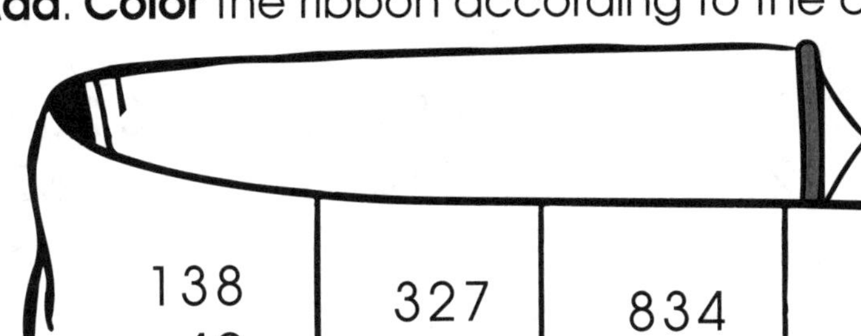

138 + 49	327 + 513	834 + 128	108 + 146	506 + 91	249 + 128

If the sum is in the:

100's — green
200's — yellow
300's — red
400's — blue
500's — purple
600's — orange
700's — pink
800's — gold
900's — silver

367 + 424	724 + 39	704 + 283	691 + 205	265 + 319

432 + 249	528 + 349	924 + 56	306 + 248	226 + 165

826 + 164	328 + 145	426 + 261	747 + 143

0-7696-8513-7

Name ______________________

Cotton Pickin' Math

Solve the problems.

7,215 62 141 +2,015	4,621 35 1,318 + 9	6,117 24 315 +2,136	2,481 2,514 2 + 43	3,204 182 23 + 5
8,143 60 235 +1,423	35 242 6 +1,203	7,006 242 9 + 31	521 3,134 64 + 243	496 8,172 83 + 199
6,201 325 41 +2,136	5,242 342 8 + 51	4,162 328 41 + 503	6,425 41 324 + 3	
4,205 81 3 + 414	2,516 310 82 + 3	5,426 310 512 + 4		

Name ____________________

Palindrome Sums

A **number palindrome** is similar to a word palindrome in that it reads the same backward or forward.

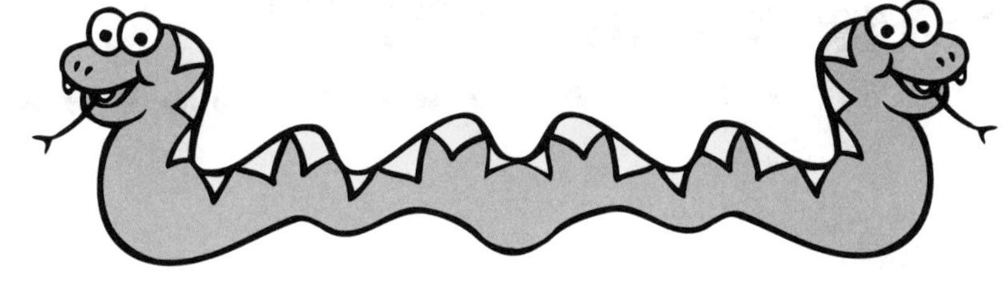

Examples:
75,457
1,689,861

Create number palindromes using addition.

Your Number

To do this, choose any number: ____________________

652

Then, **reverse** that number's digits: ____________________

256

and **add** the two numbers together: ____________________

652 + 256 = 908

If the sum is not a palindrome, **reverse** the digits in that sum and add as you did in the first step: ____________________

908 + 809 = 1717

Continue in this manner until the sum is a palindrome. ____________________

1717 + 7171 = 8888

____

____

____

The example required three steps to produce a palindrome.
How many steps did it take for you to create a number palindrome? __________

Subtraction

20 - 16 =

8 - 5 = 3

8 - 1 = 7

Name ______________________________

Stay on Track

Add or **subtract**. **Write** each answer in the puzzle.

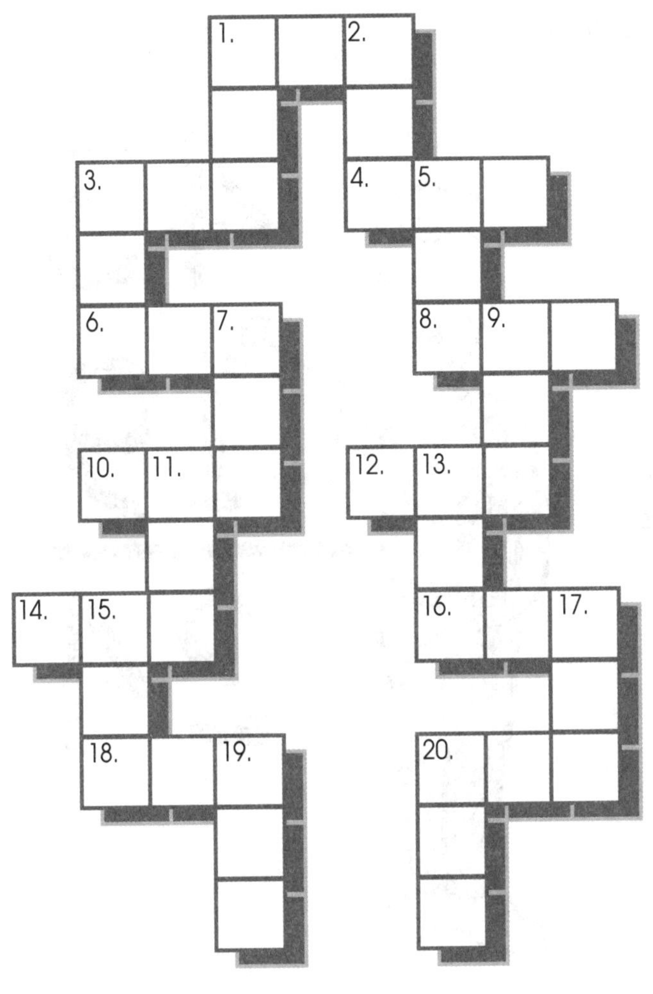

Across

1. 413 + 312

3. 102 + 415

4. 223 + 103

6. 131 + 253

8. 324 + 321

10. 207 + 222

12. 105 + 214

14. 315 + 400

16. 121 + 503

18. 451 + 421

20. 312 + 281

Down

1. 859 − 112

2. 985 − 402

3. 887 − 344

5. 789 − 583

7. 699 − 240

9. 589 − 100

11. 767 − 512

13. 497 − 321

15. 259 − 151

17. 974 − 511

19. 689 − 450

20. 797 − 236

 0-7696-8513-7

Name ____________________

Subtracting Two-Digit Numbers
With Regrouping

Step 1: Decide whether to regroup. In the ones column, 3 is less than 9 so, regroup 4 tens 3 ones to 3 tens 13 ones.

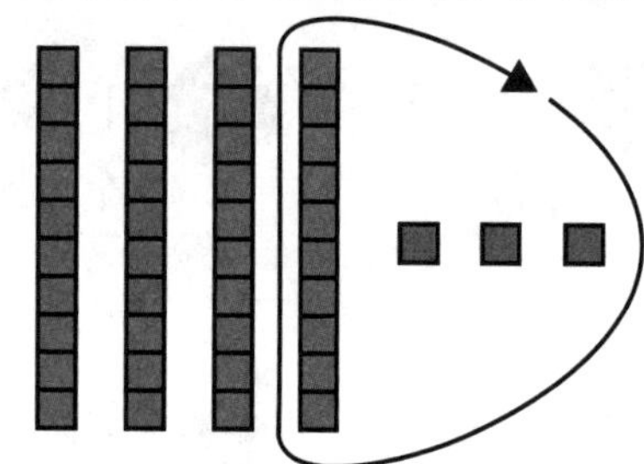

Step 2: Subtract the ones.

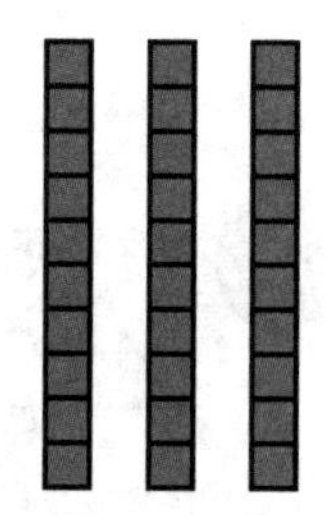

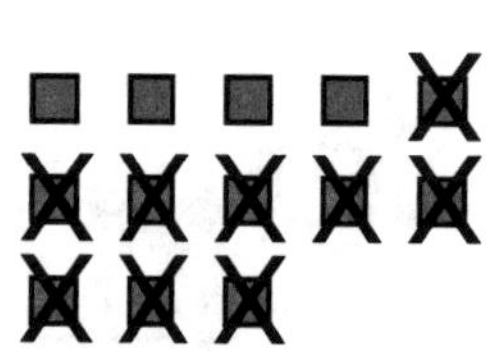

Step 3: Subtract the tens.

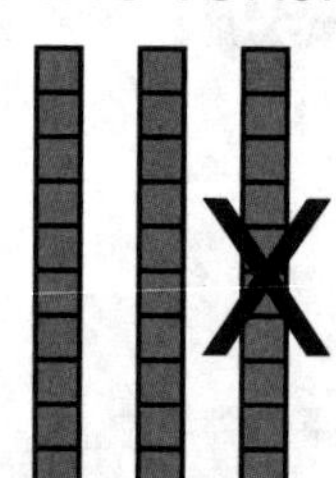

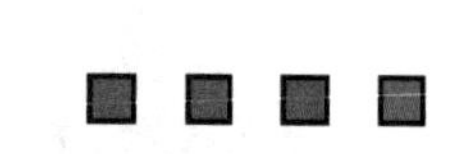

Subtract to find the difference. **Regroup**, if needed.

67	85	86	91	44	61
−34	−12	−47	−48	−27	−34

32	97	60	52	71	83
−14	−36	−45	−22	−19	−15

Name ________________________________

Soaring to the Stars

Connect the dots in order and form two stars. Begin one star with the subtraction problem whose difference is 100 and end with the problem whose difference is 109. Begin the other star with 110 and end with 120. Then, **color** the pictures.

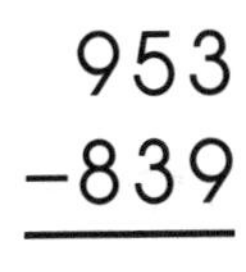

953
−839

774
−658

493
−378

364
−247

751
−638

844
−726

839
−728

570
−458

446
−327

384
−279

383
−273

696
−576

590
−487

575
−471

653
−547

493
−386

359
−257

862
−754

190
− 89

359
−259

585
−476

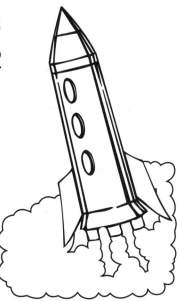

Name ____________________

Paint by Number

Solve each problem. **Color** each shape according to the key below.

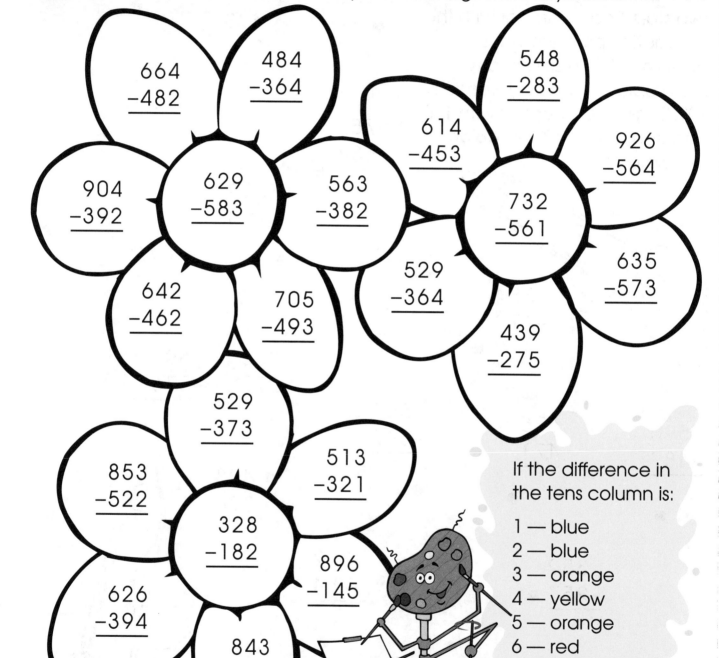

664 − 482 = ____

484 − 364 = ____

904 − 392 = ____

629 − 583 = ____

563 − 382 = ____

642 − 462 = ____

705 − 493 = ____

548 − 283 = ____

614 − 453 = ____

926 − 564 = ____

732 − 561 = ____

529 − 364 = ____

635 − 573 = ____

439 − 275 = ____

529 − 373 = ____

853 − 522 = ____

513 − 321 = ____

328 − 182 = ____

896 − 145 = ____

626 − 394 = ____

843 − 392 = ____

If the difference in the tens column is:

1 — blue
2 — blue
3 — orange
4 — yellow
5 — orange
6 — red
7 — yellow
8 — blue
9 — orange

Name ______________________________

Round and Round She Goes

When regrouping with zeros follow these steps:

1. 7 is larger than 0. Go to the tens column to regroup. Since there is a 0 in that column, you can't regroup. Go to the hundreds column.

$$\begin{array}{r} \overset{2}{\cancel{3}}\,0\,0 \\ -\,1\,4\,7 \\ \hline \end{array}$$

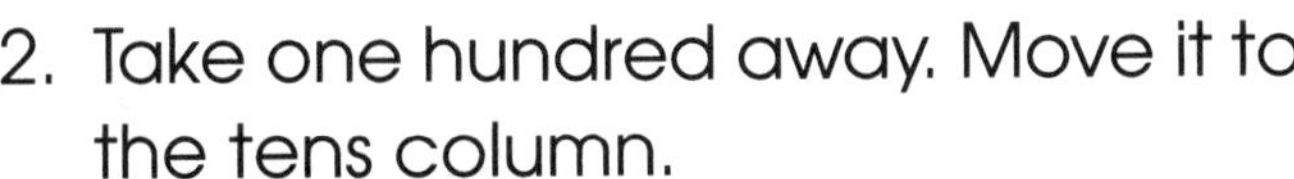

2. Take one hundred away. Move it to the tens column.

$$\begin{array}{r} \overset{2}{\cancel{3}}\,{}^{1}0\,0 \\ -\,1\,4\,7 \\ \hline \end{array}$$

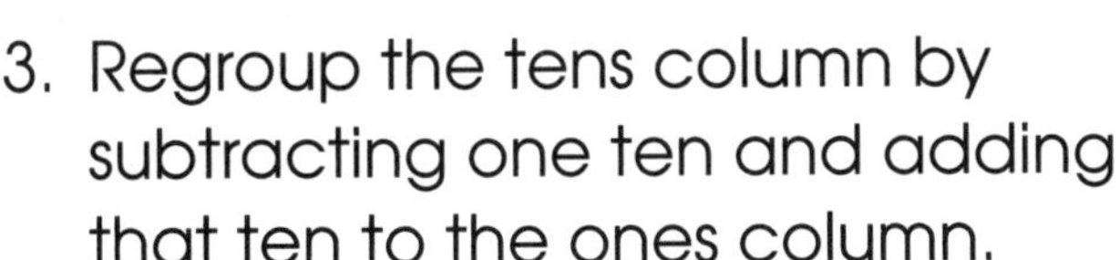

3. Regroup the tens column by subtracting one ten and adding that ten to the ones column.

$$\begin{array}{r} \overset{2}{\cancel{3}}\,{}^{1}\overset{9}{\cancel{0}}\,{}^{1}0 \\ -\,1\,4\,7 \\ \hline \end{array}$$

4. Now, subtract, starting at the ones column.

$$\begin{array}{r} \overset{2}{\cancel{3}}\,{}^{1}\overset{9}{\cancel{0}}\,{}^{1}0 \\ -\,1\,4\,7 \\ \hline 1\,5\,3 \end{array}$$

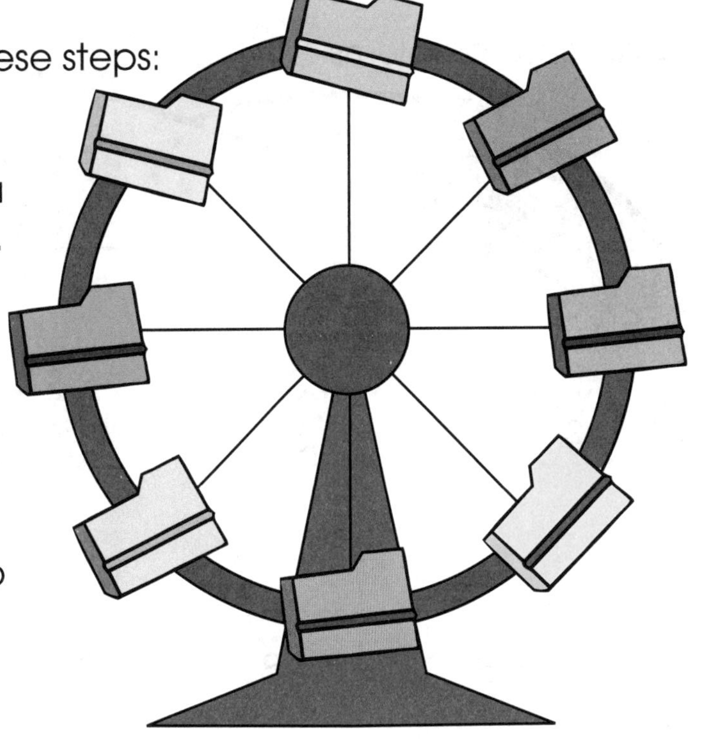

800 −736	406 −243	900 −623
200 − 82	700 −543	800 −746
400 −278	600 −432	900 −824
500 −248	400 −365	300 −284

Name ____________________

High Class Math

Solve these problems.

		$\begin{array}{r} 3,270 \\ -1,529 \\ \hline \end{array}$	$\begin{array}{r} 8,248 \\ -1,513 \\ \hline \end{array}$	
$\begin{array}{r} 7,648 \\ -3,291 \\ \hline \end{array}$	$\begin{array}{r} 4,321 \\ -1,809 \\ \hline \end{array}$	$\begin{array}{r} 8,241 \\ -3,516 \\ \hline \end{array}$	$\begin{array}{r} 3,002 \\ -1,231 \\ \hline \end{array}$	$\begin{array}{r} 9,200 \\ -3,146 \\ \hline \end{array}$
$\begin{array}{r} 5,017 \\ -2,408 \\ \hline \end{array}$	$\begin{array}{r} 8,254 \\ -3,187 \\ \hline \end{array}$	$\begin{array}{r} 7,265 \\ -2,134 \\ \hline \end{array}$	$\begin{array}{r} 3,846 \\ -1,359 \\ \hline \end{array}$	$\begin{array}{r} 8,006 \\ -3,084 \\ \hline \end{array}$
$\begin{array}{r} 3,084 \\ -1,926 \\ \hline \end{array}$	$\begin{array}{r} 6,265 \\ -4,189 \\ \hline \end{array}$	$\begin{array}{r} 4,824 \\ -1,913 \\ \hline \end{array}$	$\begin{array}{r} 6,205 \\ -1,054 \\ \hline \end{array}$	$\begin{array}{r} 5,253 \\ -4,428 \\ \hline \end{array}$
	$\begin{array}{r} 9,205 \\ -3,187 \\ \hline \end{array}$	$\begin{array}{r} 5,809 \\ -3,913 \\ \hline \end{array}$	$\begin{array}{r} 5,642 \\ -2,408 \\ \hline \end{array}$	

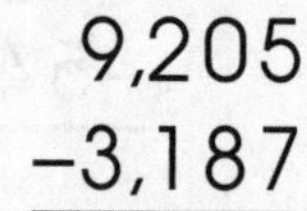

0-7696-8513-7

Multiplication

Skipping Through the Tens

Skip count by tens. Begin with the number on the first line. **Write** each number that follows.

0, ____, ____, ____, ____, ____, ____, ____, ____, ____, 100

3, ____, ____, ____, ____, 53, ____, ____, ____, ____, 103

1, ____, ____, ____, ____, ____, ____, ____, 81, ____, ____

8, ____, ____, ____, ____, ____, 68, ____, ____, ____, ____

6, ____, ____, ____, ____, ____, ____, ____, ____, ____, ____

4, ____, ____, ____, ____, ____, ____, ____, ____, ____, 104

2, ____, ____, ____, ____, ____, ____, ____, ____, 92, ____

5, ____, ____, ____, 45, ____, ____, ____, ____, ____, ____

7, ____, ____, ____, ____, ____, ____, 77, ____, ____, ____

9, ____, ____, ____, ____, ____, ____, ____, ____, ____, ____

What is ten more than . . . ?

26 ____ 29 ____

44 ____ 77 ____

53 ____ 91 ____

24 ____ 49 ____

66 ____ 35 ____

54 ____ 82 ____

Name ______________________________

Count the Legs!

Multiplication is a quick way to add. For example, count the legs of the horses below. They each have 4 legs. You could add 4 + 4 + 4. But it is quicker to say that there are 3 groups of 4 legs. In multiplication, that is 3 x 4.

Multiply to find the number of legs. **Write** each problem twice.

_____ horses x _____ legs = _____

_____ x _____ = _____

_____ ostriches x _____ legs = _____

_____ x _____ = _____

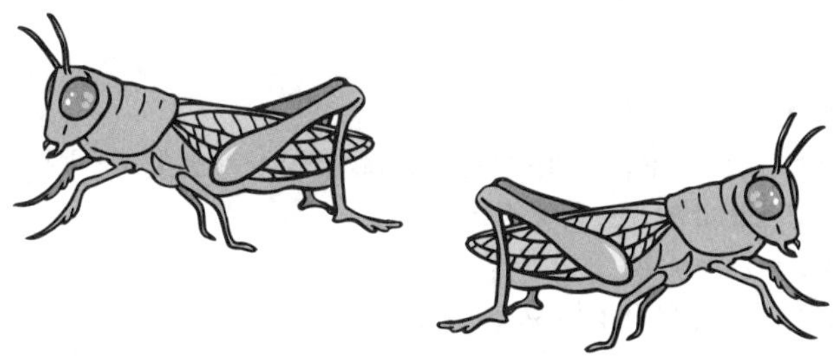

_____ insects x _____ legs = _____

_____ x _____ = _____

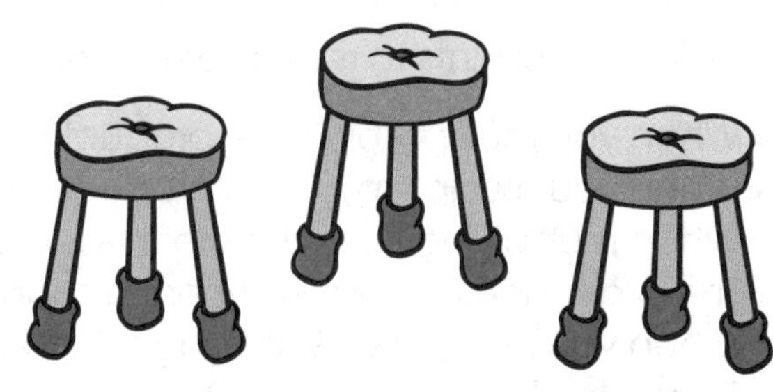

_____ stools x _____ legs = _____

_____ x _____ = _____

_____ cows x _____ legs = _____

_____ x _____ = _____

_____ birds x _____ legs = _____

_____ x _____ = _____

Name ____________________

Multiplying

Numbers to be multiplied together are called **factors**. The answer is the **product**.
Example: 3 x 6

1. The first factor tells how many groups there are. There are 3 groups.
2. The second factor tells how many are in each group. There are 6 in each group.

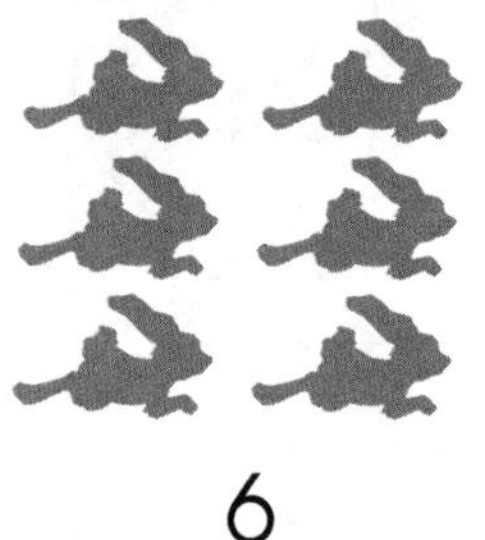

6 + 6 + 6 = 18

3 groups of 6 equal 18.
3 x 6 = 18

Some helpful hints to remember when multiplying:

- When you multiply by 0, the product is always 0. **Example:** 0 x 7 = 0
- When you multiply by 1, the product is always the factor being multiplied. **Example:** 1 x 12 = 12
- When multiplying by 2, double the factor other than 2. **Example:** 2 x 4 = 8
- The order doesn't matter when multiplying. **Example:** 5 x 3 = 15, 3 x 5 = 15
- When you multiply by 9, the digits in the product add up to 9 (until 9 x 11). **Example:** 7 x 9 = 63, 6 + 3 = 9
- When you multiply by 10, multiply by 1 and add 0 to the product. **Example:** 10 x 3 = 30
- When you multiply by 11, write the factor you are multiplying by twice (until 10). **Example:** 11 x 8 = 88

Multiply.

2	3	4	2	5	10	7	11	9
x 9	x 8	x 9	x 11	x 9	x 5	x 6	x 4	x 7
8	7	8	10	4	5	8	3	7
x 6	x 12	x 5	x 10	x 8	x 5	x 8	x 6	x 8

Name ____________________

Racing to the Finish

Multiply.

5 x 3	2 x 8	4 x 6	9 x 3	7 x 5	3 x 9
4 x 2	6 x 2	4 x 4	0 x 6	3 x 2	7 x 2
6 x 5	3 x 4	8 x 3	4 x 5	5 x 2	7 x 4
6 x 3	4 x 8	2 x 2	8 x 5	3 x 7	5 x 5
5 x 9	9 x 2	4 x 6	9 x 4		

Name ______________________________

Double Trouble

Solve each multiplication problem. Below each answer, **write** the letter from the code that matches the answer. **Read** the coded question and **write** the answer in the space provided.

1	4	9	16	25	36	49	64	81	100	121	144
E	G	H	I	N	O	S	T	U	W	X	Y

10 x10	3 x3	6 x6

4 x4	7 x7

7 x7	4 x4	8 x8	8 x8	4 x4	5 x5	2 x2

5 x5	1 x1	11 x11	8 x8

8 x8	6 x6

12 x12	6 x6	9 x9

?

Answer: ______________________________

Name ______________________________

Wacky Waldo's Snow Show

Wacky Waldo's Snow Show is an exciting and fantastic sight. Waldo has trained whales and bears to skate together on the ice. There is a hockey game between a team of sharks and a pack of wolves. Elephants ride sleds down steep hills. Horses and buffaloes ski swiftly down mountains.

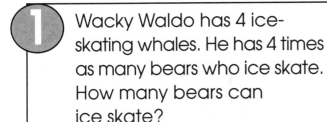

Write each problem and its answer.

1. Wacky Waldo has 4 ice-skating whales. He has 4 times as many bears who ice skate. How many bears can ice skate?

_______ x _______ = _______

2. Waldo's Snow Show has 4 shows on Thursday, but it has 6 times as many on Saturday. How many shows are there on Saturday?

_______ x _______ = _______

3. The Sharks' hockey team has 3 great white sharks. It has 6 times as many tiger sharks. How many tiger sharks does it have?

_______ x _______ = _______

4. The Wolves' hockey team has 4 gray wolves. It has 8 times as many red wolves. How many red wolves does it have?

_______ x _______ = _______

5. Waldo taught 6 buffaloes to ski. He was able to teach 5 times as many horses to ski. How many horses did he teach?

_______ x _______ = _______

6. Buff, a skiing buffalo, took 7 nasty spills when he was learning to ski. His friend Harry Horse fell down 8 times as often. How many times did Harry fall?

_______ x _______ = _______

Name ____________________

Multiplying and Regrouping

1. Multiply 3 x 8 in the ones column. Ask: Do I need to regroup?

2. Multiply 3 x 3 in the tens column. Add the 2 you carried over from the ones column. Ask: Do I need to regroup?

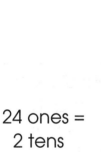

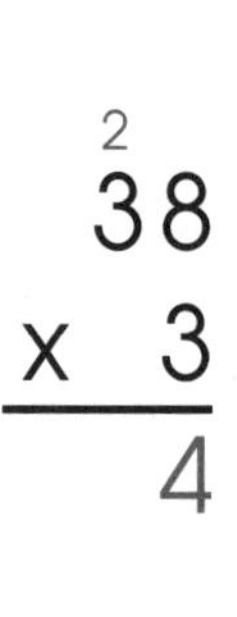

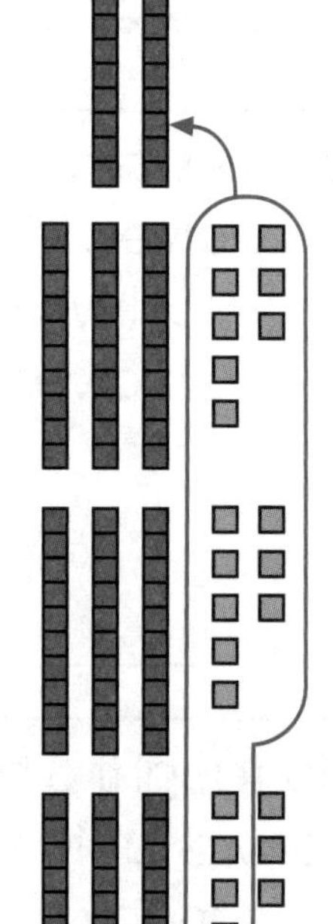

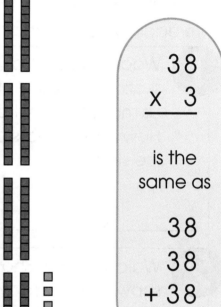

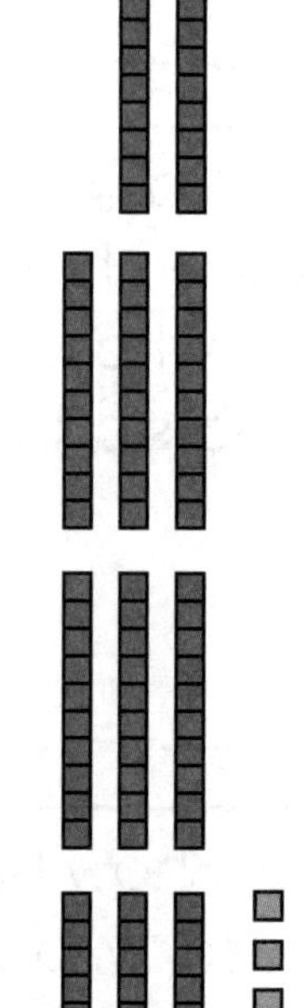

11 tens =
1 hundred
1 ten

38
x 3

is the same as

38
38
+ 38

Multiply.

29	62	39	86	43
x 3	x 4	x 4	x 7	x 6

28	48	31	25	55
x 6	x 2	x 9	x 5	x 5

Name ______________________________

Under the Big Top!

Complete this crossnumber puzzle.

43	x	4	=	
x				
2	x	58	=	
=		x		
	x	7	=	
		=		

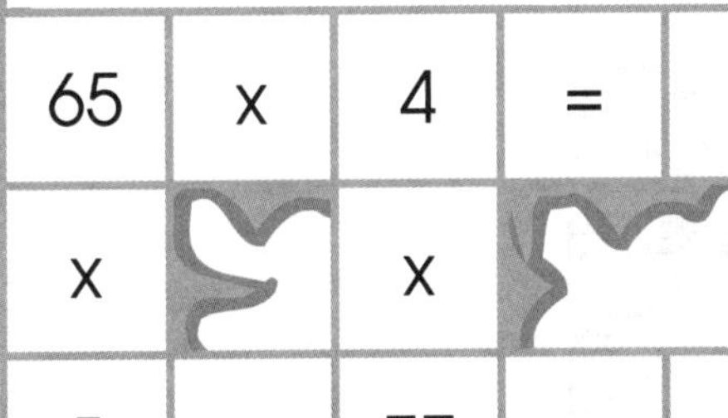

65	x	4	=	
x		x		
5	x	77	=	
=		=		

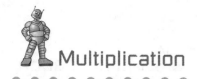

Name ______________________________

Three-Digit Regrouping

1. Multiply the ones column.
   Ask: Do I need to regroup?

$$\begin{array}{r} {}^{2} \\ 138 \\ \times\ \ 3 \\ \hline 4 \end{array}$$

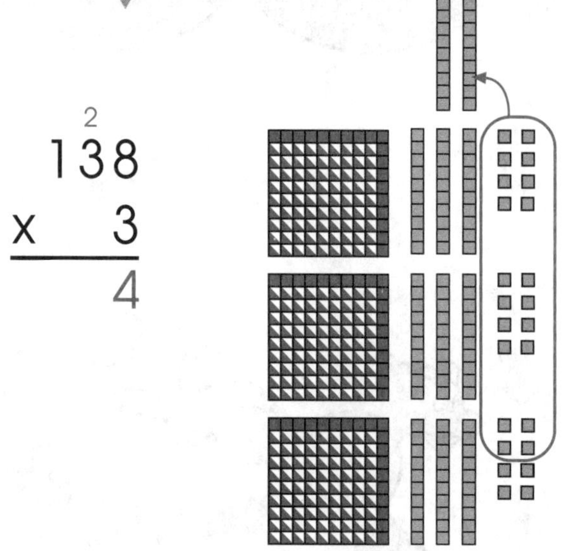

2. Multiply the tens column.
   Ask: Do I need to regroup?

$$\begin{array}{r} {}^{1}\ {}^{2} \\ 138 \\ \times\ \ 3 \\ \hline 14 \end{array}$$

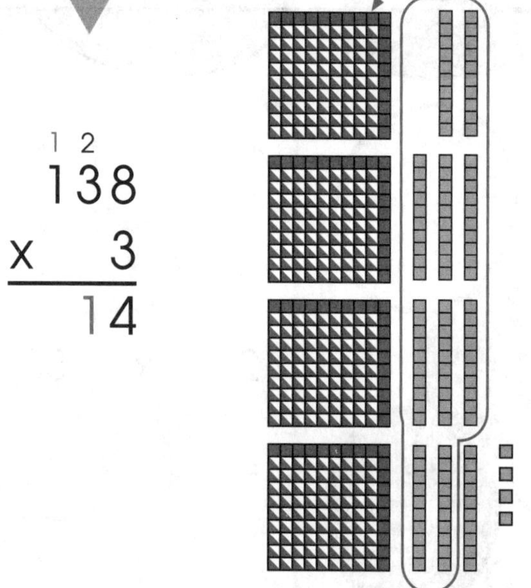

3. Multiply the hundreds column.
   Ask: Do I need to regroup?

$$\begin{array}{r} {}^{1}\ {}^{2} \\ 138 \\ \times\ \ 3 \\ \hline 414 \end{array}$$

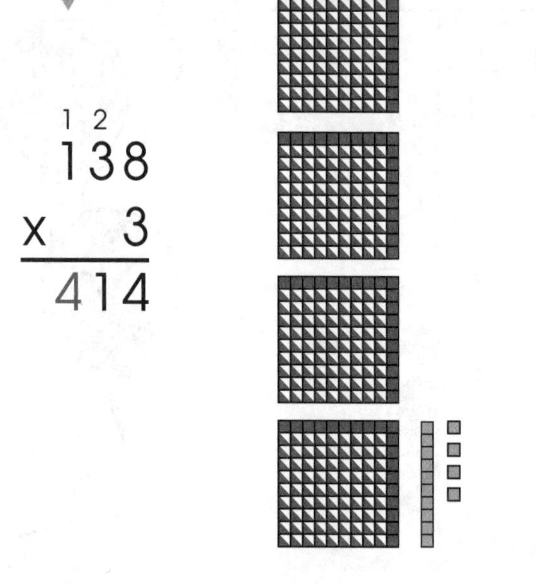

Multiply.

129 x 3	547 x 2	214 x 6
306 x 8	536 x 2	629 x 3
264 x 4	814 x 5	128 x 7

Name ____________________

Solve It!

What set of ridges and loops are different on every person?
To find out, **solve** the following problems and **write** the matching letter above each answer at the bottom of the page.

I. 303 x 3 = 9	303 x 3 = 09	303 x 3 = 909	R. 214 x 2	N. 413 x 2
N. 142 x 2			R. 211 x 4	F. 104 x 2
T. 131 x 2	P. 232 x 3		E. 301 x 2	I. 134 x 1
G. 244 x 2	S. 334 x 2			

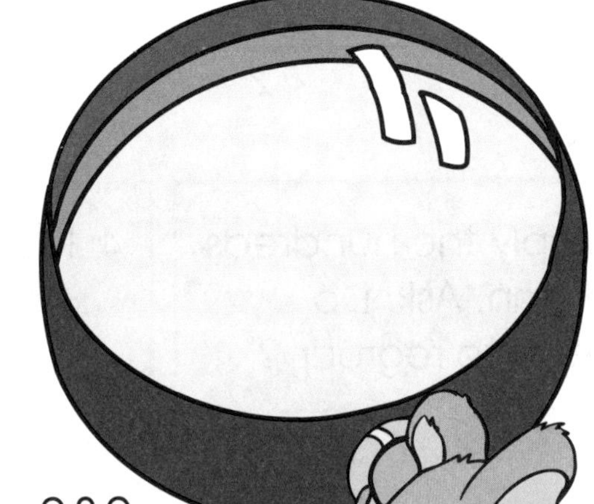

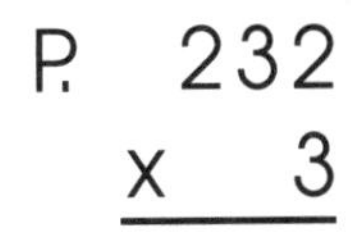

___	___	___	___	___	___	___	___	___	___	___	___
208	909	826	488	602	844	696	428	134	284	262	668

0-7696-8513-7

Name ______________________

Four-Digit Regrouping

1. Multiply the ones column. Ask: Do I need to regroup?

$$\begin{array}{r} \overset{1}{} \\ 6{,}214 \\ \times \quad 3 \\ \hline 2 \end{array}$$

12 ones =
1 ten 2 ones

2. Multiply the tens column. Ask: Do I need to regroup?

$$\begin{array}{r} 6{,}2\overset{1}{1}4 \\ \times \quad 3 \\ \hline 42 \end{array}$$

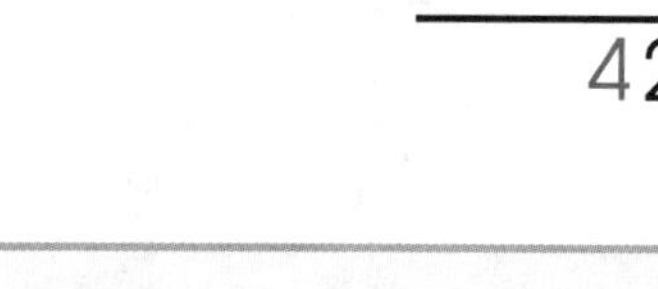

3. Multiply the hundreds column. Ask: Do I need to regroup?

$$\begin{array}{r} 6{,}2\overset{1}{1}4 \\ \times \quad 3 \\ \hline 642 \end{array}$$

4. Multiply the thousands column. Ask: Do I need to regroup?

$$\begin{array}{r} 6{,}2\overset{1}{1}4 \\ \times \quad 3 \\ \hline 18{,}642 \end{array}$$

Multiply.

4,121 x 6	7,216 x 3	2,318 x 4	4,326 x 8	2,463 x 9
6,425 x 5	7,195 x 5	8,083 x 7	5,993 x 7	6,218 x 4

Name ______________________________

Multiplying by a Two-Digit Number

Multiply.

1. Multiply by the ones place.
   3 x 2 = 6
   Ignore the 1 in the tens place.

$$\begin{array}{r} 43 \\ \times 12 \\ \hline 6 \end{array}$$

$$\begin{array}{r} 19 \\ \times 11 \\ \hline \end{array} \qquad \begin{array}{r} 32 \\ \times 31 \\ \hline \end{array}$$

2. Multiply by the ones place.
   4 x 2 = 8

$$\begin{array}{r} 43 \\ \times 12 \\ \hline 86 \end{array}$$

$$\begin{array}{r} 54 \\ \times 20 \\ \hline \end{array} \qquad \begin{array}{r} 68 \\ \times 10 \\ \hline \end{array}$$

3. Multiply by the tens. Place a zero in the ones column.
   3 x 1 = 3

$$\begin{array}{r} 43 \\ \times 12 \\ \hline 86 \\ 30 \end{array}$$

$$\begin{array}{r} 83 \\ \times 32 \\ \hline \end{array} \qquad \begin{array}{r} 42 \\ \times 24 \\ \hline \end{array}$$

4. Multiply by the tens place.
   4 x 1 = 4

$$\begin{array}{r} 43 \\ \times 12 \\ \hline 86 \\ 430 \\ \hline \end{array}$$

$$\begin{array}{r} 73 \\ \times 23 \\ \hline \end{array} \qquad \begin{array}{r} 62 \\ \times 43 \\ \hline \end{array}$$

5. Add.
   86 + 430 = 516

$$\begin{array}{r} 43 \\ \times 12 \\ \hline 86 \\ +430 \\ \hline 516 \end{array}$$

Now, **check** your answers with a calculator.

Name ____________________

Multiplying by a Two-Digit Number
With Regrouping

1. Multiply by the ones.
   8 x 7 = 56 (Carry the 5.)

```
  5
  67
 x38
   6
```

2. Multiply by the ones.
   8 x 6 = 48 + 5 = 53
   (When they are completed, cross out all carried digits.)

```
  ̶5
  67
 x38
 536
```

3. Multiply by the tens. Place a zero in the ones column.
   3 x 7 = 21 (Carry the 2.)

```
2 ̶5
  67
 x38
 536
  10
```

4. Multiply by the tens.
   3 x 6 = 18 + 2 = 20

```
 ̶2 ̶5
  67
 x38
 536
2010
```

5. Add.
   536 + 2010 = 2,546

```
 ̶2 ̶5
   67
  x38
  536
+2010
2,546
```

Multiply.

37	77
x24	x21

23	54
x45	x38

48	67
x62	x29

Now, **check** your answers with a calculator.

Multiplication Drill

Multiply. Color the picture below by matching each number with its paint brush.

134 x 22   48 x66   876 x 13   432 x 64

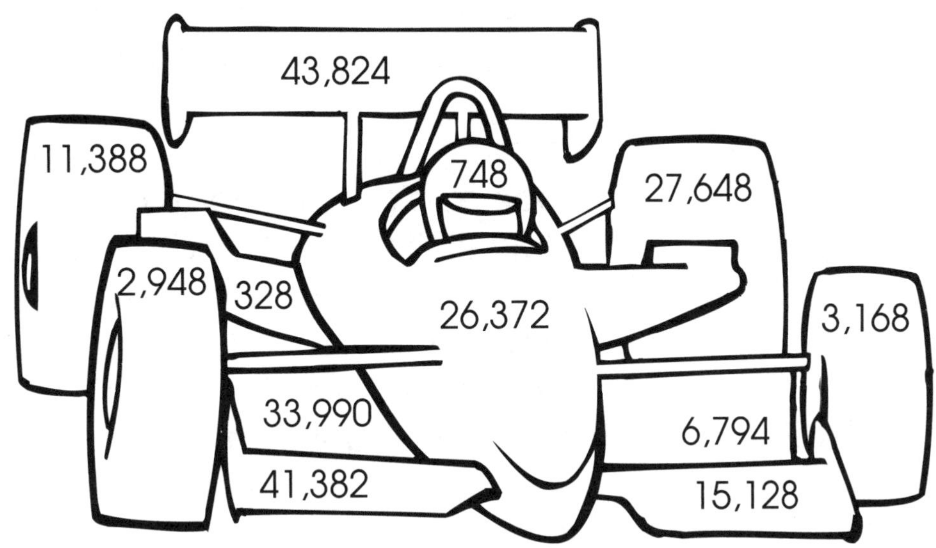

0-7696-8513-7

Name ______________________

Step by Step

Read the problems below. **Write** each answer in the space provided.

1. One battalion of ants marches with 25 ants in a row. There are 35 rows of ants in each battalion. How many ants are in one battalion?

   ____

2. The Ant Army finds a picnic! Now, they need to figure out how many ants should carry each piece of food. A team of 137 ants moves a celery stick. They need 150 ants to carry a carrot stick. A troop of 121 ants carries a very large radish. How many ants in all are needed to move the vegetables?

   ____

3. Now, the real work begins—the big pieces of food that would feed their whole colony. It takes 1,259 ants to haul a peanut butter and jelly sandwich. It takes a whole battalion of 2,067 ants to lug the lemonade back, and it takes 1,099 ants to steal the pickle jar. How many soldiers carry these big items?

   ____

4. Look-outs are posted all around the picnic blanket. It takes 53 soldiers to watch in front of the picnic basket. Another group of 69 ants watch out by the grill. Three groups of 77 watch the different trails in the park. How many ant-soldiers are on the look-out?

   ____

Work space

0-7696-8513-7

Division

Name ______________________________

Backward Multiplication

Division problems are like multiplication problems—just turned around. As you solve 8 ÷ 4, think, "how many groups of 4 make 8?" or "what number 'times' 4 is eight?"

2 x 4 = 8, so 8 ÷ 4 = **2**.

Use the pictures to help you **solve** these division problems.

9 ÷ 3 =

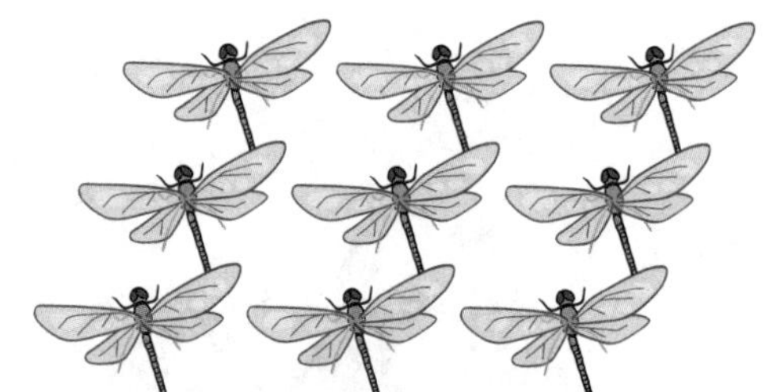

6 ÷ 2 =

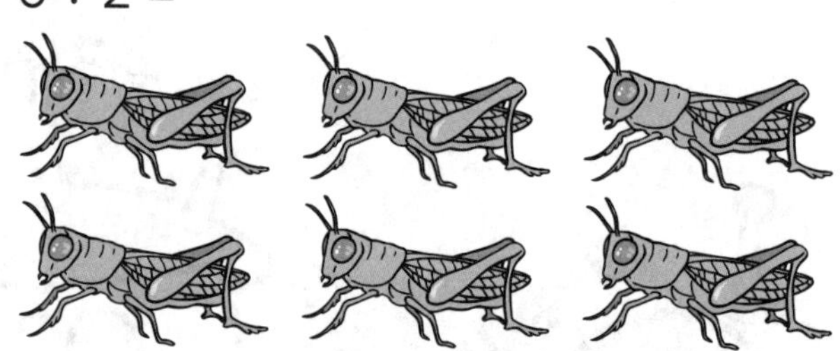

16 ÷ 4 =

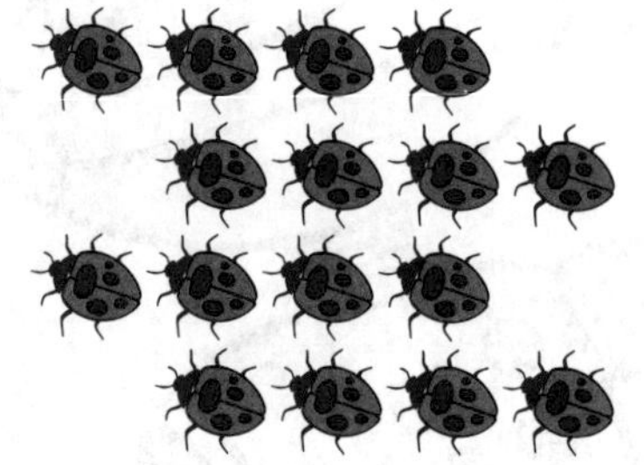

10 ÷ 5 =

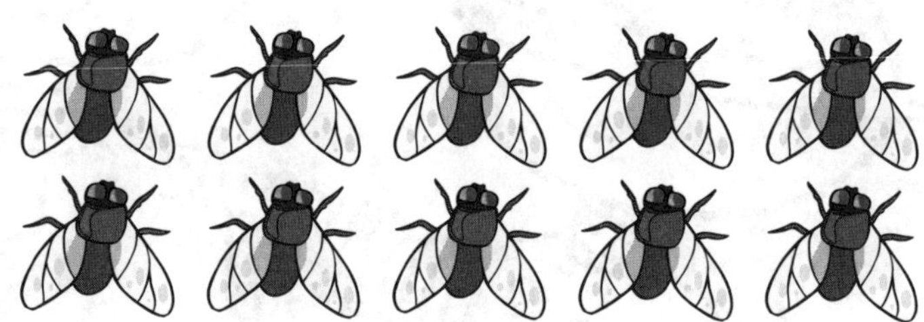

20 ÷ 1 =

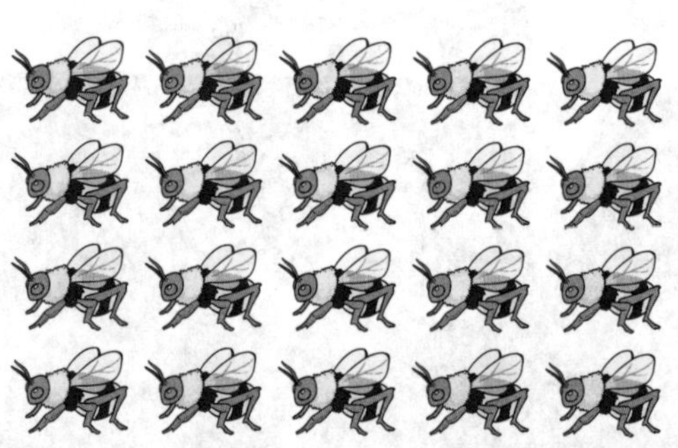

18 ÷ 3 =

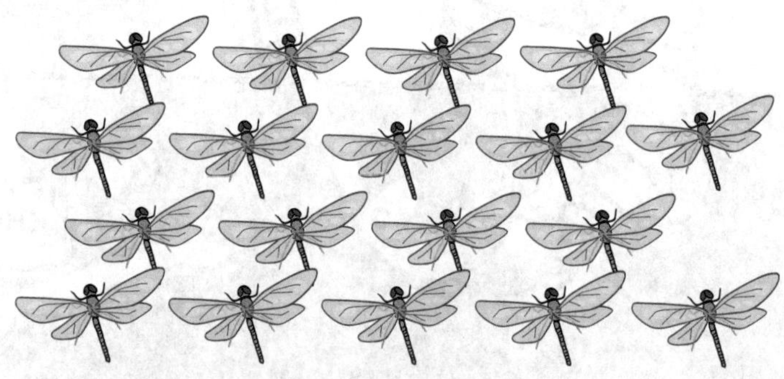

0-7696-8513-7

Name ______________________

What Exactly Is Division?

In division, you begin with an amount of something (the dividend), separate it into small groups (the divisor), then find out how many groups are created (the quotient).

Dividend		Divisor		Quotient
15	÷	3	=	5 sets
in all		in each set		

$$3\overline{)15}$$ 5 sets; 15 in all; 3 in each set

Solve these division problems.

21 ÷ 3 = ______ $3\overline{)21}$

18 ÷ 3 = ______ $3\overline{)18}$

20 ÷ 5 = ______ $5\overline{)20}$

16 ÷ 4 = ______ $4\overline{)16}$

14 ÷ 7 = ______ $7\overline{)14}$

12 ÷ 2 = ______ $2\overline{)12}$

18 ÷ 2 = ______ $2\overline{)18}$

24 ÷ 6 = ______ $6\overline{)24}$

Name ____________________

Blastoff!

Divide.

$1\overline{)6}$ $20\overline{)0}$

$2\overline{)12}$ $2\overline{)14}$

$2\overline{)16}$ $9\overline{)0}$ $9\overline{)0}$ $2\overline{)8}$ $15\overline{)0}$

$1\overline{)19}$ $2\overline{)18}$ $7\overline{)0}$ $2\overline{)10}$ $1\overline{)35}$

$1\overline{)23}$ $1\overline{)17}$ $1\overline{)7}$ $2\overline{)4}$ $12\overline{)0}$

$2\overline{)6}$ $1\overline{)11}$ $1\overline{)5}$

Name ______________________________

Division Tic–Tac–Toe

Solve the problems. **Draw** an **X** on the odd (9, 7, 5, 3) answers. **Draw** an **O** on the even (8, 6, 4, 2) answers.

$4\overline{)36}$	$4\overline{)24}$	$10 \div 5$
$5\overline{)40}$	$32 \div 4$	$25 \div 5$
$35 \div 5$	$20 \div 4$	$12 \div 4$

$4\overline{)32}$	$12 \div 4$	$5\overline{)30}$
$4\overline{)28}$	$4\overline{)20}$	$20 \div 4$
$20 \div 5$	$10 \div 5$	$15 \div 5$

$24 \div 4$	$5\overline{)45}$	$28 \div 4$
$5\overline{)45}$	$5\overline{)20}$	$8 \div 4$
$4\overline{)16}$	$5\overline{)15}$	$30 \div 5$

$25 \div 5$	$4\overline{)8}$	$16 \div 4$
$32 \div 4$	$5\overline{)20}$	$5\overline{)35}$
$40 \div 5$	$4\overline{)12}$	$15 \div 5$

$5\overline{)10}$	$4\overline{)8}$	$24 \div 4$
$4\overline{)36}$	$5\overline{)35}$	$4\overline{)32}$
$45 \div 5$	$5\overline{)30}$	$4\overline{)12}$

$8 \div 4$	$45 \div 5$	$4\overline{)16}$
$5\overline{)25}$	$36 \div 4$	$4\overline{)24}$
$5\overline{)10}$	$25 \div 5$	$4\overline{)36}$

$4\overline{)12}$	$5\overline{)10}$	$5\overline{)45}$
$30 \div 5$	$5\overline{)25}$	$35 \div 5$
$4\overline{)32}$	$8 \div 4$	$5\overline{)20}$

$36 \div 4$	$4\overline{)28}$	$16 \div 4$
$24 \div 4$	$5\overline{)35}$	$5\overline{)40}$
$5\overline{)25}$	$8 \div 4$	$36 \div 4$

$28 \div 4$	$5\overline{)30}$	$45 \div 5$
$16 \div 4$	$32 \div 4$	$15 \div 5$
$4\overline{)20}$	$4\overline{)12}$	$4\overline{)8}$

Name ______________________________

Lizzy the Lizard Bags Her Bugs

Lizzy the Lizard separates her bugs into separate bags so that her lunch is ready for the week. Help her decide how to divide the bugs.

1. Lizzy caught 45 cockroaches. She put 5 into each bag. How many bags did she use?

   _______ ÷ _______ = _______

2. Lizzy found 32 termites. She put 4 into each bag. How many bags did she need?

   _______ ÷ _______ = _______

3. Lizzy captured 49 stinkbugs. She put them into 7 bags. How many stinkbugs were in each bag?

   _______ ÷ _______ = _______

4. Lizzy bagged 27 horn beetles. She used 3 bags. How many beetles went into each bag?

   _______ ÷ _______ = _______

5. Lizzy lassoed 36 butterflies. She put 9 into each bag. How many bags did she need?

   _______ ÷ _______ = _______

6. Lizzy went fishing and caught 48 water beetles. She used 6 bags for her catch. How many beetles went into each bag?

   _______ ÷ _______ = _______

Name ____________________

Two-Digit Quotients

Steps:

1. Ask: Is the tens digit large enough to divide into? (Yes.) Divide. Multiply the partial quotient (2) by the divisor (4) and subtract from the partial dividend (8).

$$\begin{array}{r} 2 \\ 4\overline{)84} \\ -8 \\ \hline 0 \end{array} \quad 4 \times 2$$

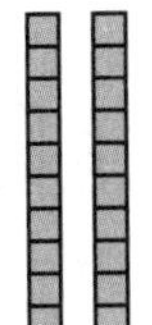
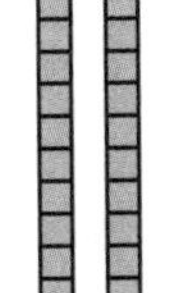
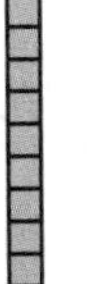

8 tens divided into 4 groups. How many are in each group? (2)

2. Carry down the 4 in the ones column. Ask: How many groups of 4 are there in 4? (1) Divide. Multiply the partial quotient (1) by the divisor (4) and subtract from the partial dividend (4).

$$\begin{array}{r} 21 \\ 4\overline{)84} \\ -8 \\ \hline 04 \\ -\ 4 \\ \hline 0 \end{array} \quad 4 \times 1$$

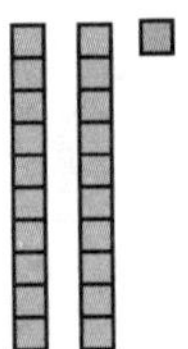
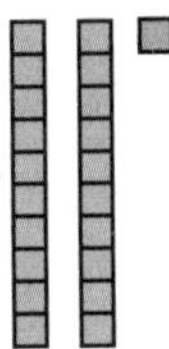
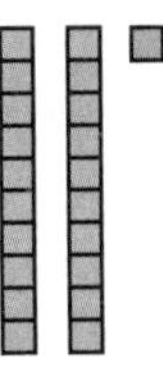

3. When 84 things are divided into 4 groups, there will be 21 in each group.

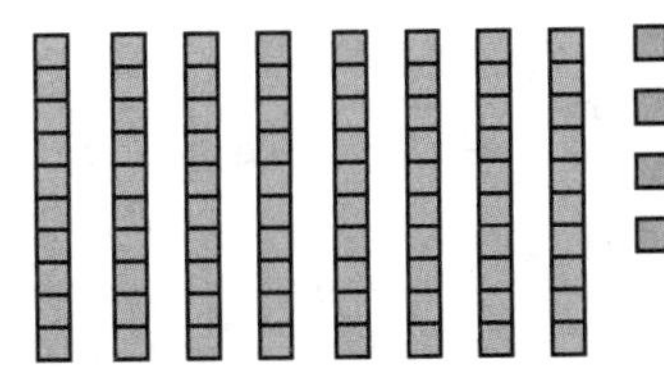 = 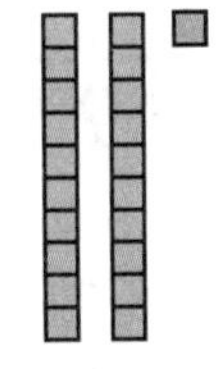 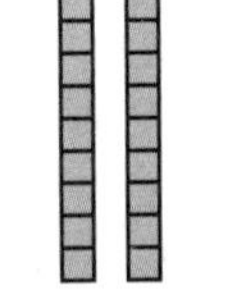 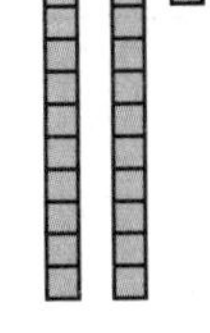 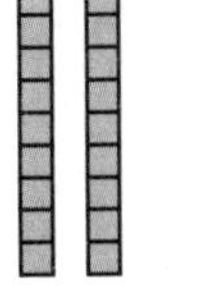 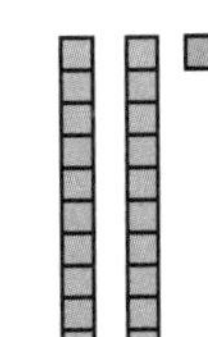

84 ÷ 4 = 21 + 21 + 21 + 21

$$\begin{array}{r} 21 \\ 4\overline{)84} \\ -8 \\ \hline 04 \\ -\ 4 \\ \hline 0 \end{array}$$

Divide.

$3\overline{)63}$ $\quad$ $2\overline{)72}$

$4\overline{)48}$ $\quad$ $2\overline{)56}$

$3\overline{)96}$ $\quad$ $2\overline{)82}$

Name ____________________

Snowball Bash

Divide this mound of giant snowballs!

7)84 5)75

3)45 9)99 4)88 5)80

4)64 3)57 3)78 3)72 8)96

2)86 2)38 6)66 5)65 4)52

4)68 6)78 7)91 2)42 6)72

 0-7696-8513-7

Name ______________________

Three-Digit Quotients

Steps:

1. Ask: Is the hundreds digit large enough to divide into? (Yes.) Divide. Multiply the partial quotient by the divisor and subtract from the partial dividend.

```
    1
7 | 938
   -7
    2
```

2. Ask: Can I divide the remaining 2 by 7? (No.) Bring down the 3 tens.

```
    1
7 | 938     2 hundreds
   -7       + 3 tens
    23      = 23 tens
```

3. Divide the 23 tens by 7. Multiply the partial quotient by the divisor and subtract.

```
    13
7 | 938
   -7
    23
   -21
     2
```

4. Ask: Can I divide the remaining 2 by 7? (No.) Bring down 8 ones.

```
    13
7 | 938
   -7       2 tens
    23      + 8 ones
   -21      = 28 ones
     28
```

5. Divide the 28 ones by 7. Multiply the partial quotient by the divisor and subtract.

```
    134
7 | 938
   -7
    23
   -21
     28
   - 28
      0
```

Divide.

6 | 888 2 | 542

3 | 693 4 | 544

7 | 896 5 | 635

 0-7696-8513-7

Name ____________________

On-Stage Division

Divide.

$6\overline{)888}$	$2\overline{)956}$	$2\overline{)712}$	$4\overline{)860}$	$5\overline{)845}$
$6\overline{)750}$	$9\overline{)999}$	$8\overline{)968}$	$3\overline{)774}$	$5\overline{)735}$

$8\overline{)920}$

$8\overline{)984}$ $4\overline{)500}$ $2\overline{)846}$ $4\overline{)712}$

Name ______________________

Zeros in the Quotient

Steps:

1. Decide where to place the first digit in the quotient.
   - 3 can go into 4.

   480 ÷ 3

2. Divide. Then, multiply.
   - 4 ÷ 3 = 1
   - 3 x 1 = 3

   $3\overline{)480}$

3. Subtract and compare.
   - 4 – 3 = 1
   - Is 1 less than 3? (Yes.)

   $$\begin{array}{r} 1 \\ 3\overline{)480} \\ -3 \\ \hline 1 \end{array}$$

4. Bring down. Repeat the steps.
   - Bring down 8.
   - 18 ÷ 3 = 6
   - 6 x 3 = 18
   - 18 – 18 = 0
   - Bring down 0.
   - 3 cannot go into 0.
   - 0 x 3 = 0

   $$\begin{array}{r} 160 \\ 3\overline{)480} \\ -3 \\ \hline 18 \\ -18 \\ \hline 00 \\ -0 \\ \hline 0 \end{array}$$

Steps:

1. Decide where to place the first digit in the quotient.
   - 3 can go into 3.

   327 ÷ 3

2. Divide. Then, multiply.
   - 3 ÷ 3 = 1
   - 3 x 1 = 3

   $3\overline{)327}$

3. Subtract and compare.
   - 3 – 3 = 0
   - Is 0 less than 3? (Yes.)

   $$\begin{array}{r} 1 \\ 3\overline{)327} \\ -3 \\ \hline 0 \end{array}$$

4. Bring down. Repeat the steps.
   - Bring down the 2.
   - 3 cannot go into 2.
   - 0 x 3 = 0
   - 2 – 0 = 2
   - Bring down the 7.
   - 27 ÷ 3 = 9
   - 9 x 3 = 27
   - 27 – 27 = 0

   $$\begin{array}{r} 109 \\ 3\overline{)327} \\ -3 \\ \hline 02 \\ -0 \\ \hline 27 \\ -27 \\ \hline 0 \end{array}$$

Divide.

$3\overline{)624}$ $4\overline{)680}$ $2\overline{)722}$ $6\overline{)648}$ $2\overline{)814}$ $3\overline{)912}$

Name ______________________________

Yum! Yum!

What edible fungus is occasionally found on pizzas or in omelets? To find out, **solve** the following problems and **write** the matching letter above the answer at the bottom of the page.

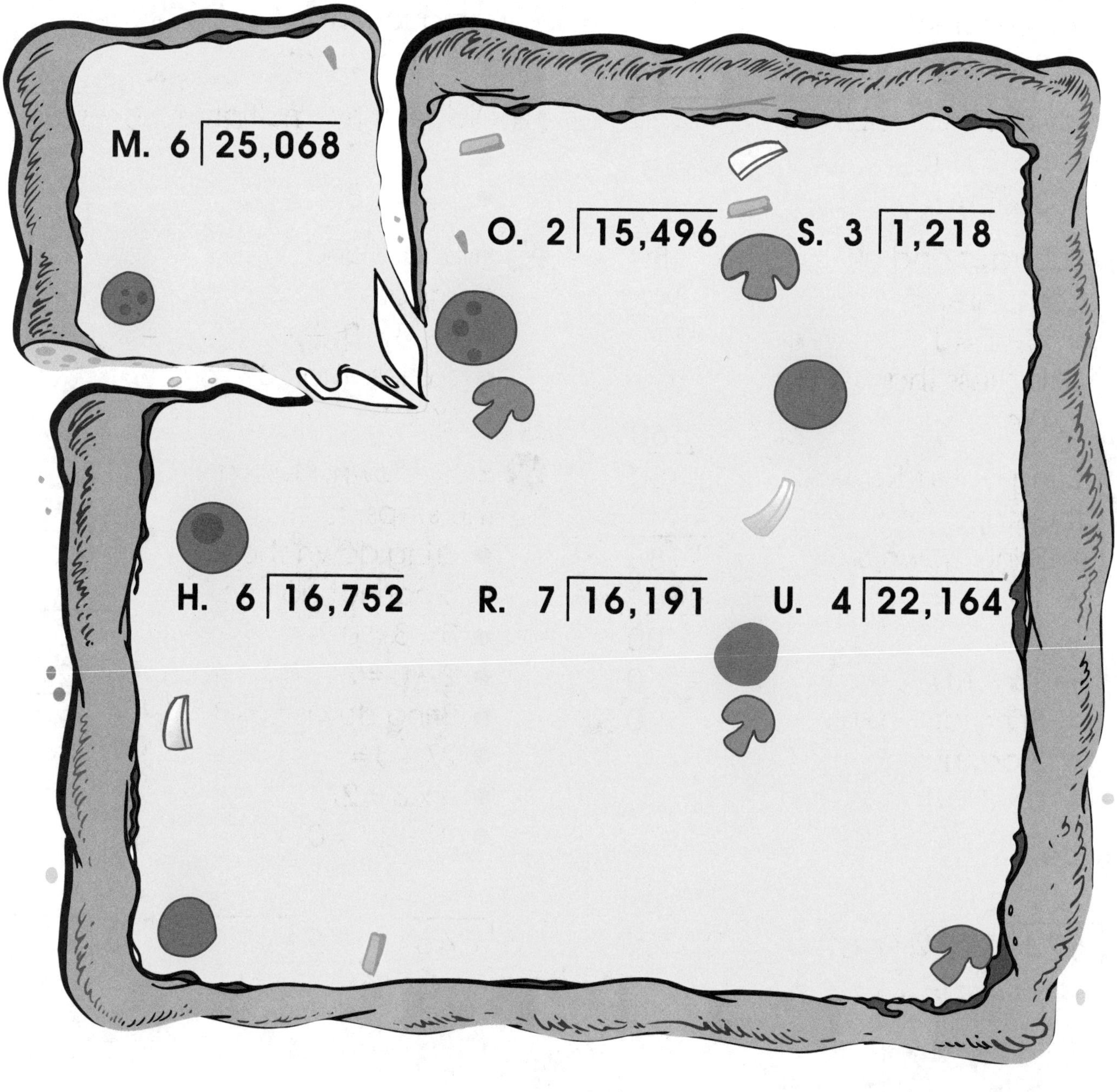

M. $6\overline{)25,068}$

O. $2\overline{)15,496}$

S. $3\overline{)1,218}$

H. $6\overline{)16,752}$

R. $7\overline{)16,191}$

U. $4\overline{)22,164}$

___	___	___	___	___	___	___	___	___
4,178	5,541	406	2,792	2,313	7,748	7,748	4,178	406

Name ______________________

Two-Digit Quotients
With Remainders

Steps:

1. Ask: Is the tens digit large enough to divide into? (Yes.) Divide. Multiply the partial quotient (1) by the divisor (3) and subtract from the partial dividend (4)

$$\begin{array}{r} 1 \\ 3\overline{)44} \\ -3 \\ \hline 1 \end{array} \quad 3 \times 1$$

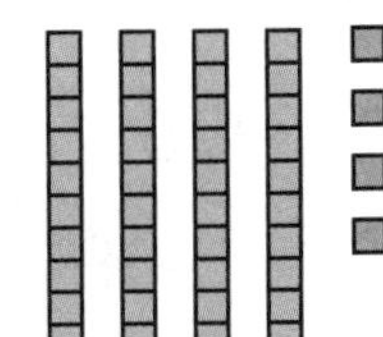

2. Ask: Can I divide the remaining 1 by 3? (No.) Bring down the 4. You now have 14 ones.

$$\begin{array}{r} 1 \\ 3\overline{)44} \\ -3 \\ \hline 14 \end{array}$$

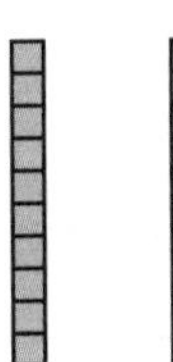
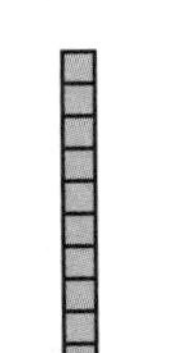
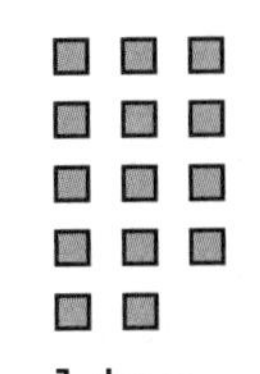

1 ten
+ 4 ones
= 14 ones

3. Divide the 14 ones by 3. Multiply the partial quotient by the divisor and subtract.

$$\begin{array}{r} 14 \\ 3\overline{)44} \\ -3 \\ \hline 14 \\ -12 \\ \hline 2 \end{array} \quad 3 \times 4$$

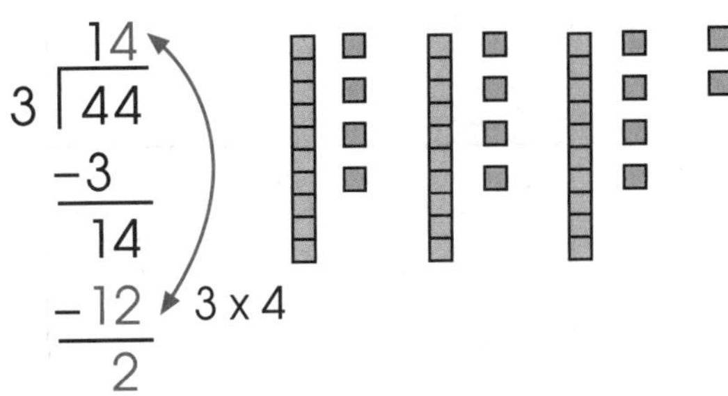

4. Ask: Can I divide the remaining 2 by 3? (No.) Make it a remainder.

$$\begin{array}{r} 14 \text{ R}2 \\ 3\overline{)44} \\ -3 \\ \hline 14 \\ -12 \\ \hline 2 \end{array}$$

Divide.

$5\overline{)64}$ $\quad$ $3\overline{)73}$ $\quad$ $2\overline{)53}$ $\quad$ $4\overline{)91}$ $\quad$ $6\overline{)74}$ $\quad$ $3\overline{)76}$

Name ____________________

Looking to the Stars

Solve the problems. To find the path to the top, your answers should match the problem number. **Color** the path.

	27. $3\overline{)63}$	28. $3\overline{)84}$	29. $4\overline{)97}$	30. $6\overline{)74}$		
	22. $4\overline{)74}$	23. $2\overline{)46}$	24. $2\overline{)48}$	25. $3\overline{)75}$	26. $6\overline{)96}$	
15. $5\overline{)92}$	16. $3\overline{)41}$	17. $3\overline{)57}$	18. $4\overline{)84}$	19. $4\overline{)76}$	20. $7\overline{)86}$	21. $5\overline{)72}$
8. $5\overline{)57}$	9. $3\overline{)65}$	10. $2\overline{)87}$	11. $5\overline{)55}$	12. $7\overline{)84}$	13. $3\overline{)87}$	14. $7\overline{)93}$
1. $3\overline{)96}$	2. $6\overline{)94}$	3. $5\overline{)93}$	4. $9\overline{)36}$	5. $2\overline{)97}$	6. $6\overline{)84}$	7. $3\overline{)68}$

Name ______________________________

Three-Digit Quotients
With Remainders

Steps:

1. Ask: Is the hundreds digit large enough to divide into? (Yes.) Divide. Multiply the partial quotient by the divisor and subtract from the partial dividend.

```
   2
4)854
 -8
  0
```

2. Bring down the 5 tens. Ask: Can I divide 5 by 4? (Yes.) Multiply the partial quotient by the divisor and subtract.

```
   21
4)854
 -8
  05
 - 4
   1
```

3. Ask: Is the difference of 1 less than the divisor 4? (Yes.) Bring down the 4 ones.

1 ten + 4 ones = 14 ones

```
   21
4)854
 -8
  05
 - 4
   14
```

4. Divide the 14 ones by 4. Multiply the partial quotient by the divisor and subtract.

```
   213
4)854
 -8
  05
 - 4
   14
 - 12
    2
```

5. Ask: Is the remaining difference of 2 less than the divisor? (Yes.) Make 2 a remainder.

```
   213 R2
4)854
 -8
  05
 - 4
   14
 - 12
    2
```

Divide.

$2\overline{)631}$ $\quad 6\overline{)945}$ $\quad 3\overline{)860}$ $\quad 5\overline{)914}$ $\quad 4\overline{)927}$ $\quad 8\overline{)972}$

Name ______________________

Puzzling Problems

Solve the following problems. **Write** the answers in the puzzle.

Across

2. $2\overline{)917}$

4. $6\overline{)830}$

7. $4\overline{)975}$

8. $2\overline{)859}$

12. $2\overline{)779}$

14. $3\overline{)475}$

16. $3\overline{)680}$

17. $8\overline{)988}$

18. $3\overline{)971}$

19. $5\overline{)927}$

Down

1. $3\overline{)776}$

3. $7\overline{)948}$

5. $3\overline{)740}$

6. $7\overline{)897}$

9. $4\overline{)751}$

10. $5\overline{)714}$

11. $4\overline{)639}$

13. $6\overline{)749}$

15. $5\overline{)634}$

Name ____________________

Four-Digit Quotients

With Remainders

Steps:

1. Decide where to place the first digit in the quotient.
- 6 cannot go into 1.
- 6 can go into 14.

2. Divide. Then, multiply.
- 14 ÷ 6 = 2
- 6 x 2 = 12

3. Subtract and compare.
- 14 – 12 = 2
- Is 2 less than 6? (Yes.)

4. Bring down. Repeat the steps.
- Bring down the 6.
- 26 ÷ 6 = 4
- 6 x 4 = 24
- 26 – 24 = 2
- Is 2 less than 6? (Yes.)
- Bring down the 4.
- 24 ÷ 6 = 4
- 6 x 4 = 24
- 24 – 24 = 0
- Is 0 less than 6? (Yes.)
- Bring down the 8.
- 8 ÷ 6 = 1
- 6 x 1 = 6
- 8 – 6 = 2
- Is 2 less than 6? (Yes.)
- No more numbers, so 2 is the remainder.

14,648 ÷ 6

$6\overline{)14{,}648}$

$$\begin{array}{r} 2 \\ 6\overline{)14{,}648} \\ -12 \\ \hline 2 \end{array}$$

$$\begin{array}{r} 2{,}441 \text{ R2} \\ 6\overline{)14{,}648} \\ -12 \\ \hline 26 \\ -24 \\ \hline 24 \\ -24 \\ \hline 08 \\ -6 \\ \hline 2 \end{array}$$

Divide.

$5\overline{)22{,}464}$ $6\overline{)23{,}445}$

$3\overline{)14{,}458}$ $8\overline{)50{,}469}$

$3\overline{)23{,}767}$ $4\overline{)23{,}303}$

Name ____________________

To Catch a Butterfly

Solve the problems. **Draw** a line to connect each net to the butterfly with the correct answer.

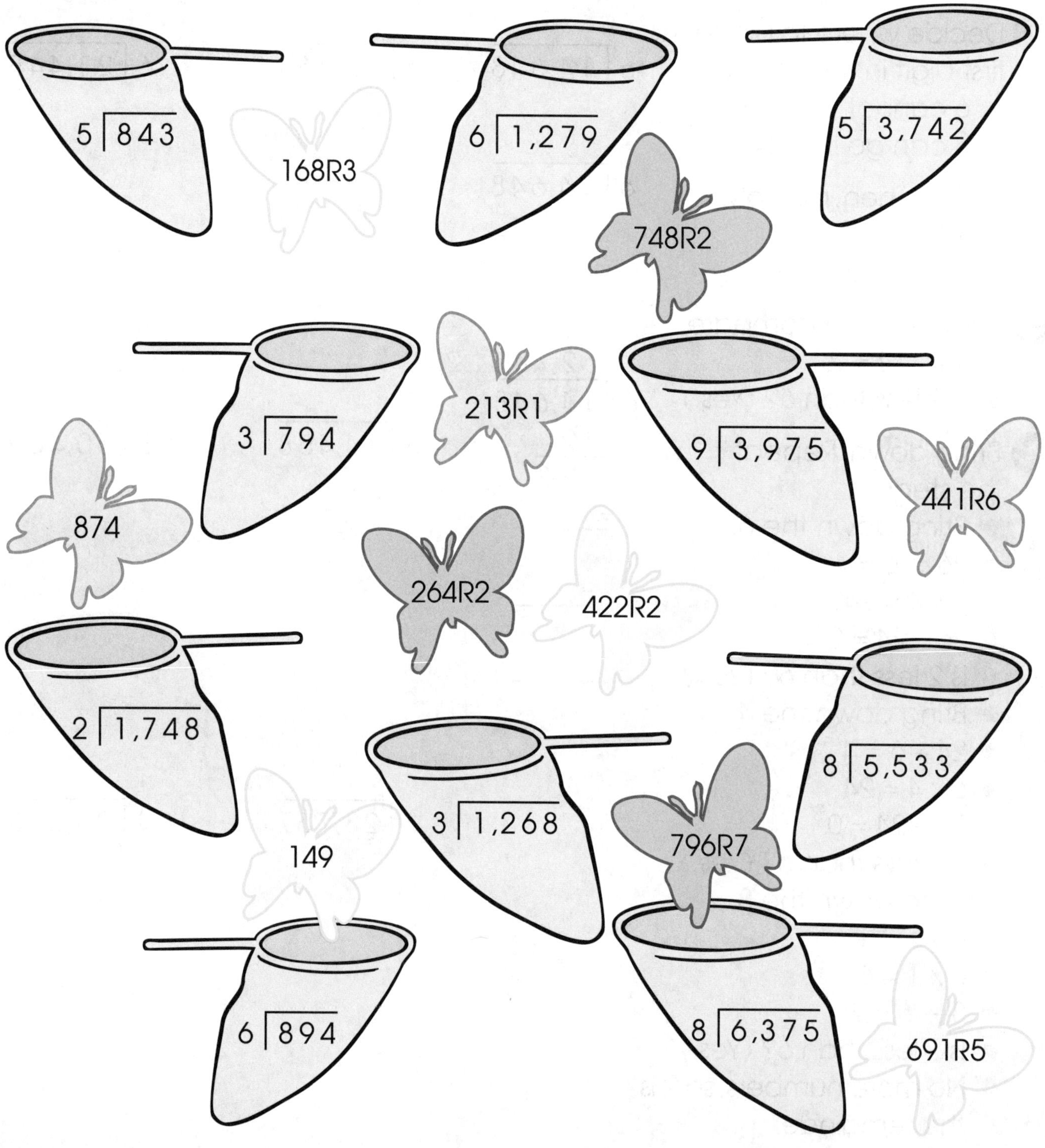

$5\overline{)843}$

168R3

$6\overline{)1,279}$

$5\overline{)3,742}$

748R2

$3\overline{)794}$

213R1

$9\overline{)3,975}$

874

441R6

264R2

422R2

$2\overline{)1,748}$

$8\overline{)5,533}$

$3\overline{)1,268}$

149

796R7

$6\overline{)894}$

$8\overline{)6,375}$

691R5

Name ______________________________

Two-Digit Divisors

With Remainders

Steps:

1. Decide where to place the first digit in the quotient. $240 \div 26$
   - 26 cannot go into 2. $26\overline{)240}$
   - 26 cannot go into 24.
   - 26 can go into 240.

2. Divide. Then, multiply.
   - $240 \div 26 = 9$
   - $9 \times 26 = 234$

   $$\begin{array}{r} 9 \\ 26\overline{)240} \\ -234 \\ \hline \end{array}$$

3. Subtract and compare.
   - $240 - 234 = 6$
   - Is 6 less than 26? (Yes.)
   - No more numbers, so 6 is the remainder.

   $$\begin{array}{r} 9 \text{ R6} \\ 26\overline{)240} \\ -234 \\ \hline 6 \end{array}$$

4. Check division with multiplication. Multiply the quotient by the divisor and add the remainder. If you divided correctly, your answer will be the dividend!

   $$\begin{array}{r} 26 \\ \times\ 9 \\ \hline 234 \\ +\ 6 \\ \hline 240 \end{array}$$

Steps:

1. Decide where to place the first digit in the quotient. $180 \div 25$
   - 25 cannot go into 1. $25\overline{)180}$
   - 25 cannot go into 18.
   - 25 can go into 180.

2. Divide. Then, multiply.
   - $180 \div 25 = 7$
   - $7 \times 25 = 175$

   $$\begin{array}{r} 7 \\ 25\overline{)180} \\ -175 \\ \hline \end{array}$$

3. Subtract and compare.
   - $180 - 175 = 5$
   - Is 5 less than 25? (Yes.)
   - No more numbers, so 5 is the remainder.

   $$\begin{array}{r} 7 \text{ R5} \\ 25\overline{)180} \\ -175 \\ \hline 5 \end{array}$$

4. Check.

   $$\begin{array}{r} 25 \\ \times\ 7 \\ \hline 175 \\ +\ 5 \\ \hline 180 \end{array}$$

Divide.

$14\overline{)77}$ $\quad 34\overline{)70}$ $\quad 13\overline{)80}$ $\quad 24\overline{)82}$ $\quad 17\overline{)140}$ $\quad 47\overline{)290}$

Name ____________________

Hoppin' Division

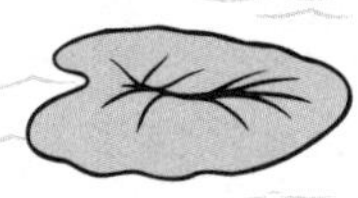

Solve these division problems.

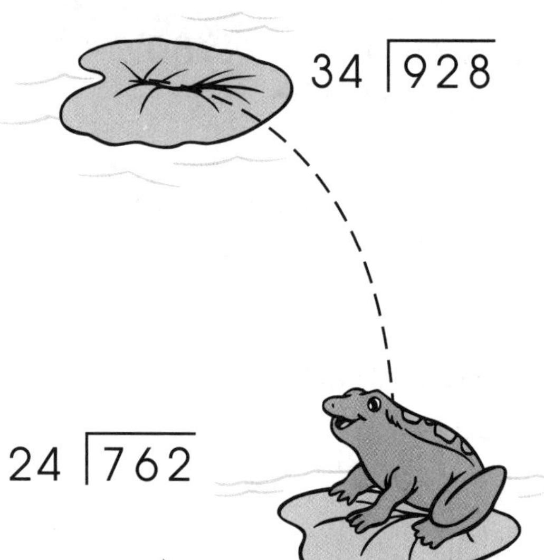

34)928   25)329   15)730   35)825

24)762

27)380   16)340   17)699

33)864   22)290   32)876   18)766

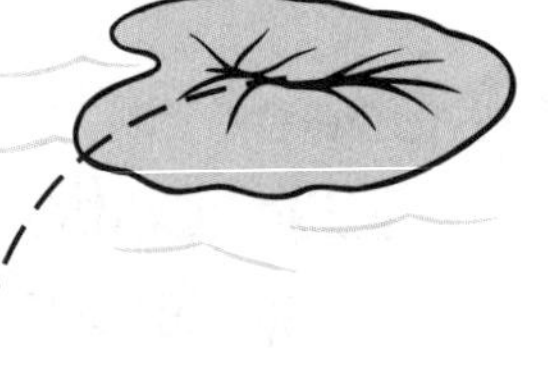

23)375   13)678   26)607   14)884

Name ________________________________

Which Problem Is Correct?

Circle the equation on the left you should use to solve the problem. Then, **solve** the problem. Remember the decimal point in money questions.

1. $\begin{array}{r} 56 \\ +17 \\ \hline \end{array}$ $\begin{array}{r} 56 \\ -17 \\ \hline \end{array}$ Bill and his friends collect baseball cards. Bill has 17 fewer cards than Mack. Bill has 56 cards. How many baseball cards does Mack have?

2. $\begin{array}{r} 54 \\ \times\ 3 \\ \hline \end{array}$ $3\overline{)54}$ Amos bought 54 baseball cards. He already had 3 times as many. How many baseball cards did Amos have before his latest purchase?

3. $\begin{array}{r} 3.80 \\ +3.50 \\ \hline \end{array}$ $\begin{array}{r} 3.80 \\ -3.50 \\ \hline \end{array}$ Joe paid \$3.50 for a Mickey Mantle baseball card. Ted Williams cost him \$3.80. How much more did he pay for Ted Williams than for Mickey Mantle?

4. $\begin{array}{r} 3.60 \\ \times\ \ 9 \\ \hline \end{array}$ $9\overline{)3.60}$ Will bought 9 baseball cards for \$3.60. How much did he pay per (for each) card?

5. $\begin{array}{r} 8.00 \\ +\ .50 \\ \hline \end{array}$ $\begin{array}{r} 8.00 \\ -\ .50 \\ \hline \end{array}$ Babe Ruth baseball cards were selling for \$8.00. Herb Score baseball cards sold for 50 cents. Herb Score cards sold for how much less than Babe Ruth cards?

6. $\begin{array}{r} 0.75 \\ \times\ \ 8 \\ \hline \end{array}$ $8\overline{)0.75}$ Andy bought 8 baseball cards at 75 cents each. How much did Andy pay in all?

Name ____________________

On the Average . . .

Division is good for finding averages. An **average** is a number that tells about how something is normally.

The children on the 6-on-6 basketball team made the following number of baskets:

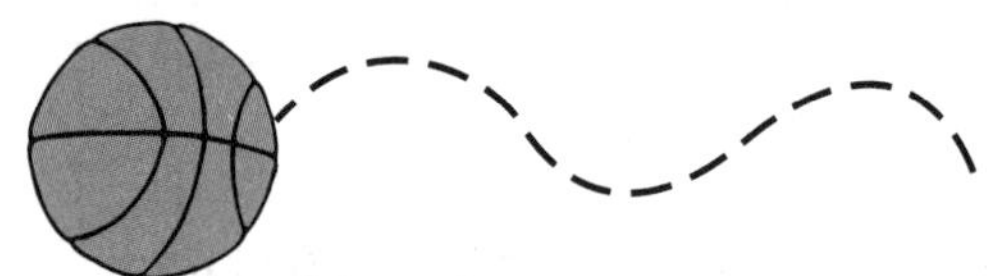

April 1
Beth 3
Colton 3
Ryan 1
Jen 2
J.J. 2

The school paper wants to write about the game, but they don't have room for such a long list. Instead the reporter will find the average by following the steps below.

Steps:

1. **Add** all the team members' baskets together.

   _____ + _____ + _____ + _____ + _____ + _____ = _____

2. **Count** to find out how many team members there were.

   _____

3. **Divide** your answer for step 1 by the number in step 2.

   _____ ÷ _____ = _____

The paper will report that each team member normally makes an average of 2 baskets each. Remember—add, count, divide.

Find the average for the following problem:
In their last 3 games, the Longlegs scored 24 points, 16 points and 20 points.

1) Add. 2) Count. 3) Divide.

What was their average? ____________

Geometry

Name ______________________________

Geometry Match-Ups

A **polygon** is a closed shape with straight sides.

Directions: Cut out each polygon on the next page. To make them more durable, glue them onto cardboard or oaktag. Use the shapes to fill out the table below. (Keep the shapes for other activities as well.)

Game: Play this game with a partner. Put the shapes in a bag or cover them with a sheet of paper. Player One pulls out a shape and tells how many sides and angles it has. Without showing the shape, he/she puts the polygon back. Player Two should name the shape. Then, Player Two puts his/her hand in the bag and, without looking, tries to find the polygon from the description. Then, switch roles. Continue the game until all the polygons have been identified.

When you finish playing, **complete** the chart below.

Drawing of the shape (or polygon)	Shape name	Number of sides	Number of angles (or corners)
	triangle		
	square		
	pentagon		
	rectangle		
	hexagon		

Name ______________________________

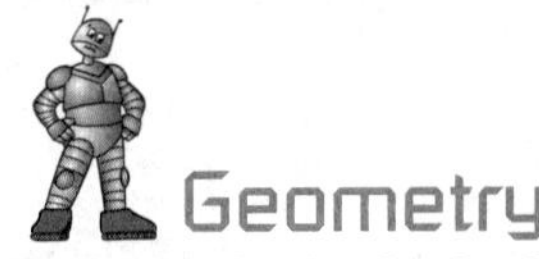

Shapes

hexagon

pentagon

square

triangle

rectangle

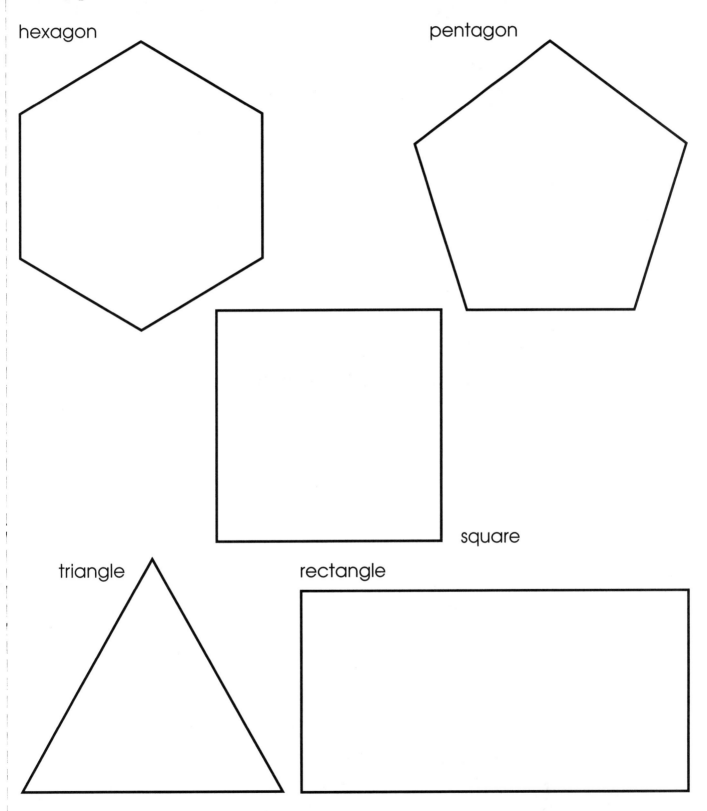

This page intentionally left blank.

Name ____________________

A Native American Wall Hanging

Congruent figures have the same size and shape. They do not have to be the same color or in the same position.

Congruent figures

Not congruent figures

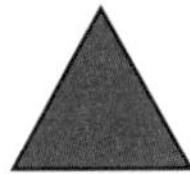  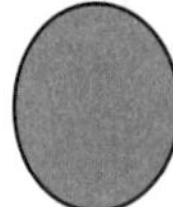 

Directions: Draw two congruent figures to create a new shape. You can use triangles, squares, rectangles, pentagons, hexagons, octagons, semicircles, quarter-circles or trapezoids to make the shape. Use the new shape to create a wall hanging design. Connect the two congruent figures at one side. Color each part of the congruent pairs. Display your hanging on a wall of your house.

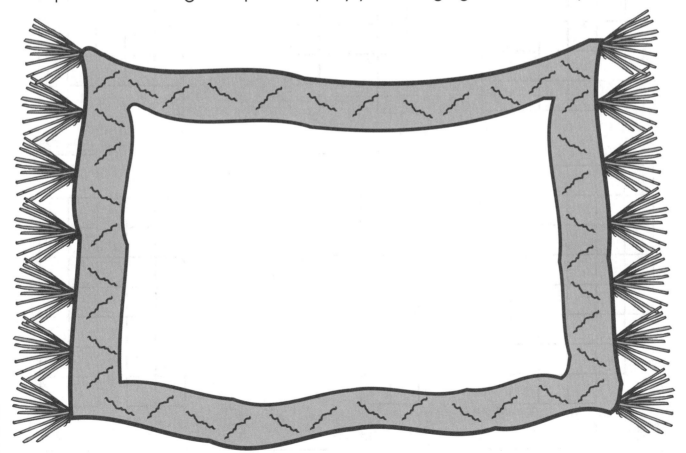

Name ____________________

Perimeter Problems

The **perimeter** is the distance around the outside of a shape. **Find** the perimeters for the figures below by adding the lengths of all the sides.

Example:

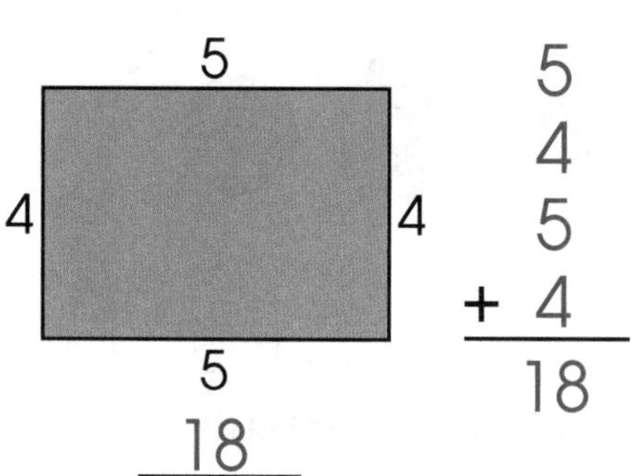

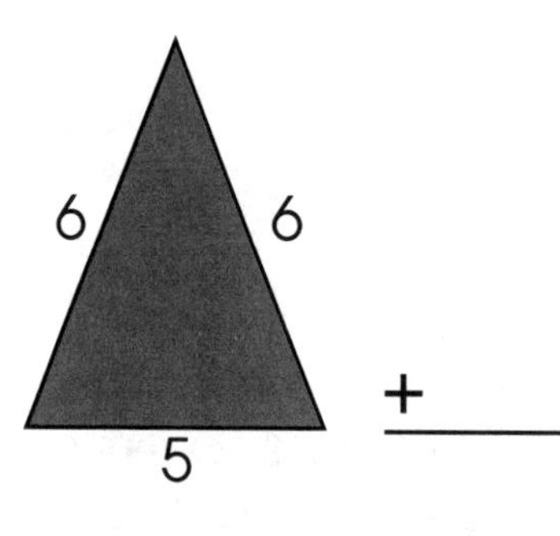

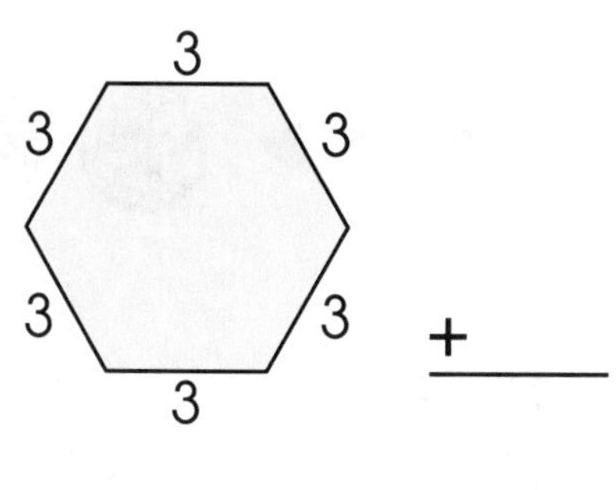

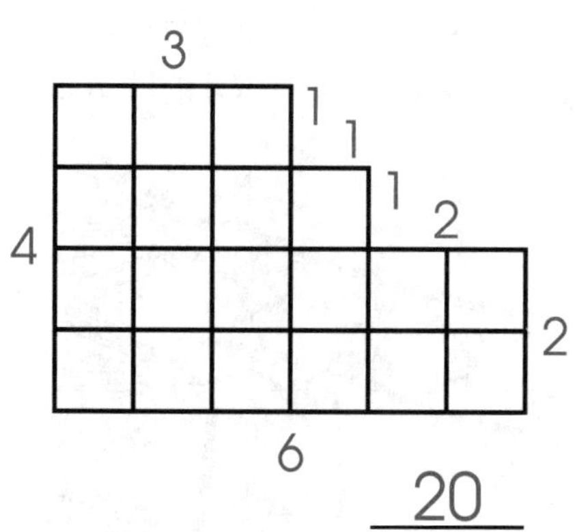

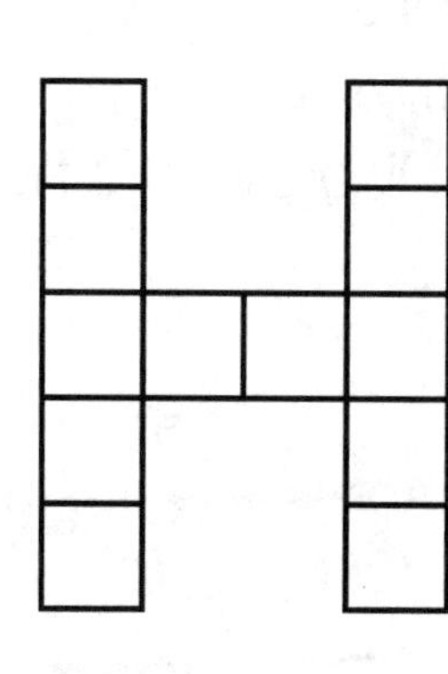

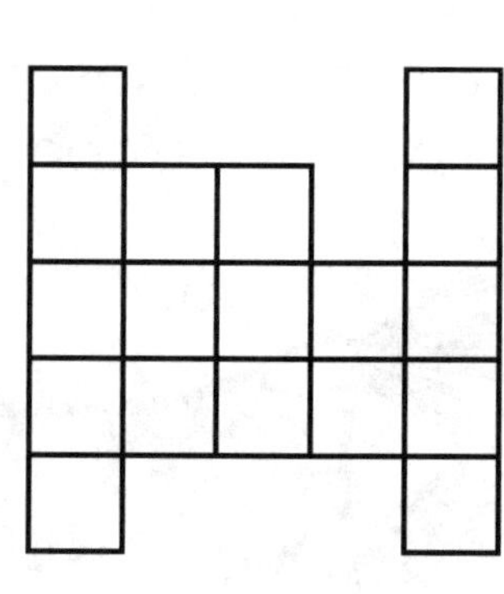

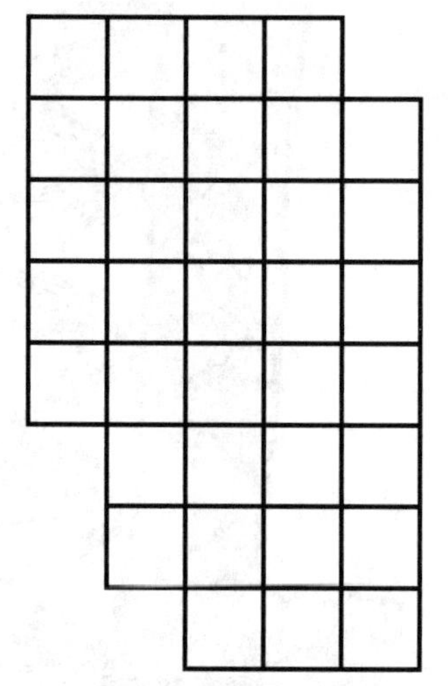

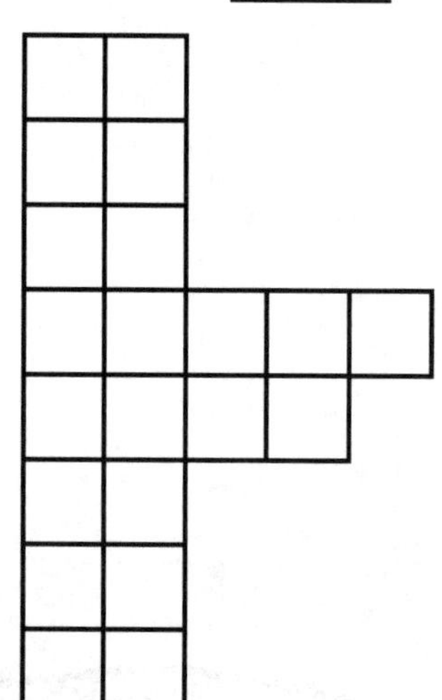

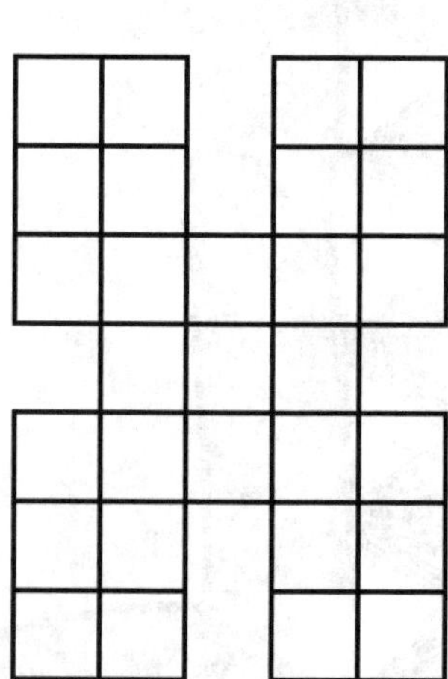

Name ______________________

A Square Activity

The **area** is the number of square units covering a flat surface. **Find** the area by counting the square units.

Example: 2 squares x 5 squares = 10 squares

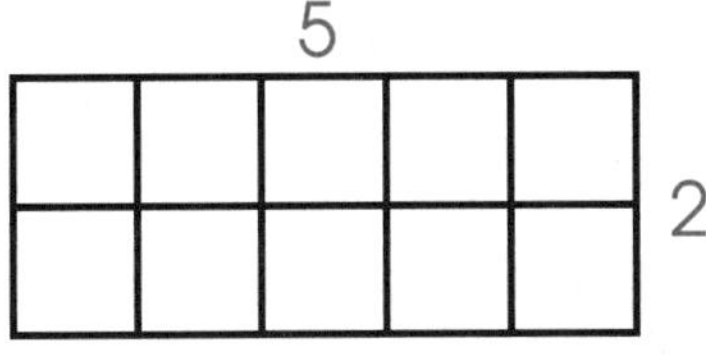

10

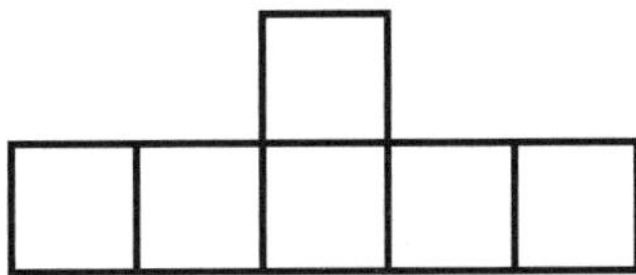

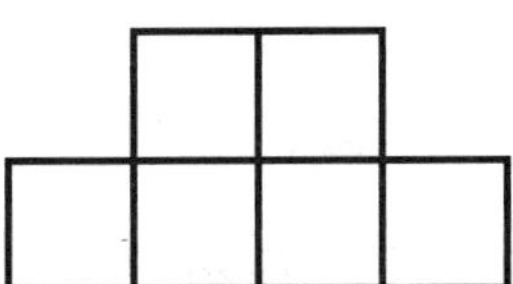

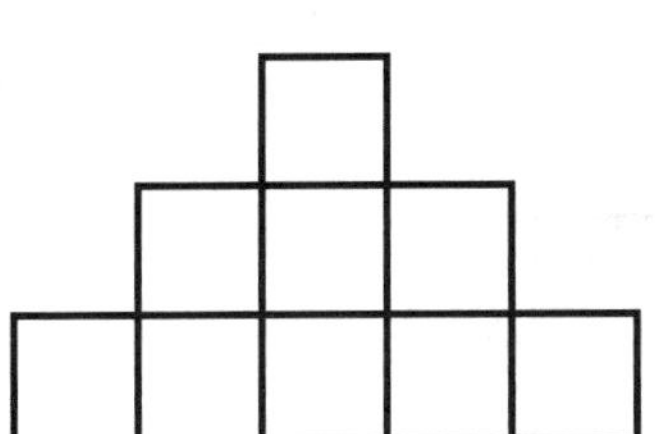

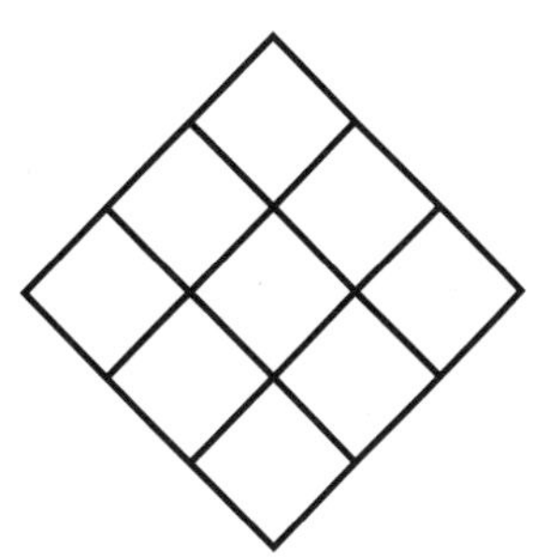

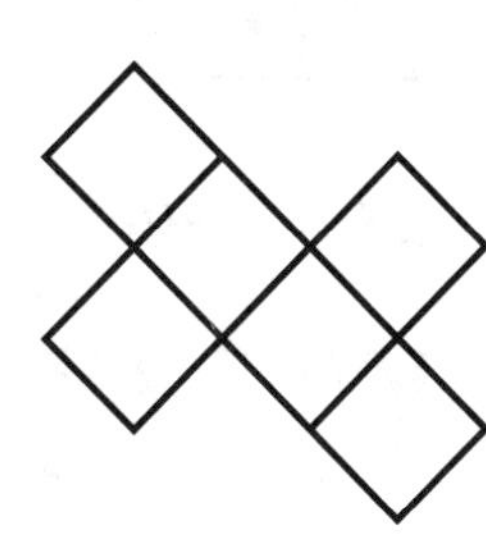

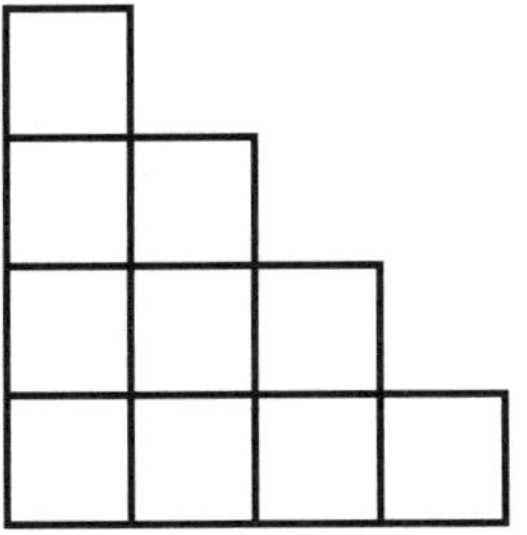

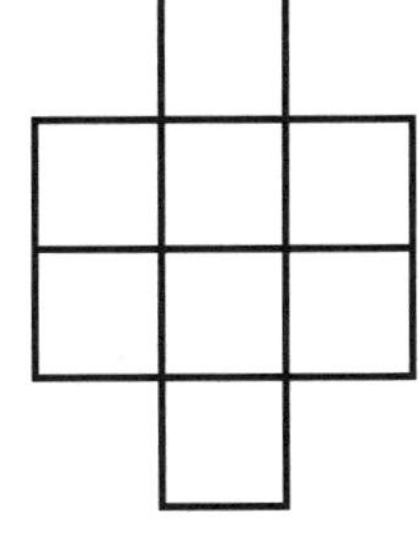

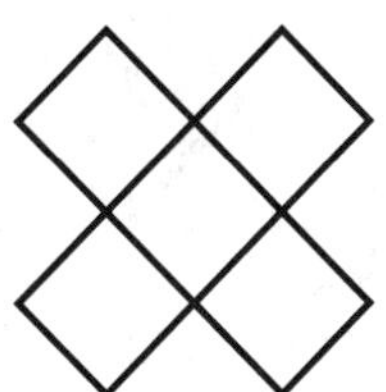

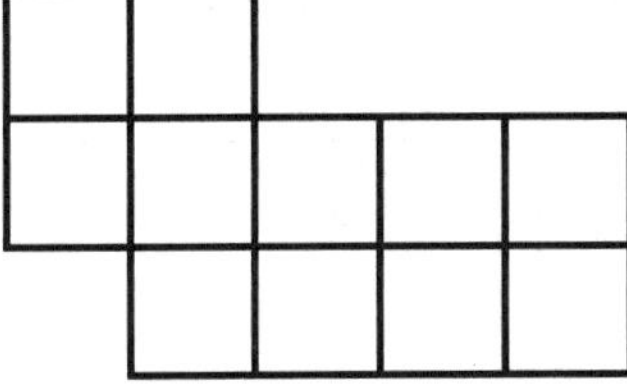

Name ______________________________

Quilt Math

The area of a rectangle is calculated by multiplying the length of one side by the width of another side. **Find** the perimeter and area of each quilt.

1\.

perimeter ______ area ______

2\. 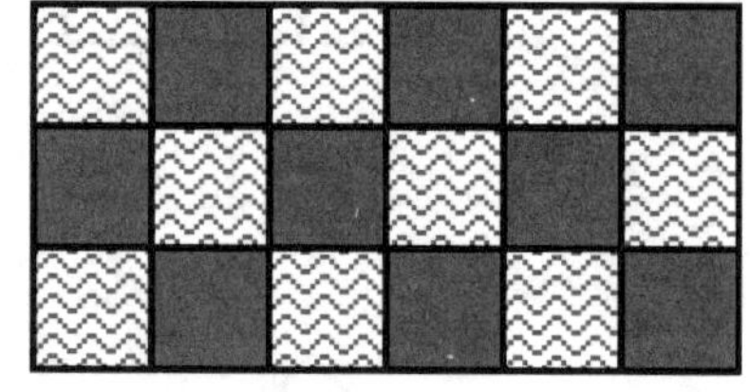

perimeter ______ area ______

3\. 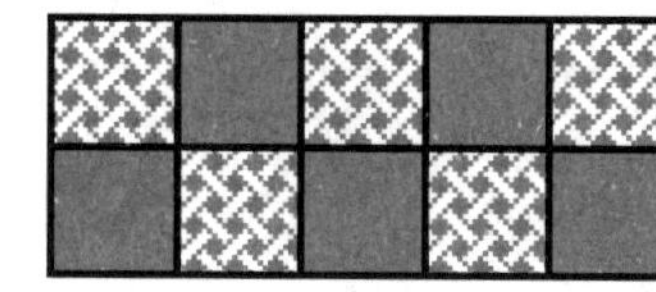

perimeter ______ area ______

4\. 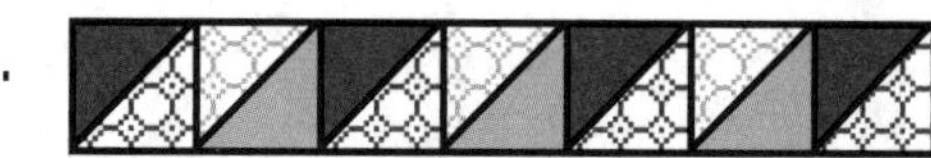

perimeter ______ area ______

5\. 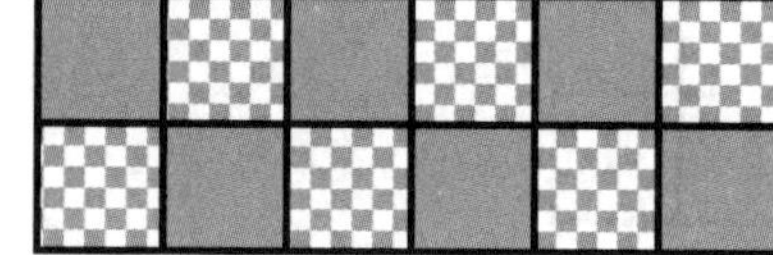

perimeter ______ area ______

6\. 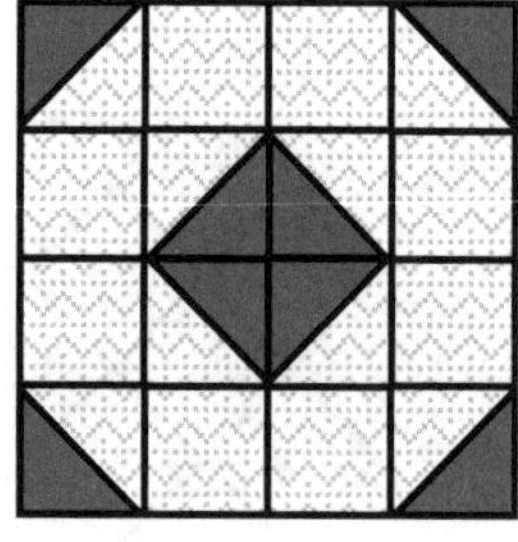

perimeter ______ area ______

7\. 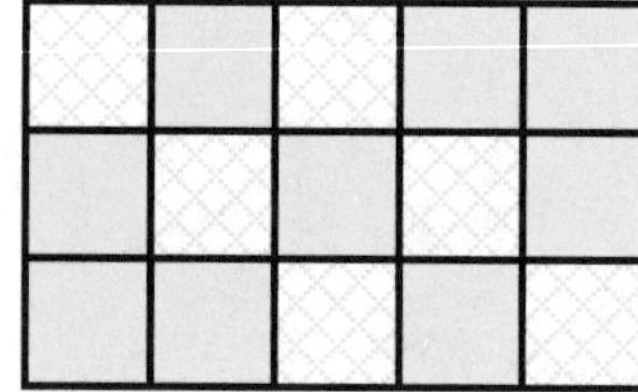

perimeter ______ area ______

8. What did you notice about the perimeter in problems 4, 5, 6 and 7?

____

9. On another sheet of paper, lay out, then sketch a quilt that has 30 blocks in it.
10. On another sheet of paper, lay out, then sketch a quilt that has a perimeter of 14 units.

Name ____________________

"State"istics

Choose ten states. Then, **research** their "lengths" and "heights" and **multiply** them to find their areas.

State Name	Approximate Miles E–W	Approximate Miles N–S	Area in Square Miles

Name ______________________

Turn Up the Volume

The **volume** is the measure of the inside of a shape. **Find** the volume of these shapes by counting the boxes. You might not be able to see all the boxes, but you can tell that they are there.

Example:

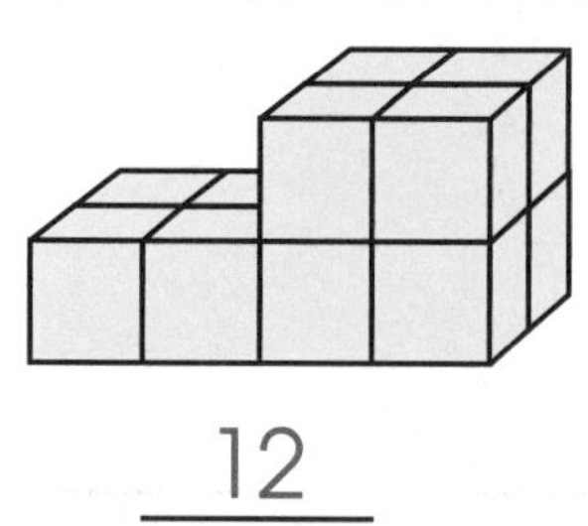

12

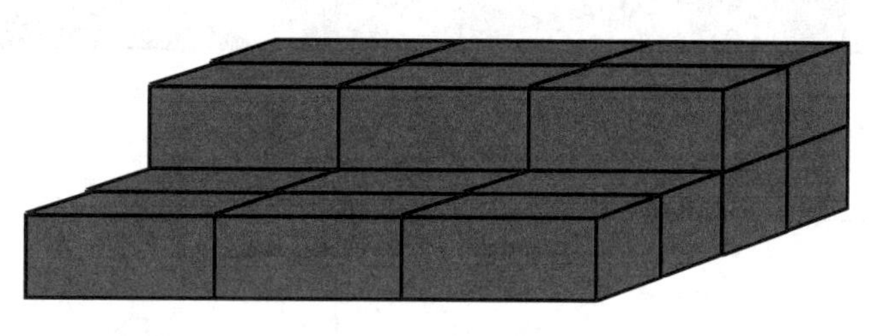

______ ______

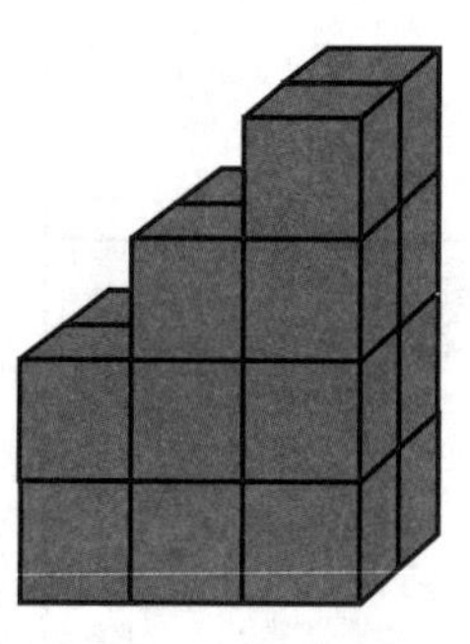

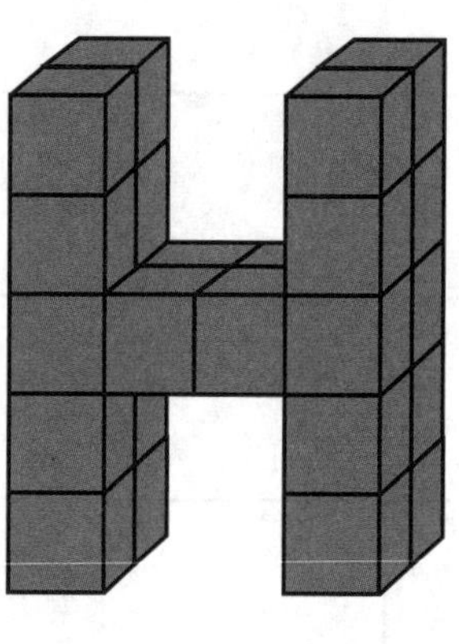

______ ______ ______

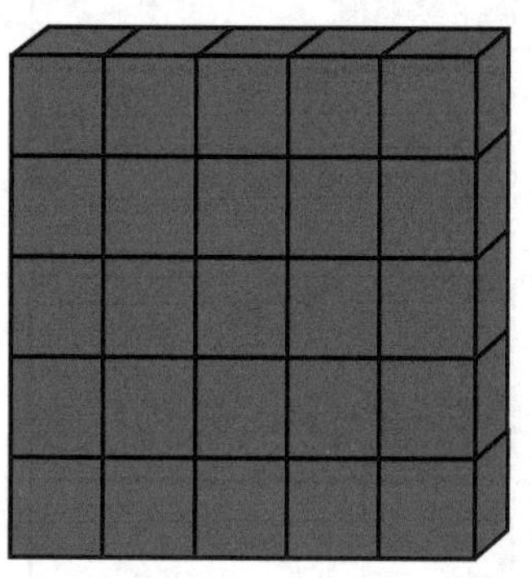

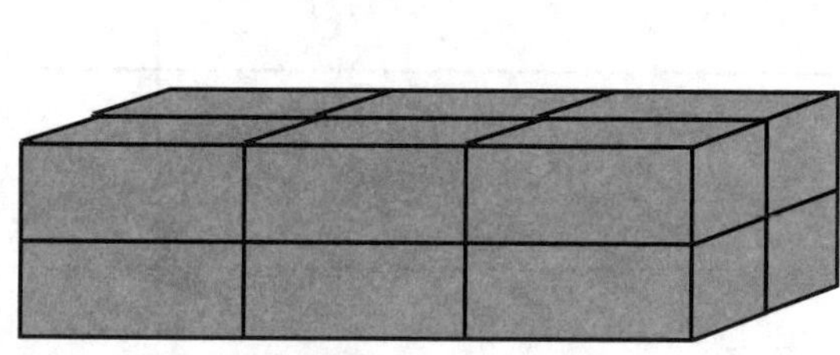

______ ______ ______

Name ______________________

How Much Can a Container Contain?

To find volume: Multiply length x width x height

1. Select four food boxes and draw and color one in each box below.
2. Measure the width, length and height (the sides) of each box and record it next to its picture.
3. Find the volume of each box and record it next to its picture.

H = ____
W = ____
L = ____

Name ______________________

Going in Circles

A **circle** is a round, closed figure. It is named by its center. A **radius** is a line segment from the center to any point on the circle. A **diameter** is a line segment with both points on the circle. The diameter always passes through the center of the circle.

Name the radius, diameter and circle.

Example:

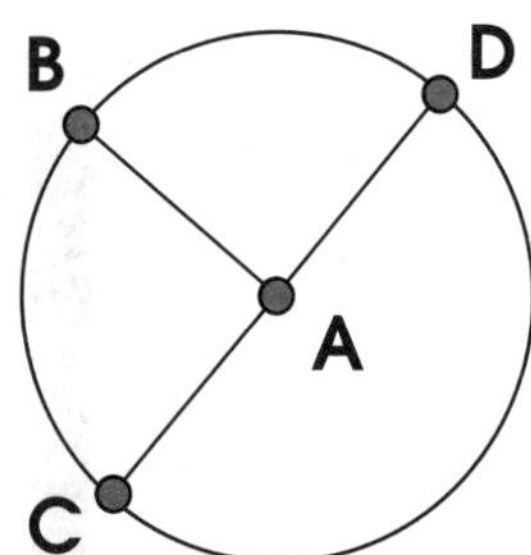

circle A

radius AB

diameter CD

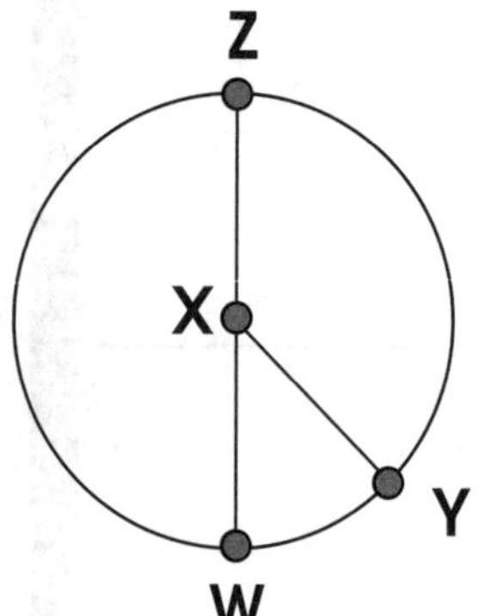

circle ______

radius ______

diameter ______

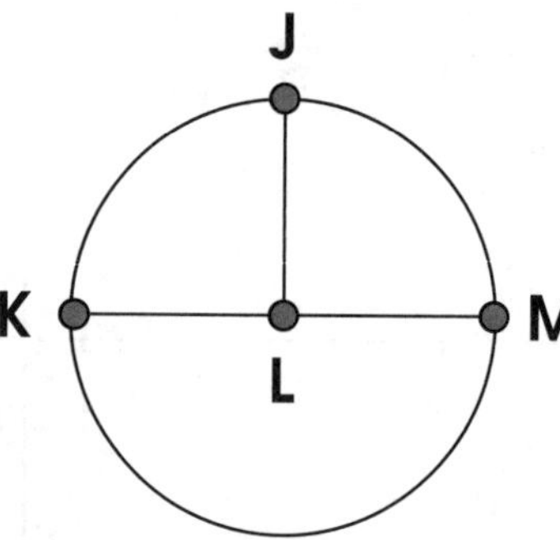

circle ______

radius ______

diameter ______

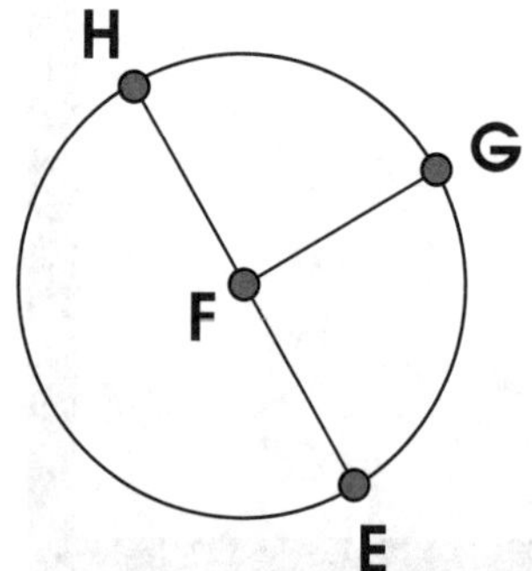

circle ______

radius ______

diameter ______

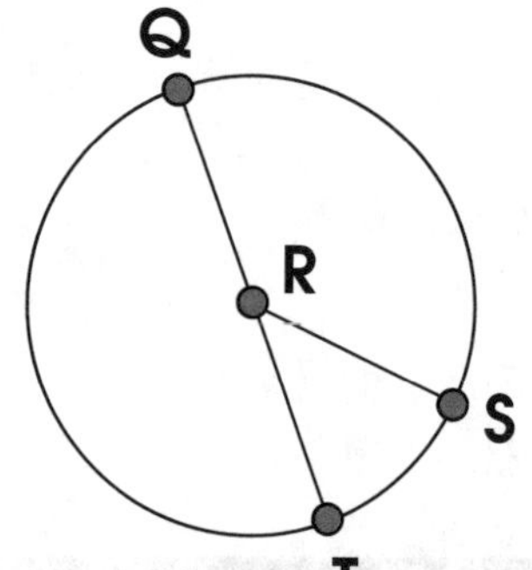

circle ______

radius ______

diameter ______

Name ____________________

Perfect Symmetry

A figure that can be separated into two matching parts is **symmetric**. The **line of symmetry** is the line that divides the shape in half.

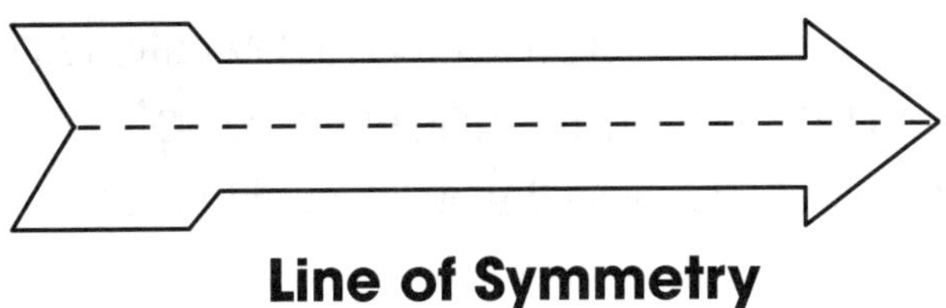

Line of Symmetry

Is the dotted line shown a line of symmetry?

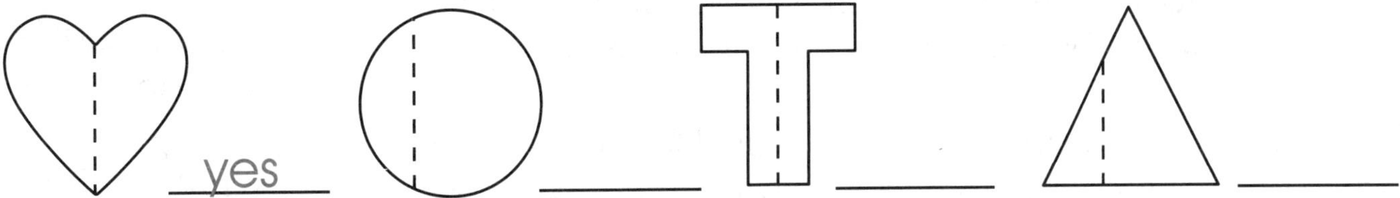

Draw each matching part.

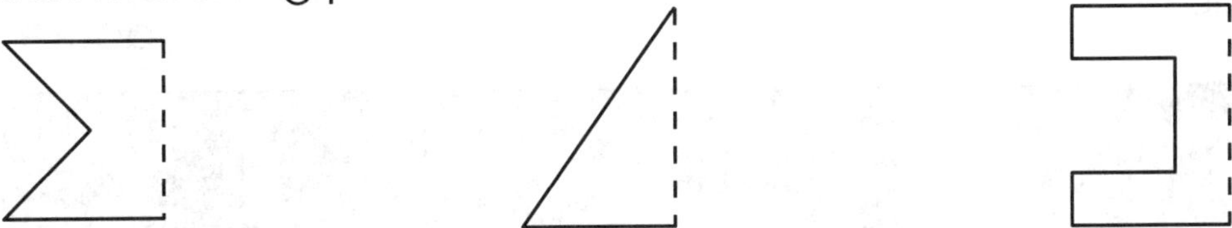

Complete the letters to make symmetric words.

Make two symmetric words of your own.

Name ____________________

Look at the World From a Different Angle

Lines come together in many different ways. The point where two lines meet is called an **angle**. You may have to look at the things around you in a different way to find these angles.

perpendicular

Use the table below to **record** your observations from around the house. Look for objects that illustrate each category on the chart. **Draw** a sketch of each object and **label** it. **Find** as many objects for each category as possible.

Challenge: Look around the house and find one object that illustrates all five geometric categories. Sketch the object and label the various types of angles, lines or shapes that it has.

acute

right	acute	obtuse	straight	perpendicular

Fractions

RECIPES

INGREDIENTS
1/4 NUTS
1/4 MOTOR OIL
1/4 BUTTONS
1/4 SCREWS

OIL

Name ____________________

Graham Cracker Denominator

Find a cracker. If possible, use one that has four pieces. Break your crackers into as many or as few pieces as desired but make each piece the same size.

With fractions, the number of pieces into which an object is broken is how the bottom number, the **denominator**, obtains its numerical value. Remember that you started with one cracker that is in pieces now. **Write** the number of pieces as a denominator.

☐ ← numerator
―
denominator → ☐

To determine the top number, the **numerator**, eat part of the cracker. In the diagram at the right, cross out the part you ate. This is the numerator.

Write two fractions—a fraction to show what is left and a fraction to show what was eaten.

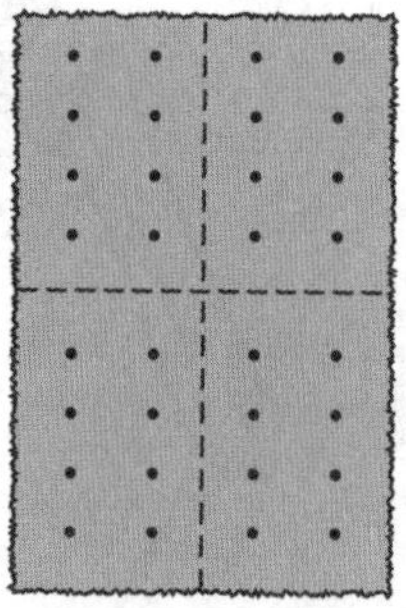

numerator ☐ / demoninator ☐ of the cracker is left. numerator ☐ / denominator ☐ of the cracker is gone.

Eat another piece of the cracker. **Cross out** the part you ate in the diagram. Now, **write** how much is left.

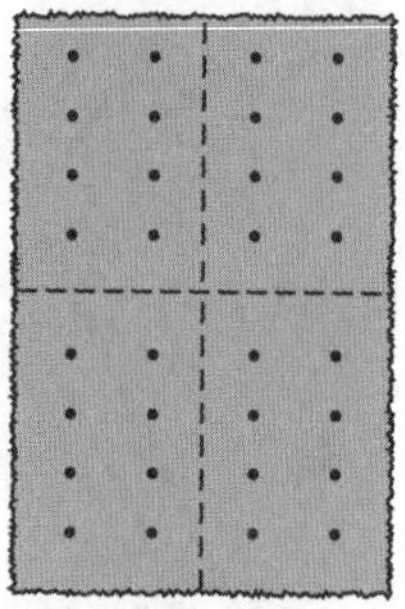

numerator ☐ / denominator ☐ of the cracker is left. numerator ☐ / denominator ☐ of the cracker is gone.

Eat another piece of the cracker. **Cross out** the part you ate in the diagram. Now, **write** how much is left.

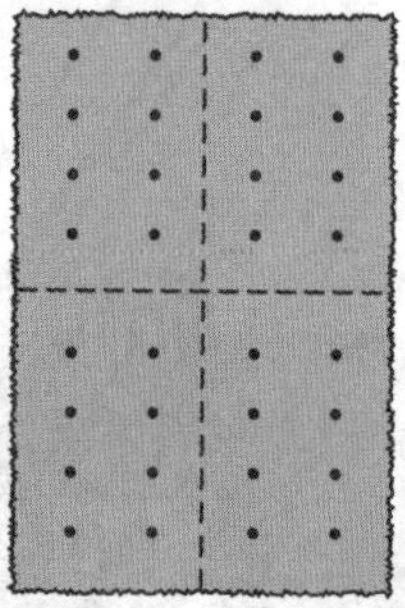

numerator ☐ / denominator ☐ of the cracker is left. numerator ☐ / denominator ☐ of the cracker is gone.

Which part changes, the numerator or the denominator?

Name ______________________________

What Fraction Am I?

Identify the fraction for each shaded section.

Example: There are 5 sections on this figure. 2 sections are shaded. 2/5 of the sections are shaded. 3 sections are not shaded. 3/5 of the sections are not shaded.

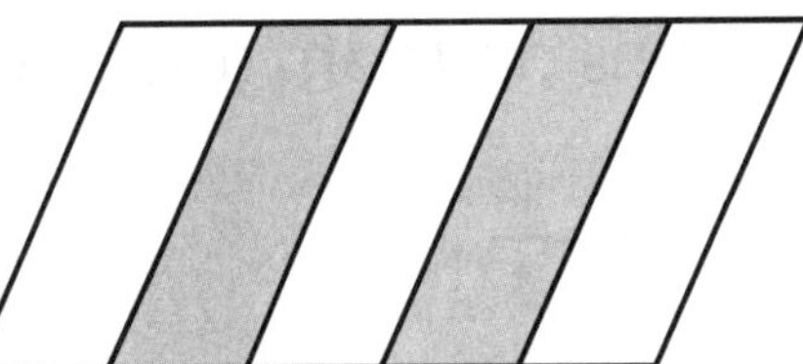

A. ________

B. ________

C. ________

D. ________

E. ________

F. ________

G. ________

H. ________

I. ________

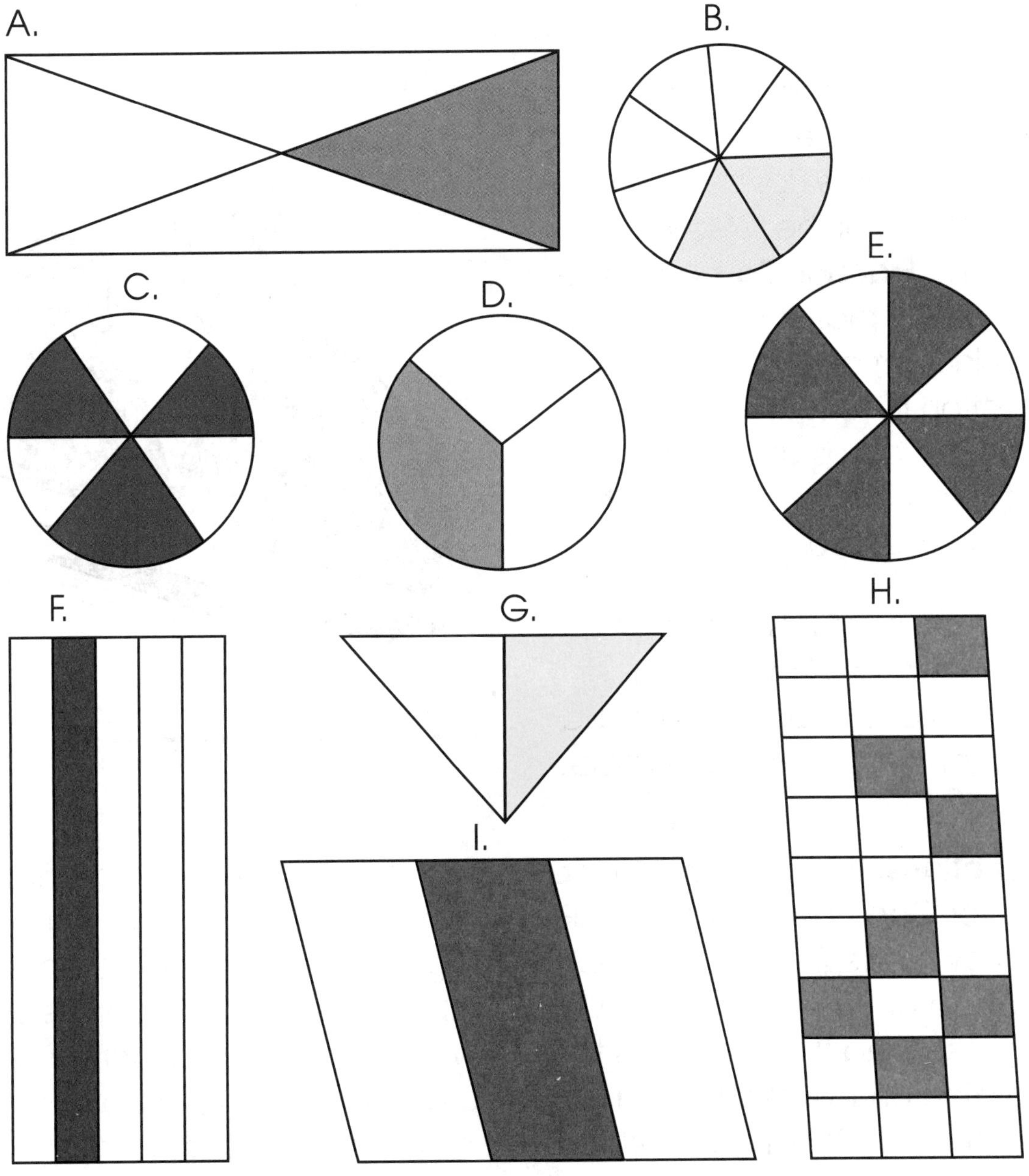

A.

B.

C.

D.

E.

F.

G.

H.

I.

Name ____________________

The Whole Thing

Preparation: Cut 14 index cards in half. Write three copies of the following fractions on them (one per card): $-\frac{1}{3}$, $+\frac{1}{3}$, $-\frac{1}{6}$, $+\frac{1}{6}$, $-\frac{1}{2}$, $+\frac{1}{2}$, $-\frac{1}{4}$, $+\frac{1}{4}$.

On four more cards, write $+\frac{1}{3}$, $+\frac{1}{6}$, $+\frac{1}{2}$, $+\frac{1}{4}$.

Rules: This game involves 2–4 players. Put the stack of fraction cards upside down in the middle of the playing area. Use the **Fraction Bars** on page 167. Each player puts a whole bar in front of him/her and the fraction bars to the side. Fraction cards are always returned to the bottom of the stack after use.

The object of this game is to build a whole bar using a set of fractions. Players may build as many as four sets at a time.

Directions: Player One draws a fraction card. If a minus card is drawn and Player One has no bar, then Player One loses his/her turn. If an addition card is drawn, the fraction bar representing the fraction named on the card is placed on the whole bar. When a subtraction fraction card is drawn, the bar representing the fraction is taken away. If no fraction bar representing the fraction on the minus card is placed above the bar, the player simply loses his/her turn. The first player to build a whole bar is the winner.

Name ______________________

Working With Fractions

Use the fraction bars to help you **find** the smallest fraction in each row. **Circle** it.

1. $\frac{1}{2}$ $\frac{2}{3}$ $\frac{1}{6}$ $\frac{1}{3}$
2. $\frac{2}{3}$ $\frac{2}{6}$ $\frac{3}{3}$ $\frac{3}{6}$
3. $\frac{2}{2}$ $\frac{3}{6}$ $\frac{2}{3}$ $\frac{1}{3}$
4. $\frac{5}{6}$ $\frac{4}{6}$ $\frac{1}{2}$ $\frac{2}{3}$
5. $\frac{6}{6}$ $\frac{2}{3}$ $\frac{5}{6}$ $\frac{2}{2}$

1 Whole					
$\frac{1}{2}$			$\frac{2}{2}$		
$\frac{1}{3}$		$\frac{2}{3}$		$\frac{3}{3}$	
$\frac{1}{6}$	$\frac{2}{6}$	$\frac{3}{6}$	$\frac{4}{6}$	$\frac{5}{6}$	$\frac{6}{6}$

Use the fraction bars to help you **find** the greatest fraction in each row. **Circle** it.

1 Whole							
$\frac{1}{2}$				$\frac{2}{2}$			
$\frac{1}{4}$		$\frac{2}{4}$		$\frac{3}{4}$		$\frac{4}{4}$	
$\frac{1}{8}$	$\frac{2}{8}$	$\frac{3}{8}$	$\frac{4}{8}$	$\frac{5}{8}$	$\frac{6}{8}$	$\frac{7}{8}$	$\frac{8}{8}$

1. $\frac{1}{2}$ $\frac{3}{4}$ $\frac{6}{8}$ $\frac{8}{8}$
2. $\frac{1}{4}$ $\frac{1}{8}$ $\frac{7}{8}$ $\frac{1}{2}$
3. $\frac{1}{8}$ $\frac{1}{2}$ $\frac{1}{4}$ $\frac{2}{8}$
4. $\frac{1}{4}$ $\frac{3}{8}$ $\frac{5}{8}$ $\frac{3}{4}$
5. $\frac{2}{8}$ $\frac{1}{8}$ $\frac{1}{4}$ $\frac{6}{8}$

Name ____________________

More Fractions

Compare the fractions below. **Write** < or > in each box.

Examples:

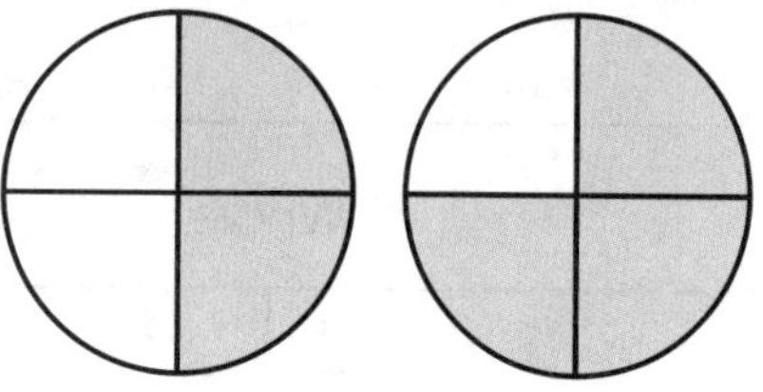

$\frac{2}{4}$ [<] $\frac{3}{4}$

less than

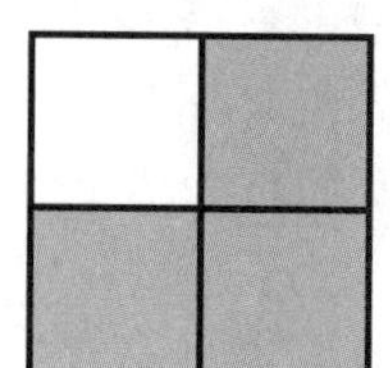 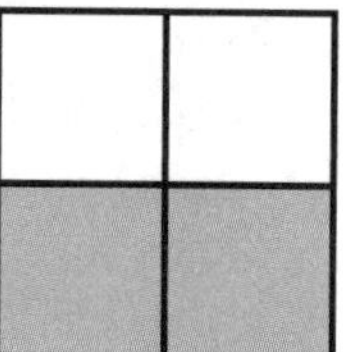

$\frac{3}{4}$ [>] $\frac{2}{4}$

greater than

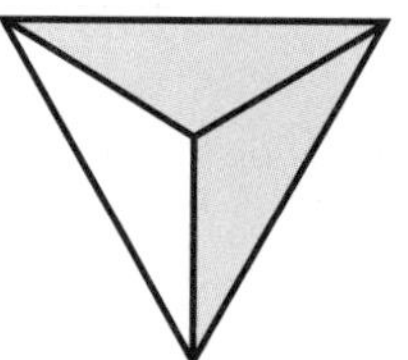 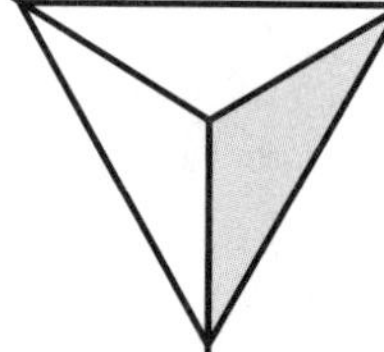

$\frac{2}{3}$ ☐ $\frac{1}{3}$

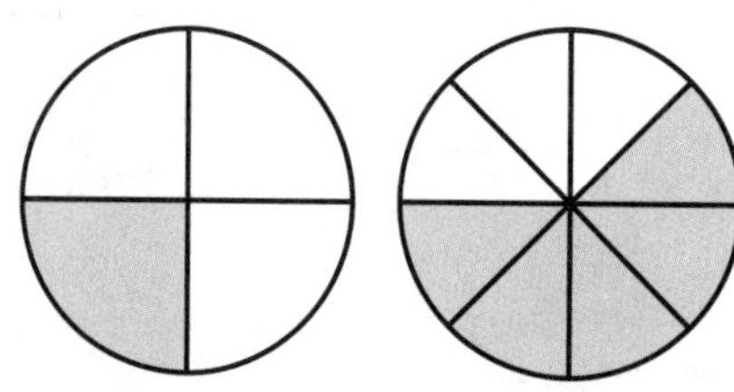

$\frac{1}{4}$ ☐ $\frac{5}{8}$

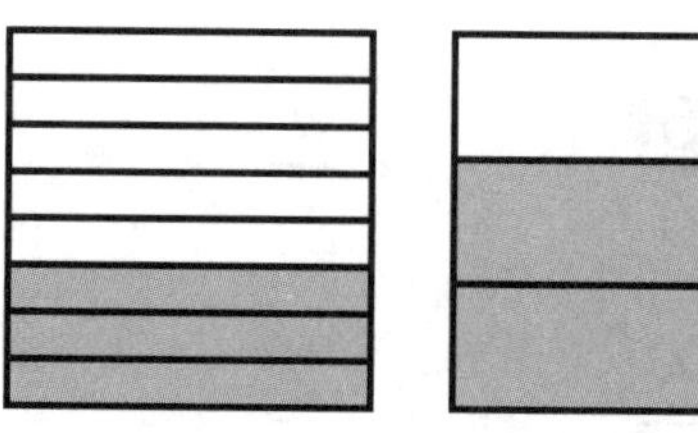

$\frac{3}{8}$ ☐ $\frac{2}{3}$

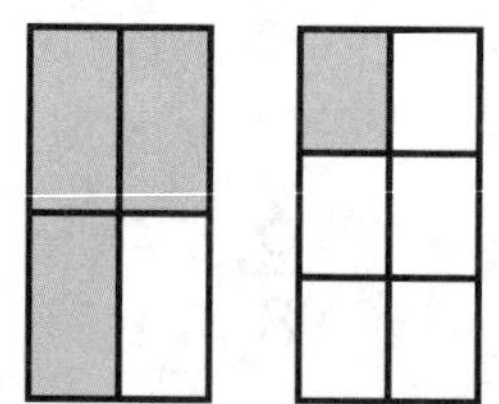

$\frac{3}{4}$ ☐ $\frac{1}{6}$

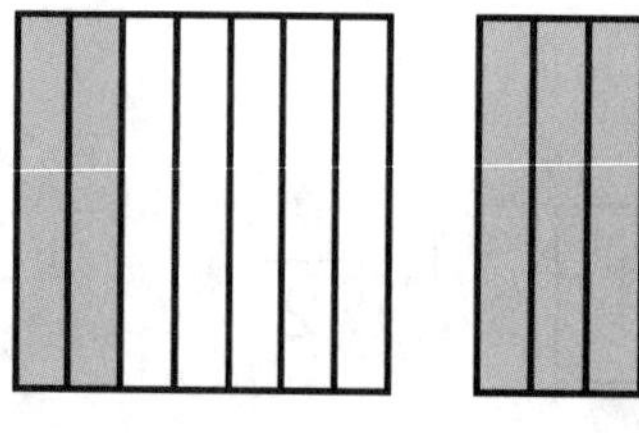

$\frac{2}{7}$ ☐ $\frac{4}{7}$

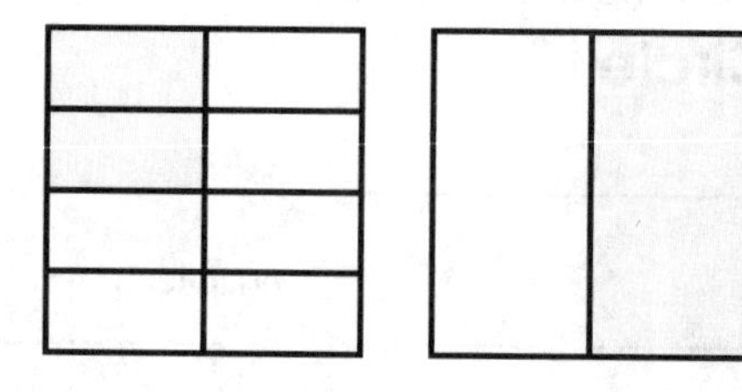

$\frac{2}{8}$ ☐ $\frac{1}{2}$

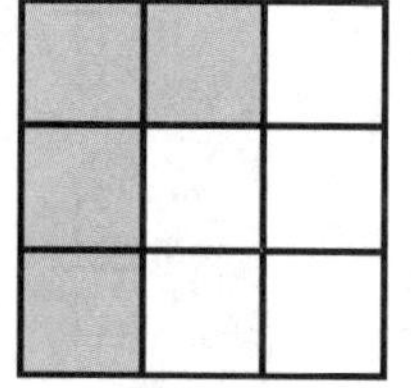

$\frac{4}{9}$ ☐ $\frac{2}{3}$

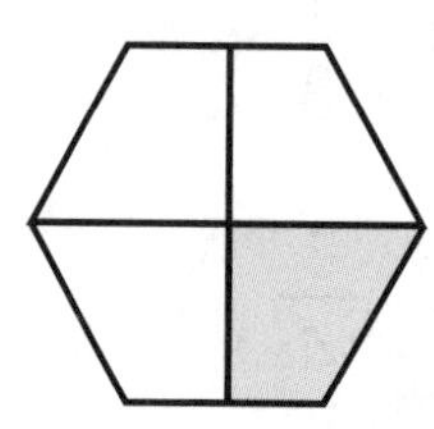

$\frac{1}{4}$ ☐ $\frac{3}{6}$

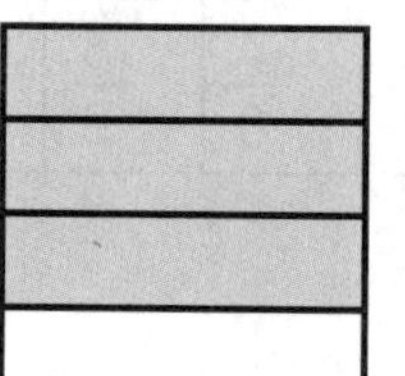 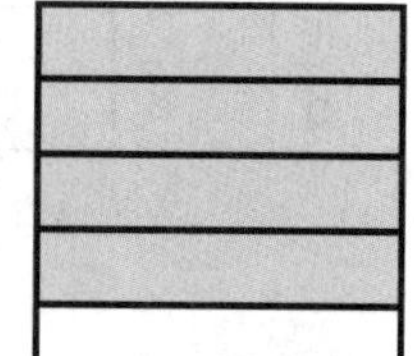

$\frac{3}{4}$ ☐ $\frac{4}{5}$

Name ______________________

Exploring Equivalent Fractions

Equivalent fractions are two different fractions which represent the same number. For example, on page 172, the picture shows that 1/2 and 3/6 are the same or equivalent fractions.

Complete these equivalent fractions. **Use** your fraction bars.

1. $\frac{1}{3} = \frac{}{6}$ 2. $\frac{1}{2} = \frac{}{4}$ 3. $\frac{3}{4} = \frac{}{8}$ 4. $\frac{1}{3} = \frac{}{9}$

Circle the figure that shows a fraction equivalent to the first figure. **Write** the fractions for the shaded area under each figure.

5. 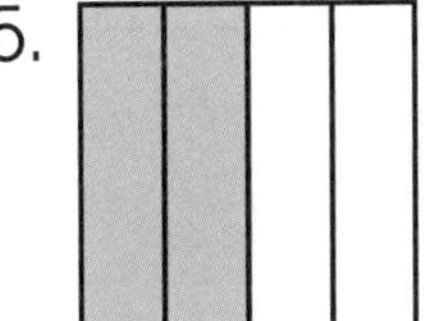 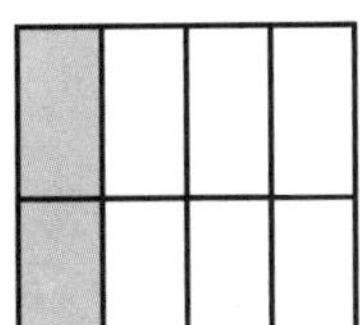 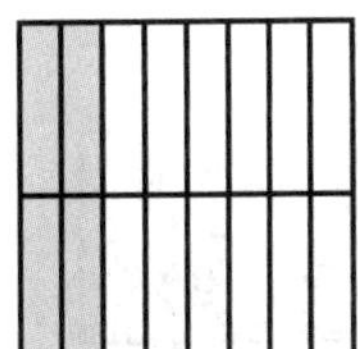 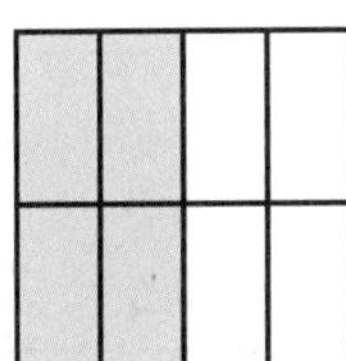

______ ______ ______ ______

6. 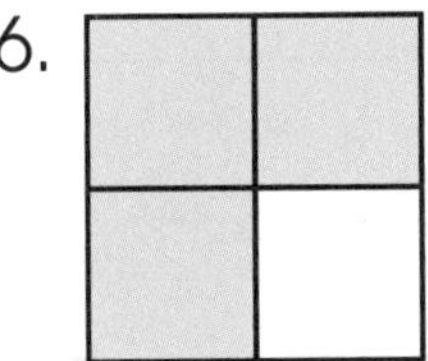 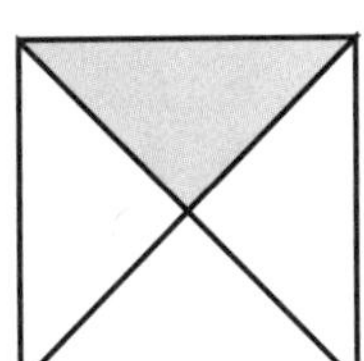 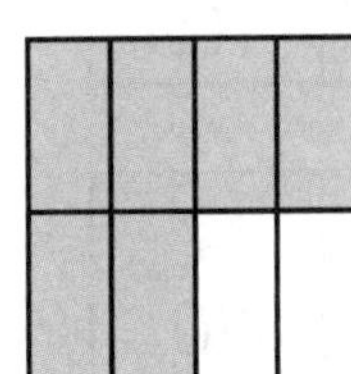 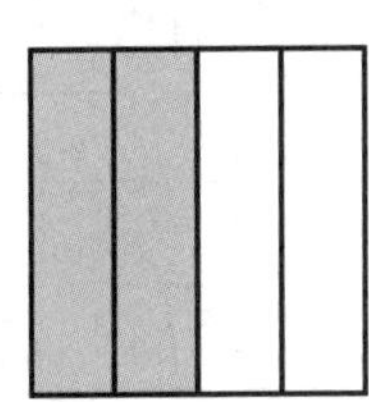

______ ______ ______ ______

Write two equivalent fractions for each fraction.

7. $\frac{1}{4}$, ___, ___ 8. $\frac{1}{5}$, ___, ___ 9. $\frac{2}{3}$, ___, ___ 10. $\frac{3}{8}$, ___, ___

To find an equivalent fraction, **multiply** both parts of the fraction by the same number.

Example: $\frac{2}{3} \times \frac{3}{3} = \frac{6}{9}$

11. $\frac{1}{4} = \frac{}{8}$ 12. $\frac{3}{4} = \frac{}{8}$ 13. $\frac{4}{5} = \frac{8}{}$ 14. $\frac{3}{8} = \frac{}{24}$

Name ______________________

Fraction Patterns

Each row contains equivalent fractions except for one. **Find** which three fractions are equivalent for each row.
Draw an **X** on the fraction that is not equivalent. On the line, **write** a fraction that could be in the set. If necessary, **draw** a picture to help.

Example:

$\frac{1}{2}$	$\frac{2}{4}$	$\frac{3}{5}$ (crossed out)	$\frac{4}{8}$

$\frac{\text{Numerator (N) x 2}}{\text{Denominator (D) x 2}}$

New Fraction: $\frac{8}{16}$

New Fraction

1.

$\frac{1}{8}$	$\frac{2}{16}$	$\frac{2}{24}$	$\frac{4}{32}$

____

2.

$\frac{3}{4}$	$\frac{6}{8}$	$\frac{12}{16}$	$\frac{20}{30}$

____

3.

$\frac{3}{10}$	$\frac{9}{30}$	$\frac{27}{90}$	$\frac{36}{180}$

____

4.

$\frac{1}{5}$	$\frac{3}{10}$	$\frac{3}{15}$	$\frac{4}{20}$

____

5.

$\frac{3}{7}$	$\frac{6}{14}$	$\frac{8}{21}$	$\frac{12}{28}$

____

6.

$\frac{1}{2}$	$\frac{4}{8}$	$\frac{16}{32}$	$\frac{62}{128}$

____

7.

$\frac{5}{8}$	$\frac{9}{16}$	$\frac{15}{24}$	$\frac{20}{32}$

____

Write a rule to find equivalent fractions.

____

Name ____________________

More Than Peanuts

Write <, >, or = to compare the fractions below. **Draw** pictures or **write** equivalent fractions, if needed.

$\frac{3}{8}$ □ $\frac{2}{8}$ $\frac{2}{3}$ □ $\frac{3}{6}$ $\frac{3}{6}$ □ $\frac{1}{2}$

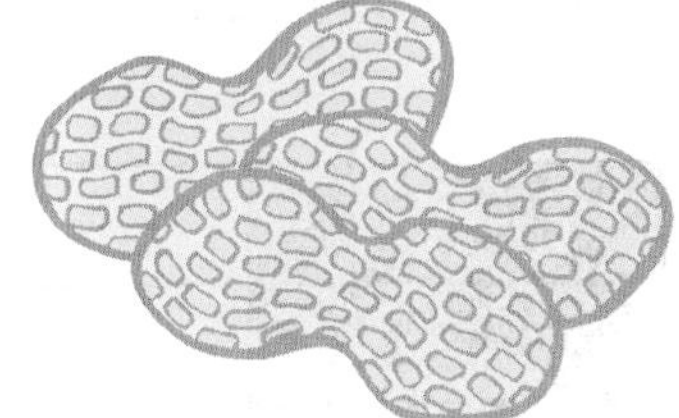

$\frac{4}{7}$ □ $\frac{4}{14}$ $\frac{1}{3}$ □ $\frac{6}{9}$ $\frac{7}{10}$ □ $\frac{2}{5}$

$\frac{8}{12}$ □ $\frac{3}{6}$ $\frac{7}{14}$ □ $\frac{1}{2}$ $\frac{4}{7}$ □ $\frac{3}{7}$ $\frac{4}{8}$ □ $\frac{8}{16}$

$\frac{1}{3}$ □ $\frac{2}{6}$ $\frac{2}{8}$ □ $\frac{1}{2}$ $\frac{1}{5}$ □ $\frac{3}{10}$ $\frac{6}{11}$ □ $\frac{5}{11}$

$\frac{6}{12}$ □ $\frac{1}{2}$ $\frac{2}{3}$ □ $\frac{2}{6}$ $\frac{7}{12}$ □ $\frac{2}{4}$ $\frac{5}{6}$ □ $\frac{1}{3}$

$\frac{7}{10}$ □ $\frac{3}{10}$ $\frac{1}{2}$ □ $\frac{8}{12}$ $\frac{1}{5}$ □ $\frac{8}{10}$ $\frac{7}{8}$ □ $\frac{2}{4}$

$\frac{3}{8}$ □ $\frac{1}{4}$ $\frac{2}{5}$ □ $\frac{5}{10}$

$\frac{5}{6}$ □ $\frac{2}{3}$ $\frac{6}{10}$ □ $\frac{2}{5}$

$\frac{6}{10}$ □ $\frac{3}{10}$ $\frac{3}{6}$ □ $\frac{6}{12}$

$\frac{1}{8}$ □ $\frac{1}{4}$ $\frac{1}{2}$ □ $\frac{1}{4}$

Name ______________________

Reduce, Reduce

To reduce a fraction, **divide** each number in the fraction by a common factor. A fraction is reduced when the numerator and the denominator have only a common factor of 1. This is called a fraction's **lowest terms**.

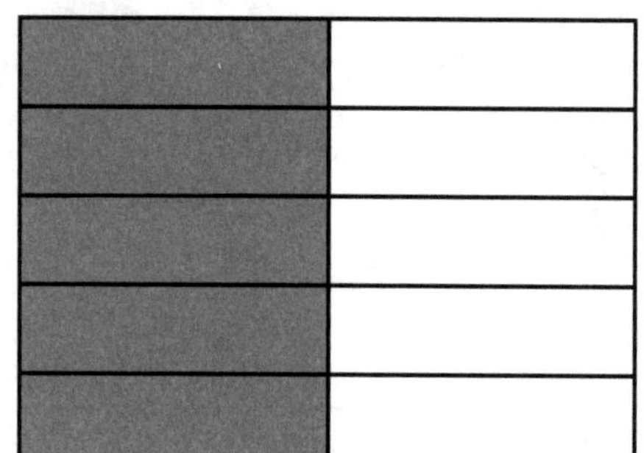

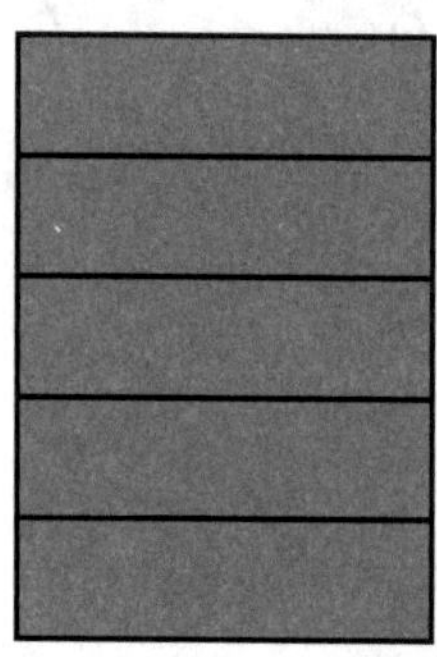

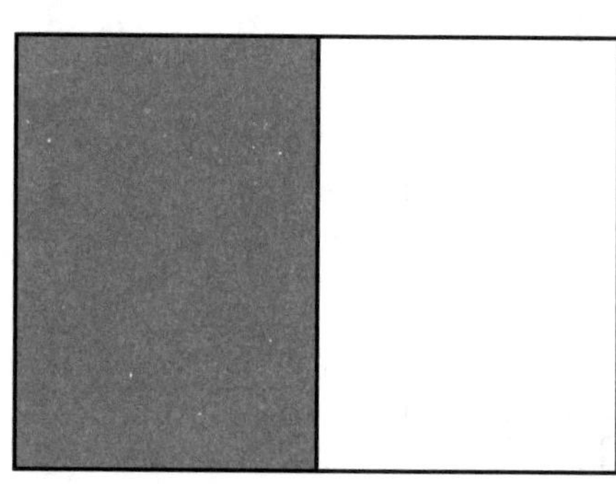

$$\frac{5}{10} \div \frac{5}{5} = \frac{1}{2}$$

5 is a common factor of 5 and 10. (It can be divided into groups of five.) Is there another number these both can be divided by? (Only the number 1.)

Example: $\frac{16}{20} \div \frac{2}{2} = \frac{8}{10}$ **Ask:** Is this the lowest? Is there another number these both can be divided by? (Yes, 2.)

$\frac{8}{10} \div \frac{2}{2} = \frac{4}{5}$ Can this still divided by a common number? (No.)

Reduce these fractions.

$\frac{9}{12} =$ $\frac{3}{15} =$ $\frac{12}{16} =$ $\frac{4}{5} =$ $\frac{2}{8} =$

$\frac{1}{8} =$ $\frac{4}{6} =$ $\frac{3}{9} =$ $\frac{7}{14} =$ $\frac{18}{24} =$

Name ______________________

Mix 'Em Up

A **mixed number** is a whole number with a fraction.

Example: $1\frac{2}{3}$ 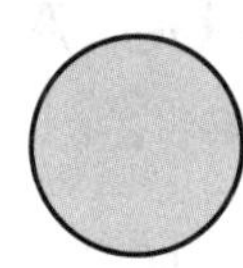 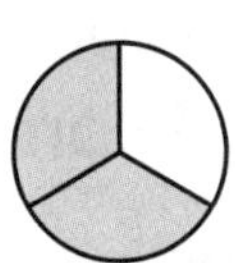

An **improper fraction** is a fraction representing a whole and a fraction. The numerator is larger than the denominator.

Example: $\frac{16}{3}$ 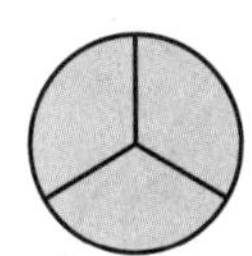   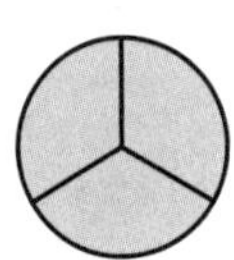 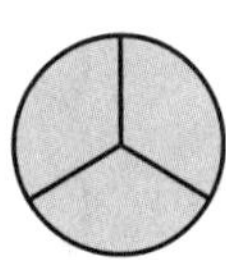 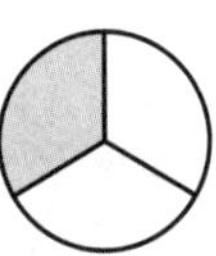

To change a mixed number to an improper fraction, **multiply** the whole number by the denominator.

Example: $2\frac{3}{4}$ 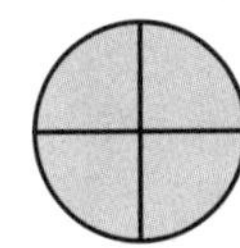 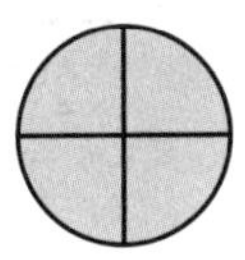 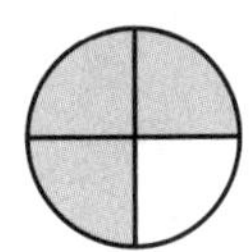 $2 \times 4 = 8$ (How many fourths?)

Add the numerator to that number. $8 + 3 = 11$

Write the fraction with the resulting number as numerator over the original denominator. $\frac{11}{4}$

$1\frac{1}{3} =$ $3\frac{2}{5} =$ $4\frac{3}{4} =$ $2\frac{2}{7} =$

To change an improper fraction to a mixed number, **divide** the numerator by the denominator. $\frac{10}{3}$

(How many wholes can be made?) $3\overline{)10}$ = 3 R1

Write the quotient as the whole number and **write** any remainder as a fraction (with the denominator from the original problem).

$3\frac{1}{3} =$

$\frac{5}{2} =$ $\frac{7}{6} =$ $\frac{4}{3} =$ $\frac{10}{4} =$

Name ____________________

Oh, My!

When the numerator is greater than the denominator (an improper fraction), write a mixed number or divide to write a whole number. A mixed number is made up of a whole number and a fraction. **Example:** $2\frac{1}{2}$

Draw the correct mouths on the animals by finding the whole or mixed number for each.

Example:

$\frac{11}{2} =$

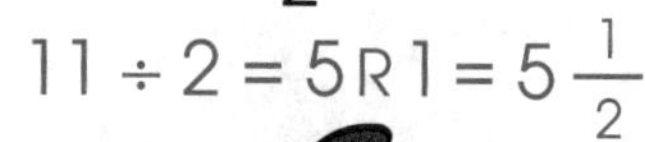

$11 \div 2 = 5R1 = 5\frac{1}{2}$

$\frac{20}{3}$

$\frac{21}{7}$

$\frac{24}{2}$

$\frac{16}{2}$

$\frac{49}{7}$

$\frac{16}{16}$

$\frac{16}{6}$

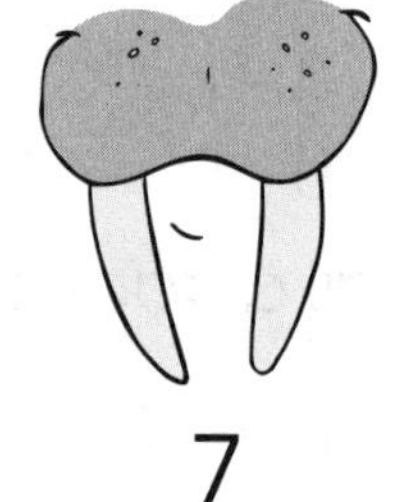

7

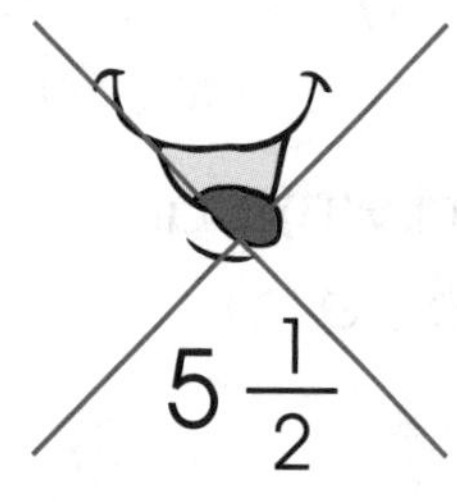

$5\frac{1}{2}$

$2\frac{4}{6}$

$6\frac{2}{3}$

3

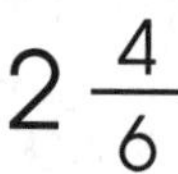

8

1

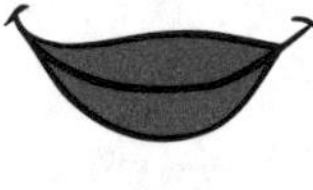

12

Sea Math

Reduce each sum to a whole number or a mixed number in the lowest terms.

$\frac{6}{9} + \frac{6}{9}$

$\frac{4}{5} + \frac{6}{5}$

$\frac{3}{4} + \frac{2}{4}$

$\frac{8}{11} + \frac{8}{11}$

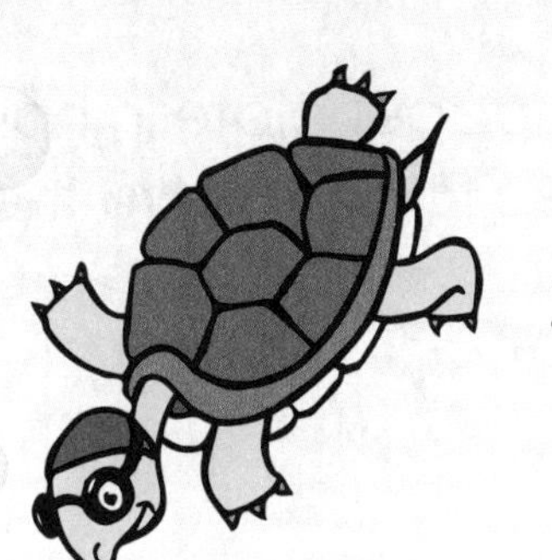

$\frac{2}{5} + \frac{3}{5}$

$\frac{8}{9} + \frac{3}{9}$

$\frac{4}{8} + \frac{6}{8}$

$\frac{5}{4} + \frac{2}{4}$

$\frac{4}{3} + \frac{2}{3}$

$\frac{5}{7} + \frac{6}{7}$

$\frac{8}{11} + \frac{3}{11}$

$\frac{3}{12} + \frac{10}{12}$

$\frac{3}{6} + \frac{3}{6}$

$\frac{6}{12} + \frac{8}{12}$

$\frac{4}{8} + \frac{4}{8}$

$\frac{5}{12} + \frac{8}{12}$

$\frac{5}{12} + \frac{10}{12}$

$\frac{7}{13} + \frac{6}{13}$

$\frac{8}{15} + \frac{14}{15}$

$\frac{5}{7} + \frac{6}{7}$

Name ____________________

Finding a Common Denominator

When adding or subtracting fractions with different denominators, find a common denominator first. A **common denominator** is a common multiple of two or more denominators.

Cut a paper plate in half. **Cut** another paper plate into eighths. Use these models to help **solve** the following addition and subtraction problems.

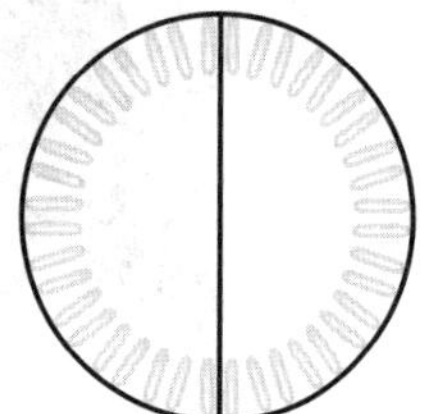

$\frac{1}{2} + \frac{2}{8} =$ The common denominator is 8 because 2 x 4 = 8; 8 x 1 = 8.

$\frac{1}{2} \times \frac{4}{4} = \frac{4}{8}$ $\qquad$ $\frac{4}{8} + \frac{2}{8} = \frac{6}{8}$

$\frac{7}{8} - \frac{1}{2} =$ The common denominator is 8 because 1 x 4 = 8; 2 x 4 = 8.

$\frac{7}{8} - \frac{4}{8} = \frac{3}{8}$

To find a common denominator of two or more fractions, follow these steps:

1. Write equivalent fractions so that the fractions have the same denominator.
2. Write the fractions with the same denominator.

Example:	Step 1	Step 2
$\frac{1}{2} + \frac{2}{6} =$	$\frac{1}{2} \times \frac{3}{3} = \frac{3}{6}$	$\frac{3}{6} + \frac{2}{6} = \frac{5}{6}$

Follow the steps above. Then, **add**. **Reduce** the answer to its lowest terms.

$\frac{5}{9} + \frac{1}{3} =$ $\qquad$ $\frac{3}{8} - \frac{1}{4} =$

$\frac{1}{3} + \frac{5}{12} =$ $\qquad$ $\frac{5}{12} - \frac{1}{6} =$

Name ____________________

Make a Wish

Solve these problems.

Example: $\frac{2}{9}$ of 27 = 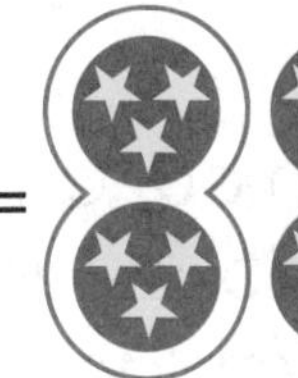    (27 ÷ 9) x 2 = 6

$\frac{7}{8}$ of 16 = $\frac{3}{7}$ of 49 = $\frac{4}{6}$ of 60 = $\frac{3}{6}$ of 54 =

$\frac{6}{8}$ of 24 = $\frac{9}{12}$ of 36 = $\frac{9}{12}$ of 24 = $\frac{2}{5}$ of 25 =

$\frac{3}{8}$ of 32 = $\frac{5}{7}$ of 42 = $\frac{3}{4}$ of 48 =

$\frac{3}{7}$ of 35 = $\frac{7}{9}$ of 36 =

$\frac{6}{8}$ of 64 = $\frac{8}{9}$ of 81 =

$\frac{3}{6}$ of 24 = $\frac{5}{6}$ of 30 =

$\frac{9}{10}$ of 40 = $\frac{6}{8}$ of 72 =

$\frac{9}{11}$ of 33 = $\frac{3}{8}$ of 48 =

Name ______________________________

Picture the Problem

Use the picture to **solve** each problem.

1. Andy had two ropes of the same length. He cut one rope into 2 equal parts and gave the 2 halves to Bill. The other rope he cut into fourths and gave 2 of the fourths to Sue. Circle who got the most rope.

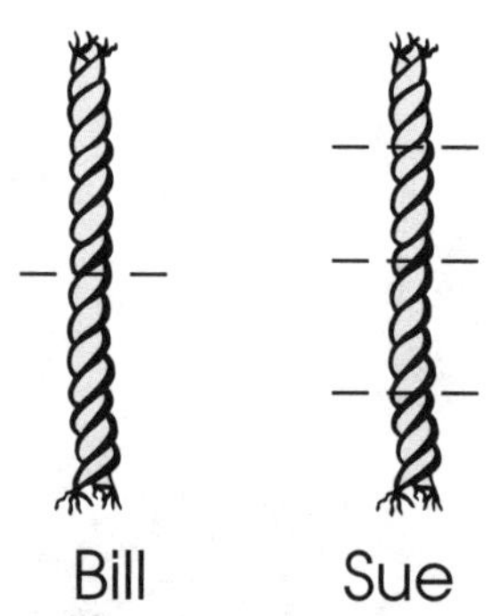

2. Mr. Johns built an office building with an aisle down the middle. He divided one side into 6 equal spaces. He divided the other side into 9 equal spaces. The Ace Company rented 5 of the ninths. The Best Company rented 4 of the sixths. Circle which company rented the larger space.

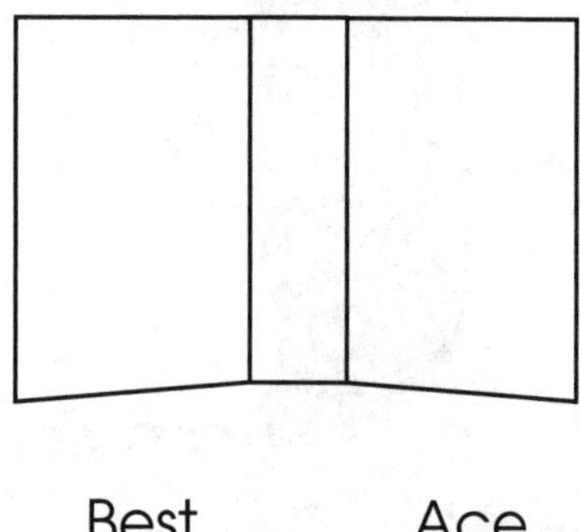

3. Hannah cut an 8-foot log into 4 equal pieces and burned 2 of them in the fireplace. Joseph cut an 8-foot log into 8 equal pieces and put 3 of them in the fireplace. Circle who put the most wood in the fireplace.

4. The 4-H Club display area at the state fair was divided into 2 equal areas. One of these sections had 12 booths, the other had 9 booths. The flower display covered 2 of the ninths, and the melon display covered 4 of the twelfths. Circle which display had the most room.

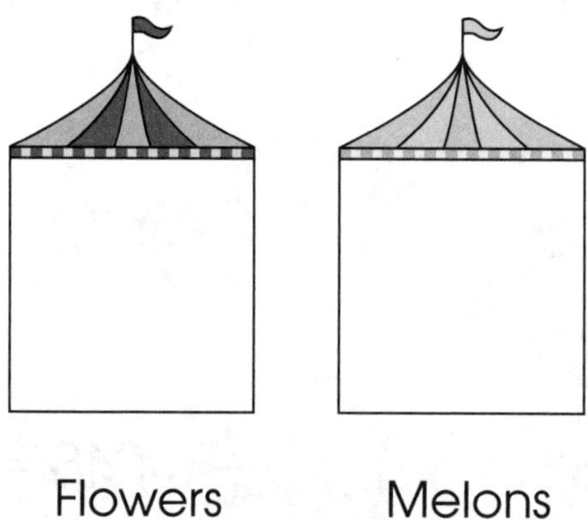

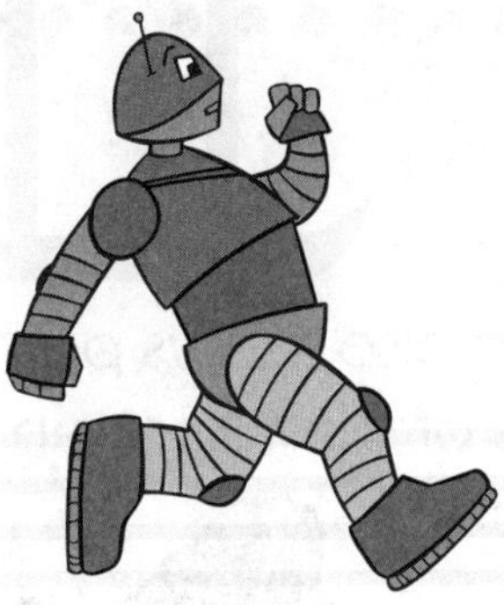

Section 8

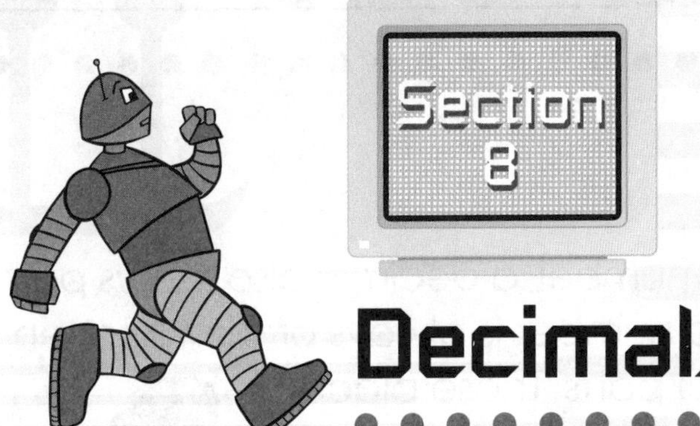

Decimals

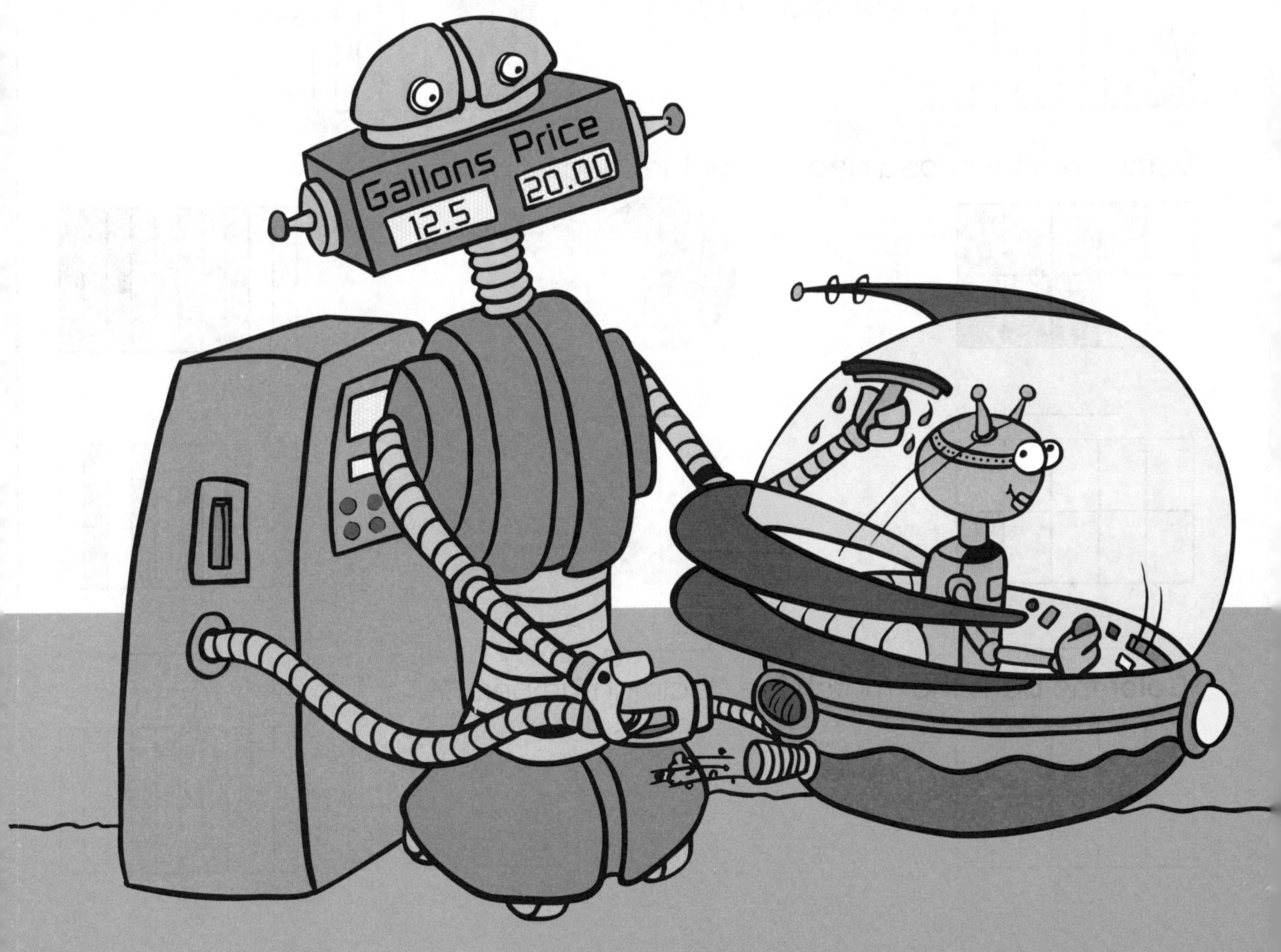

Name ______________________________

Doing Decimals

Just as a fraction stands for part of a whole number, a decimal also shows part of a whole number. And with decimals, the number is always broken into ten or a power of ten (hundred, thousand, etc.) parts. These place values are named tenths, hundredths, thousandths, etc.

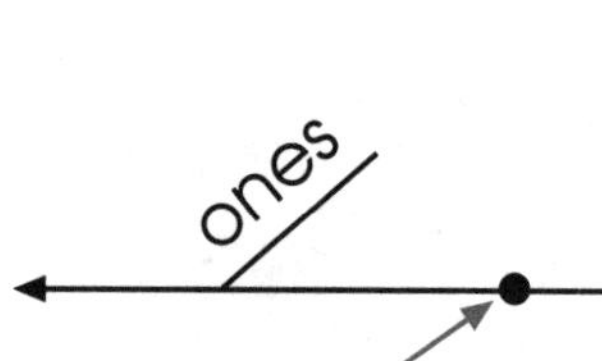

tenths hundredths thousandths

A **decimal point** is a dot placed between the ones place and the tenths place.

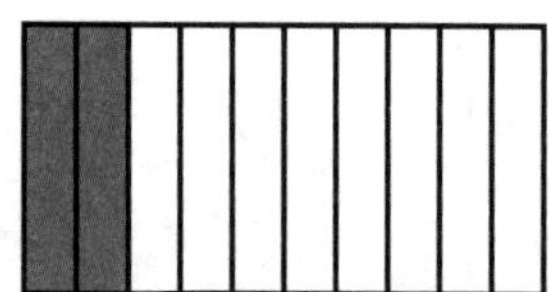

0.2 is read as "two tenths."

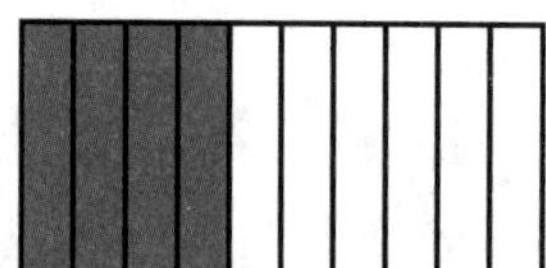

0.4 is four tenths

Write the answer as a decimal for the shaded parts.

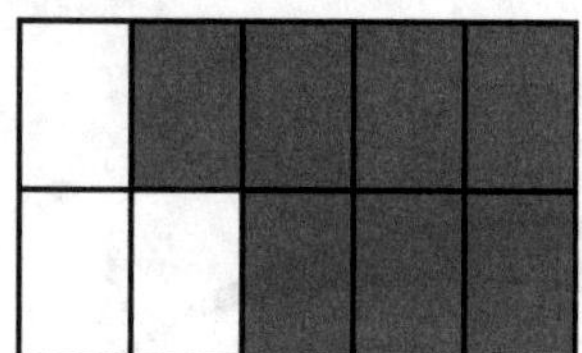

______

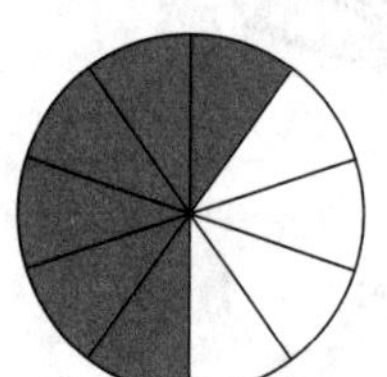

______

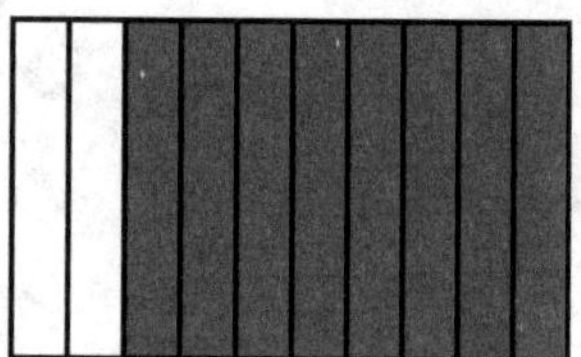

______

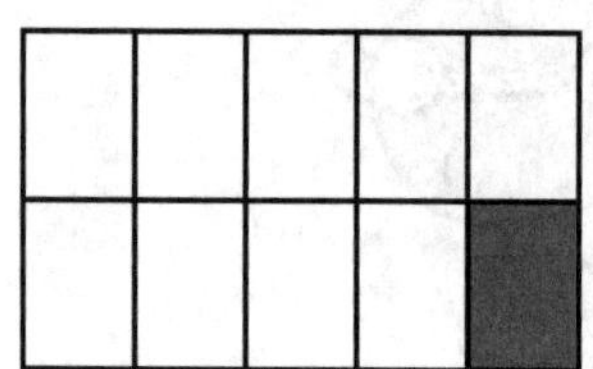

______

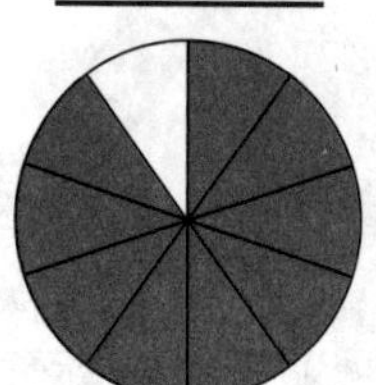

______

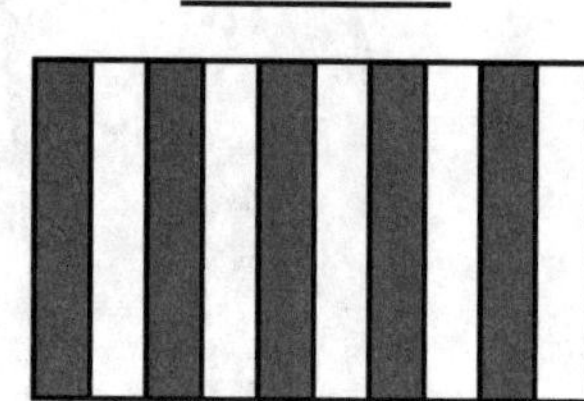

______

Color the parts that match the decimal numbers.

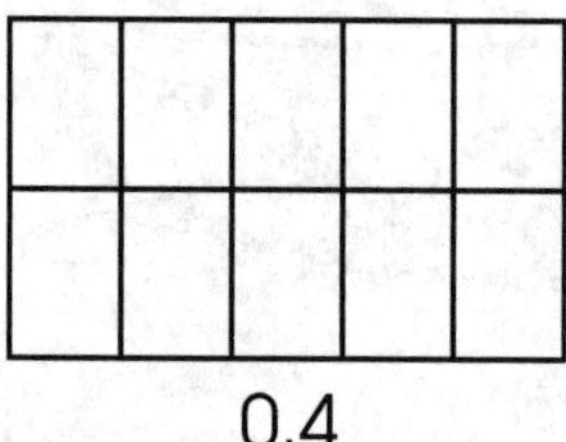

0.4

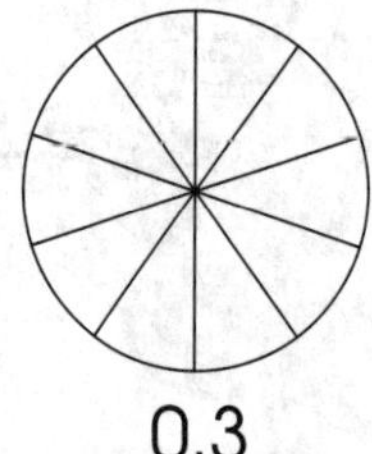

0.3

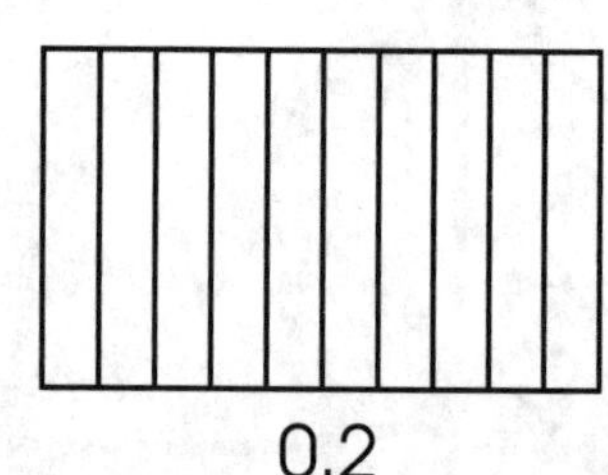

0.2

Name ______________________________

Decimal Fun

The **Hundredth Picture Grid** on page 94 is divided into one hundred parts.

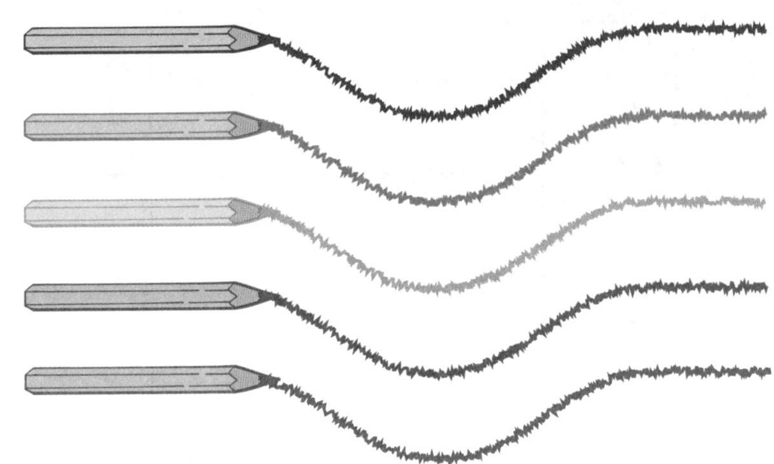

Use colored pencils to **draw** a picture of a person, animal or object on the grid. Give it a title which includes how many hundredths are colored in the drawing.

Example: "The 0.46 Flying Bird" or "A 0.82 Scuba Diver," etc.

To practice decimals, play this game with a friend.

Preparation: On index cards, write decimals in written form, such as six tenths. Then, write the decimal numbers on back.

Directions: Player One holds up either side of a card or says a decimal. Player Two writes the decimal or the words for the decimal on a sheet of paper. Player One checks his/her answer. Then, the players switch roles.

Name ______________________________

Hundredth Picture Grid

Name ____________________

Decimal Divisions

Decimals are often used with whole numbers.

Examples: 2.8

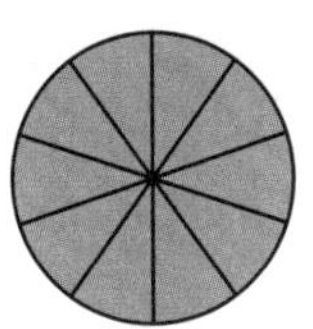
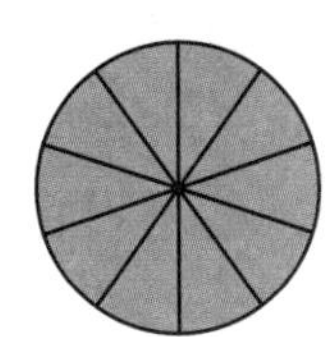
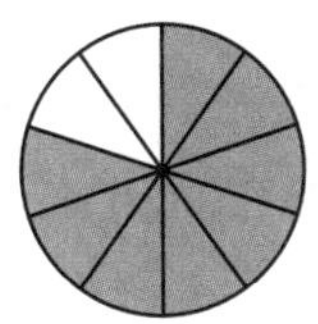

3.5

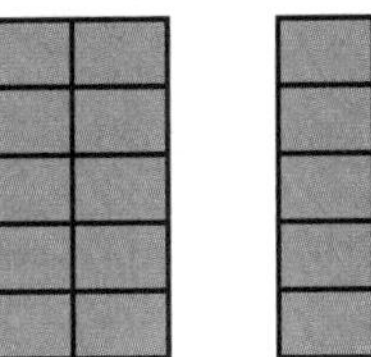
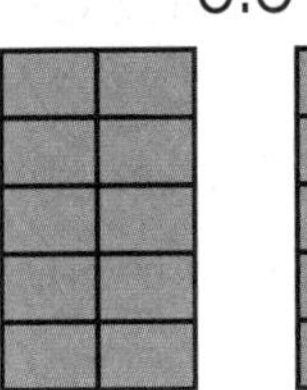
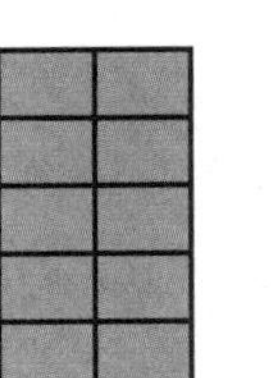
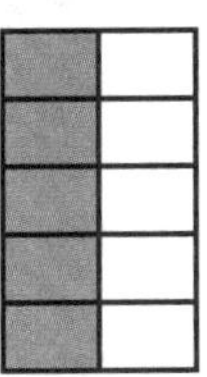

Write the decimal for each picture.

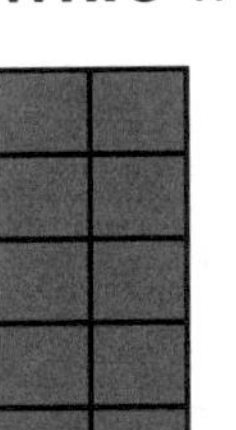
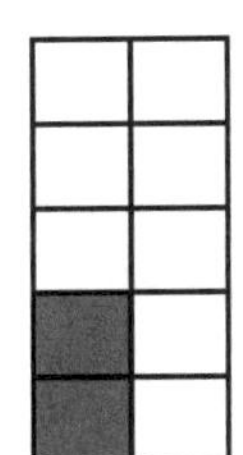
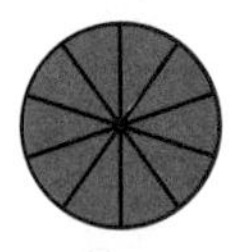
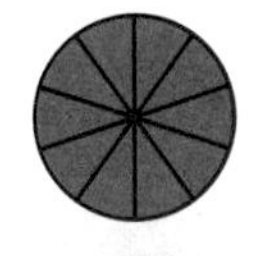

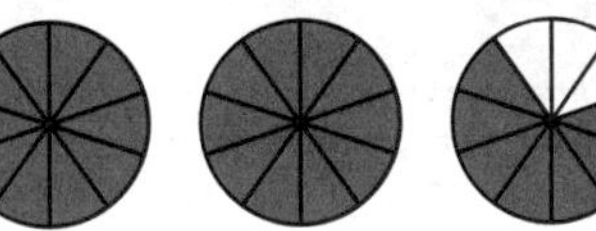
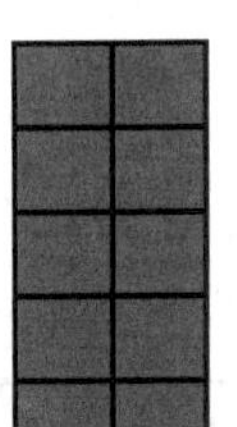
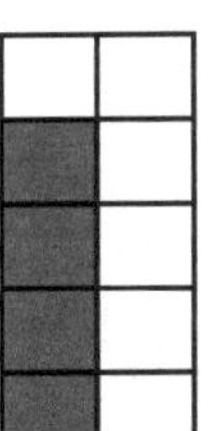
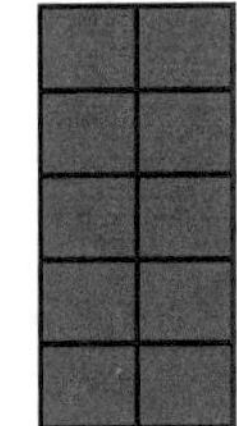

________ ________ ________

Shade in the picture to show the decimal number.

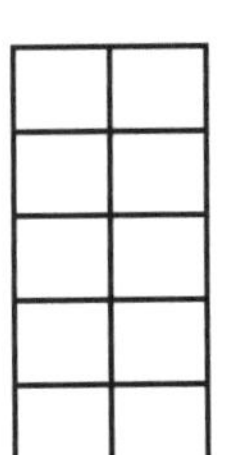
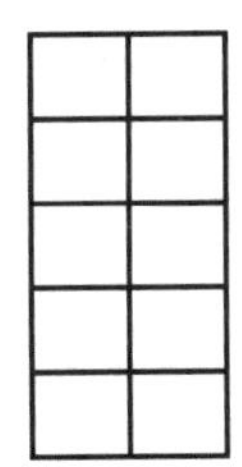

1.9

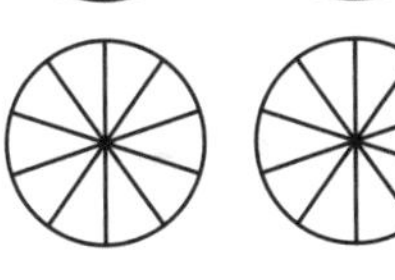

3.5

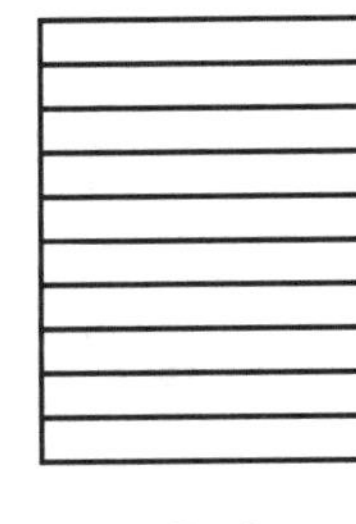

0.4

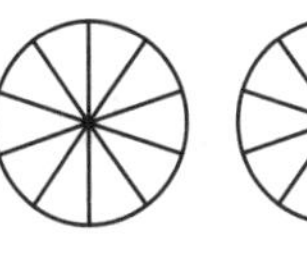
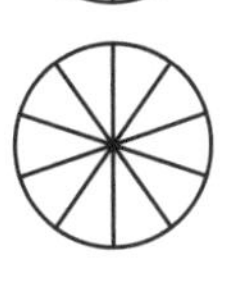
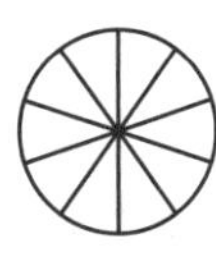

4.1

When reading decimals with whole numbers, say "point" or "and" for the decimal point.

Write the word names for each decimal from above.

1.9 ____________________ 0.4 ____________________

3.5 ____________________ 4.1 ____________________

Name ______________________________

Order in the Line

Look at the number lines below. **Cut out** the decimal number squares on the next page. First, **find** the number line on which each number is located. **Glue** the decimals in their correct positions on the correct number line.

Hint: Pay careful attention to the place value indicated on each line. A number which goes to the hundredths place will be on a number line showing hundredths place values.

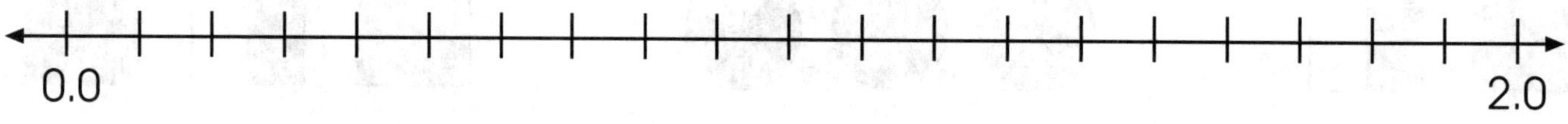

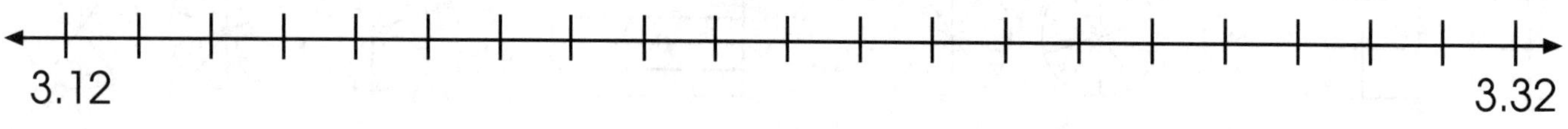

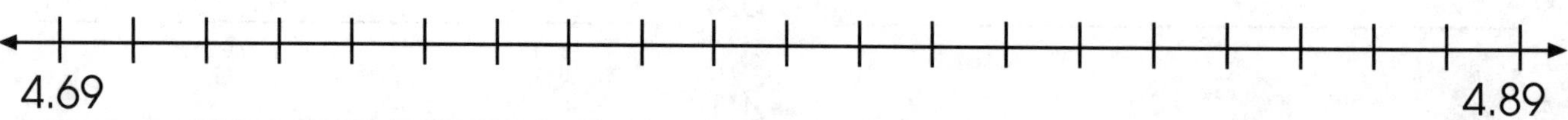

Name ______________________________

Order in the Line

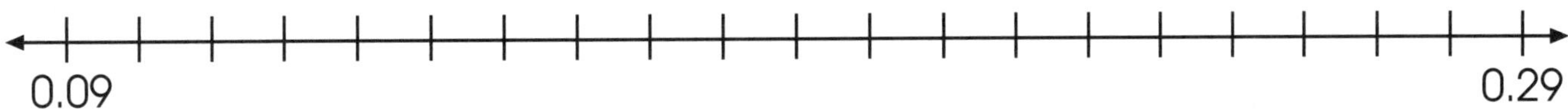

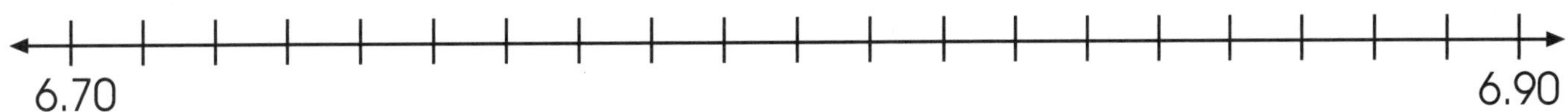

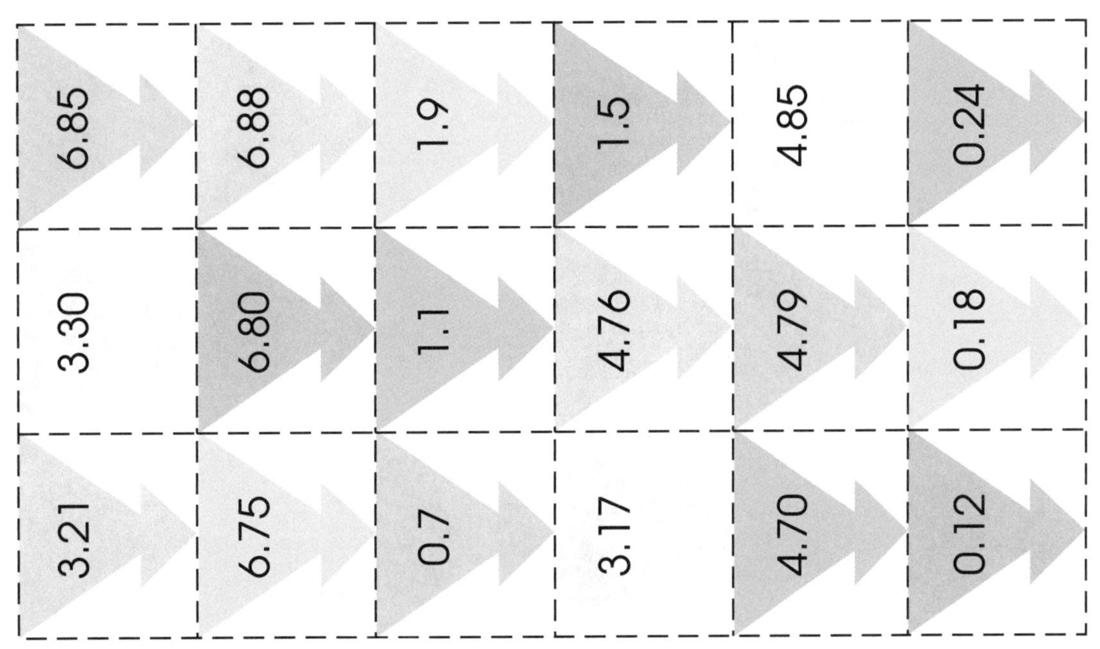

This page intentionally left blank.

Name ______________________________

Get the Point

When you add or subtract decimals, remember to include the decimal point.

Add.

$$\begin{array}{r} 3.6 \\ +3.3 \\ \hline 6.9 \end{array}$$

Subtract.

$$\begin{array}{r} 6.8 \\ -2.6 \\ \hline 4.2 \end{array}$$

Solve these problems.

$$\begin{array}{r} 4.2 \\ +5.2 \\ \hline \end{array} \quad \begin{array}{r} 6.4 \\ +1.4 \\ \hline \end{array} \quad \begin{array}{r} 3.1 \\ +7.8 \\ \hline \end{array} \quad \begin{array}{r} 4.7 \\ +3.2 \\ \hline \end{array} \quad \begin{array}{r} 4.9 \\ +2.0 \\ \hline \end{array} \quad \begin{array}{r} 4.27 \\ +5.52 \\ \hline \end{array}$$

$$\begin{array}{r} 5.9 \\ -3.2 \\ \hline \end{array} \quad \begin{array}{r} 6.7 \\ -5.6 \\ \hline \end{array} \quad \begin{array}{r} 7.8 \\ -2.5 \\ \hline \end{array} \quad \begin{array}{r} 5.8 \\ -3.3 \\ \hline \end{array} \quad \begin{array}{r} 3.9 \\ -1.5 \\ \hline \end{array} \quad \begin{array}{r} 4.86 \\ -1.76 \\ \hline \end{array}$$

$$\begin{array}{r} 0.23 \\ +0.25 \\ \hline \end{array} \quad \begin{array}{r} 0.43 \\ +0.16 \\ \hline \end{array} \quad \begin{array}{r} 0.26 \\ +0.42 \\ \hline \end{array} \quad \begin{array}{r} 0.64 \\ +0.15 \\ \hline \end{array} \quad \begin{array}{r} 0.68 \\ +0.31 \\ \hline \end{array} \quad \begin{array}{r} 6.73 \\ +1.15 \\ \hline \end{array}$$

$$\begin{array}{r} 0.87 \\ -0.42 \\ \hline \end{array} \quad \begin{array}{r} 0.98 \\ -0.35 \\ \hline \end{array} \quad \begin{array}{r} 0.79 \\ -0.15 \\ \hline \end{array} \quad \begin{array}{r} 0.87 \\ -0.67 \\ \hline \end{array} \quad \begin{array}{r} 0.83 \\ -0.12 \\ \hline \end{array} \quad \begin{array}{r} 5.86 \\ -3.83 \\ \hline \end{array}$$

$$\begin{array}{r} 3.13 \\ +2.26 \\ \hline \end{array} \quad \begin{array}{r} 4.72 \\ +1.15 \\ \hline \end{array} \quad \begin{array}{r} 6.87 \\ +2.11 \\ \hline \end{array} \quad \begin{array}{r} 4.98 \\ -2.32 \\ \hline \end{array} \quad \begin{array}{r} 5.97 \\ -2.54 \\ \hline \end{array} \quad \begin{array}{r} 6.98 \\ -1.45 \\ \hline \end{array}$$

Name ______________________

Animal Trivia

1. An earthworm is 14.9 cm long. A grasshopper is 8.7 cm long. What is the difference?

2. A pocket gopher has a hind foot 3.5 cm long. A ground squirrel's hind foot is 6.4 cm long. How much longer is the ground squirrel's hind foot?

3. A porcupine has a tail 30.0 cm long. An opossum has a tail 53.5 cm long. How much longer is the opossum's tail?

4. A wood rat has a tail which is 23.6 cm long. A deer mouse has a tail 12.2 cm long. What is the difference between the two?

5. A cottontail rabbit has ears which are 6.8 cm long. A jackrabbit has ears 12.9 cm long. How much shorter is the cottontail's ear?

6. The hind foot of a river otter is 14.6 cm long. The hind foot of a hog-nosed skunk is 9.0 cm long. What is the difference?

7. A rock mouse is 26.1 cm long. His tail adds another 14.4 cm. What is his total length from his nose to the tip of his tail?

Dueling Decimals

Preparation: To play "Dueling Decimals," you need 2 players. Each player needs a spinner and a place value card (see the example shown).

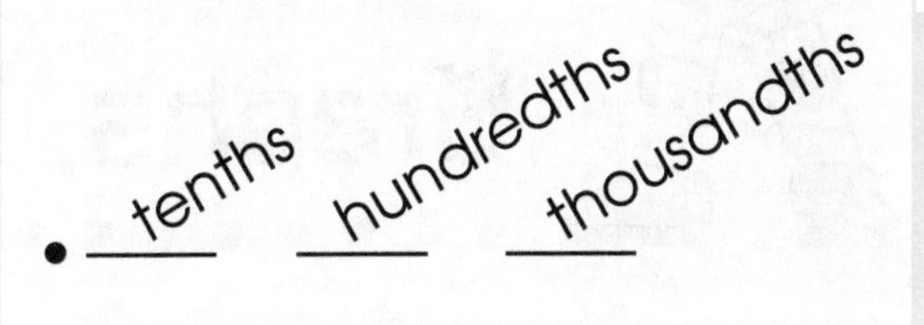

Directions: Player One should spin the spinner. The number that comes up should be recorded under the thousandths place column on the player's place value card. Player Two repeats the process. Player One then spins again, this time placing the number under the hundredths place column on his/her place value card.

Repeat until both players have a complete decimal number. Players should then compare the two numbers. The player with the larger number earns a point. Players have now completed the first round and should continue for four more rounds. The player with the most points after the fifth round wins "Dueling Decimals"!

Extension: Add your five decimal numbers. Compare the sums. Is the winner of the game also the player with a higher sum? ____________________

Why? ____________________

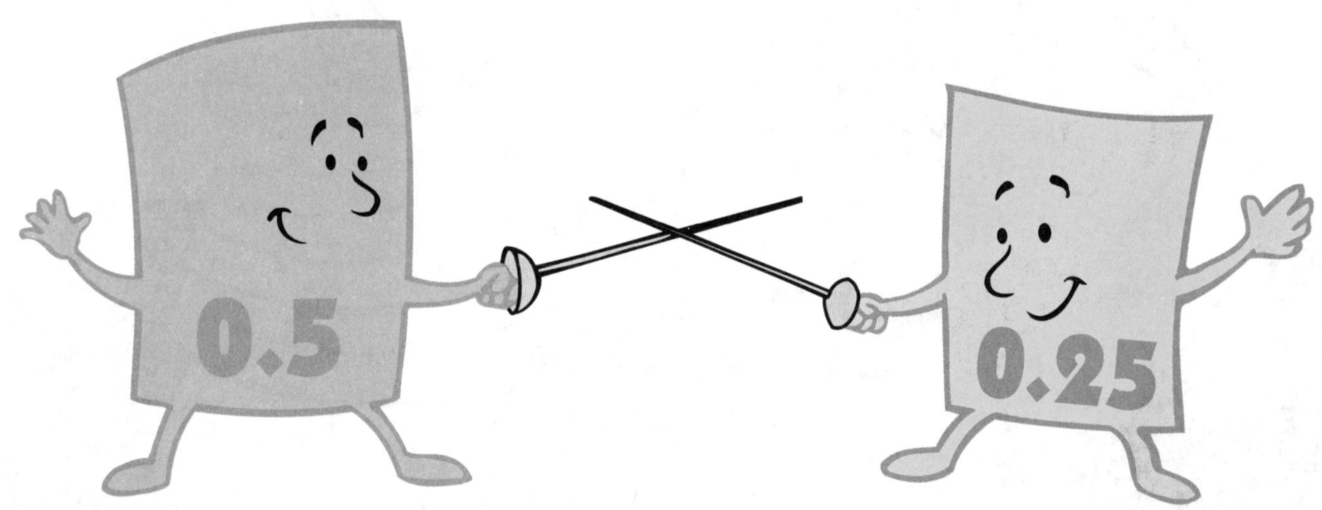

Graphs, Tables and Diagrams

BEHAVIOR
CHORES
TRASH
FEED DOG
CLEAN ROOM
DISHES
DUST

Name ______________________________

Flower Graph

A **pictograph** is a graph using pictures to give information.
Cut out the flowers and **glue** them onto the pictograph.

Daisies					
Sunflowers					
Tulips					
Roses					

How many tulips? ______

sunflowers? ______

roses? ______

daisies? ______

How many more tulips than roses? ______

How many more daisies than sunflowers? ______

How many sunflowers and tulips? ______

How many roses and daisies? ______

Each picture stands for 2 flowers.

0-7696-8513-7

This page intentionally left blank.

Name ____________________

Frog Bubbles

Complete the line graph to show how many bubbles each frog blew.

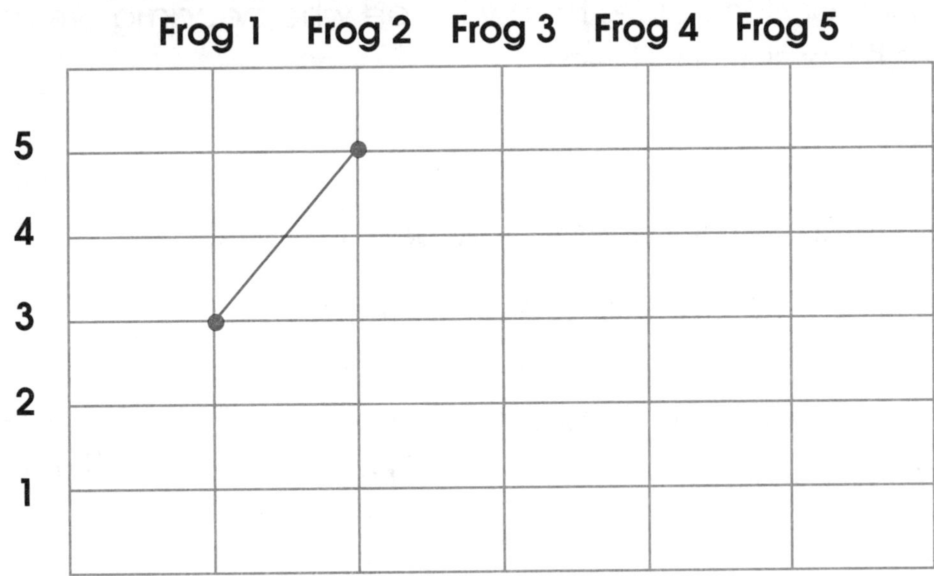

How many bubbles? Frog 1:______ 2:______ 3:______ 4:______ 5:______

Which frog blew the most bubbles?______

Which frog blew the fewest?______

Name ____________________

Vote for Me!

Middletown school had an election to choose the new members of the Student Council. Grace, Bernie, Laurie, Sherry and Sam all ran for the office of president. On the chart below are the five students' names with the number of the votes each received.

Grace	21	36	39
Bernie	47	32	26
Laurie	25	44	38
Sherry	34	37	40
Sam	48	33	29

Use the information and the clues below to see who became president and how many votes he or she received.

- The winning number of votes was an even number.
- The winning number of votes was between 30 and 40.
- The two digits added together are greater than 10.

________________ became the president of the Student Council with

________________ votes.

Who would have become president if the winning number was **odd** and the other clues remained the same?

____

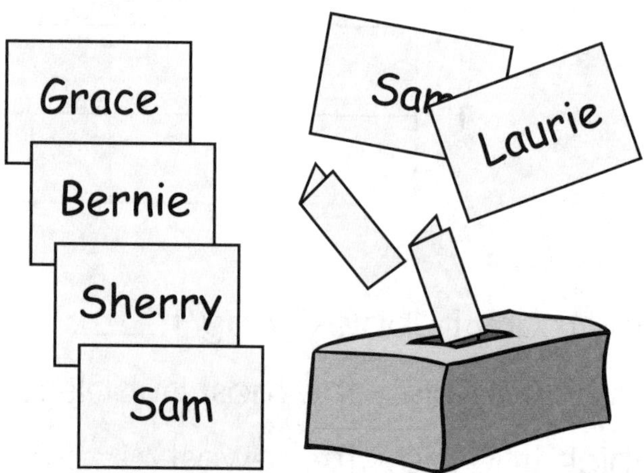

Name ______________________

School Statistics

Read each graph and follow the directions.

List the names of the students from the shortest to the tallest.

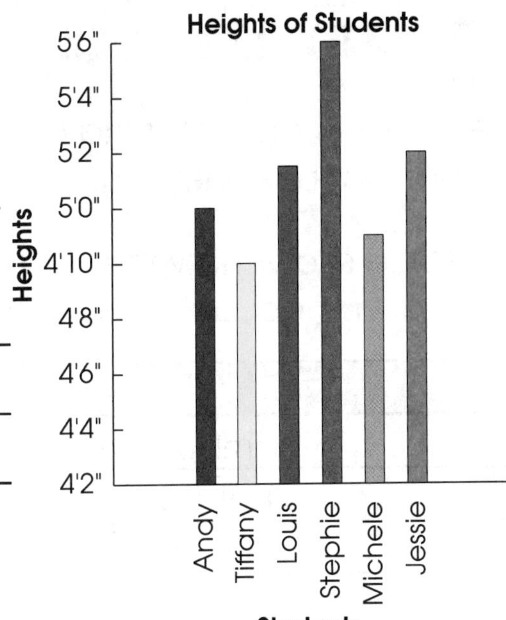

1. ____________ 4. ____________

2. ____________ 5. ____________

3. ____________ 6. ____________

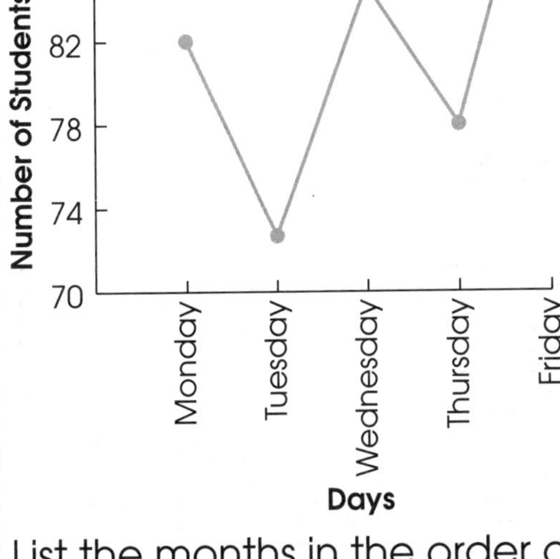

List how many lunches the students bought each day, from the day the most were bought to the least.

1. ____________ 4. ____________

2. ____________ 5. ____________

3. ____________

List the months in the order of the most number of outside recesses to the least number.

1. ____________ 6. ____________

2. ____________ 7. ____________

3. ____________ 8. ____________

4. ____________ 9. ____________

5. ____________

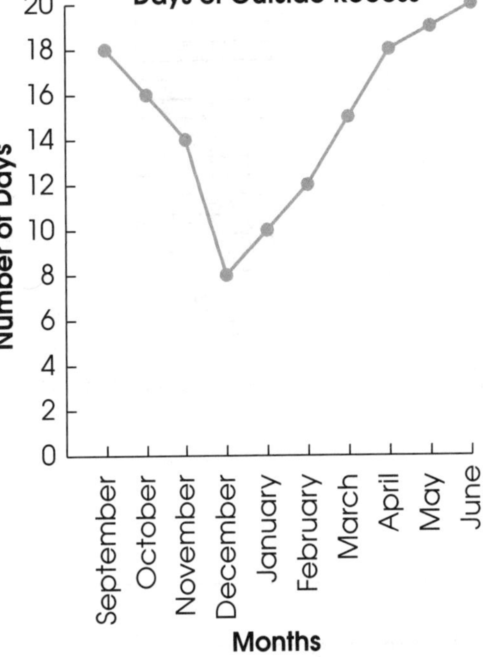

Name ______________________________

Hot Lunch Favorites

The cooks in the cafeteria asked each third- and fourth-grade class to rate the hot lunches. They wanted to know which food the children liked the best.

The table shows how the students rated the lunches.
Key: Each 🯅 equals 2 students.

Food	Number of students who liked it best
hamburgers	🯅 🯅 🯅 🯅 🯅 🯅
hot dogs	🯅 🯅 🯅 🯅 🯅 🯅 🯅
tacos	🯅 🯅 🯅 🯅 🯅
chili	
soup and sandwiches	🯅
spaghetti	🯅 🯅
fried chicken	🯅 🯅 🯅 🯅
fish sticks	🯅 🯅 🯅

Color the bar graph to show the information on the table. Remember that each 🯅 equals 2 people. The first one is done for you.

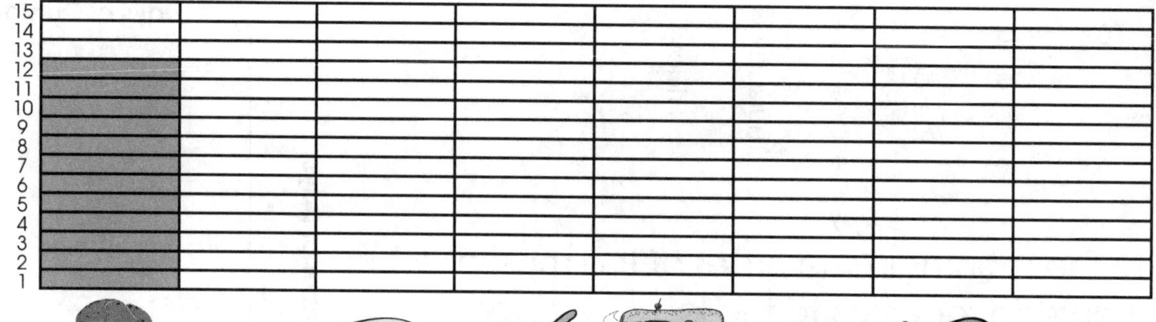

Write the food in order starting with the one that students liked most.

1. ______________________ 5. ______________________

2. ______________________ 6. ______________________

3. ______________________ 7. ______________________

4. ______________________ 8. ______________________

Name ____________________________________

Gliding Graphics

Draw the lines as directed from point to point for each graph.

Draw a line from:

- F,7 to D,1
- D,1 to I,6
- I,6 to N,8
- N,8 to M,3
- M,3 to F,1
- F,1 to G,4
- G,4 to E,4
- E,4 to B,1
- B,1 to A,8
- A,8 to D,11
- D,11 to F,9
- F,9 to F,7
- F,7 to I,9
- I,9 to I,6
- I,6 to F,7

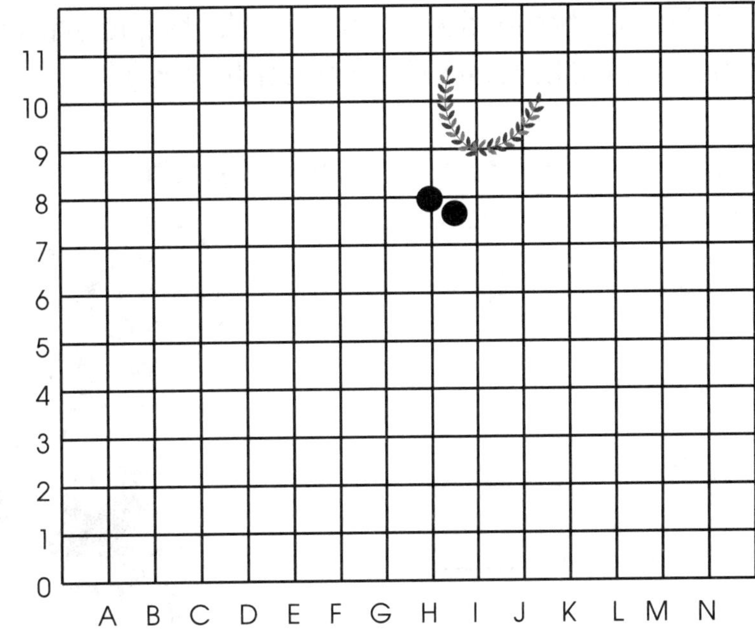

Draw a line from:

U, to Z,
Z, to X,
X, to U,
U, to S,
S, to N,
N, to N,
N, to J,
J, to L,
L, to Y,
Y, to Z,
Z, to L,
L, to J,

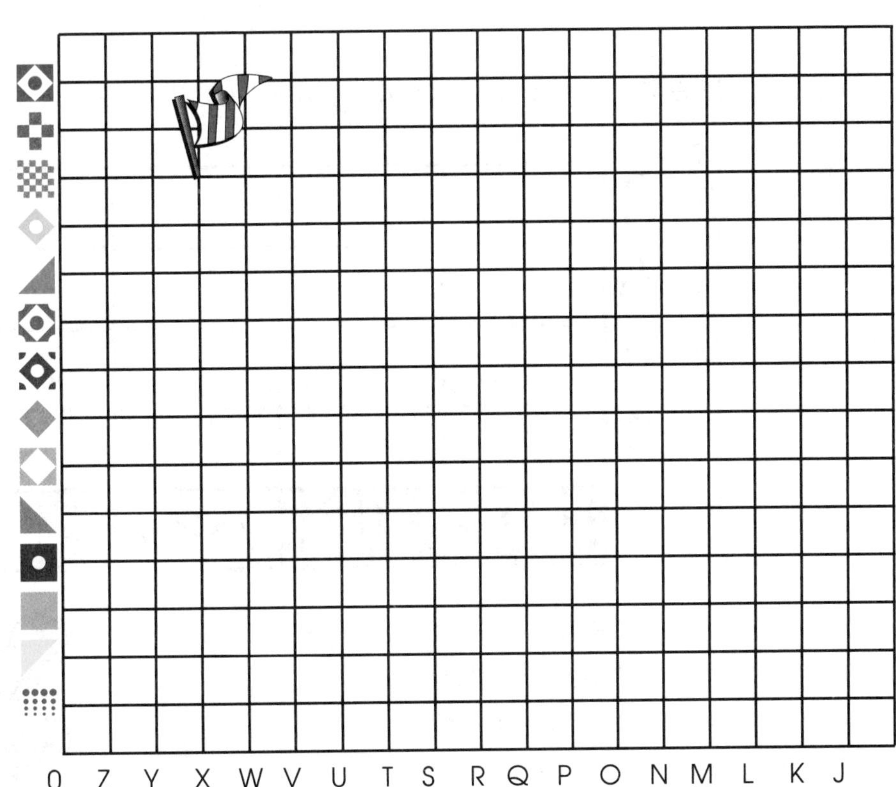

Name ______________________________

Guess the Color

Probability shows the chance that a given event will happen. To show probability, write a fraction. The number of different possibilities is the denominator. The number of times the event could happen is the numerator. (Remember to reduce fractions to the lowest terms.)

Look at the spinner. What is the probability that the arrow will land on . . .

1. red? $\frac{3}{8}$
2. blue? ________
3. yellow? ________
4. green? ________
5. orange? ________

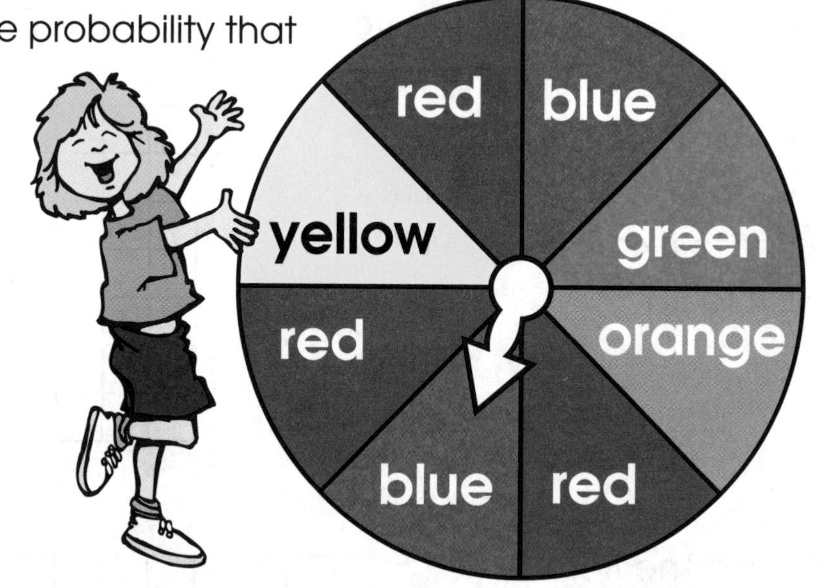

Complete the bar graph showing your answers (the data) from above.

Number of Probability					
8					
6					
4					
2					
	red	blue	yellow	orange	green

Circle the best title for the above bar graph.

a. Probability of Arrow Landing on a Color
b. Eight Turns of the Spinner
c. Which Color Is the Winner?

Name ____________________

Keep Your Heads Up!

Collect 21 pennies. **Predict** the numbers of heads and tails that will turn up before you toss the pennies. Then, **toss** the coins ten times.

Does anything change about your predictions the more you guess?

____

Toss	Guess Heads	Guess Tails	Actual Heads	Actual Tails
1				
2				
3				
4				
5				
6				
7				
8				
9				
10				

Measurement

Name ______________________________

How Does Your Home Measure Up?

Directions: Take a "measuring journey" through your house. To begin, brainstorm a list of various destinations around your house. Then, **list** five objects found in each room and **write** them on the left-hand side of a sheet of paper.

Example:

Kitchen	**Bathroom**	**Bedroom**
stove	toothbrush	books
teaspoon	hairbrush	desk/table
cookbook	soap	pillow
can opener	mirror	clock
box of cereal	bandage	hanger

Read through the objects on the list and **write** estimations of their measurements. Decide on a unit of measurement to use and whether to measure length, width or both. Then, **measure** the objects. (A tape measure or string may be used to measure the size or circumference of any oddly shaped objects.) Finally, compare your estimations with the actual measurements.

Object	Estimate	Actual

Name ______________________

Growing String Beans

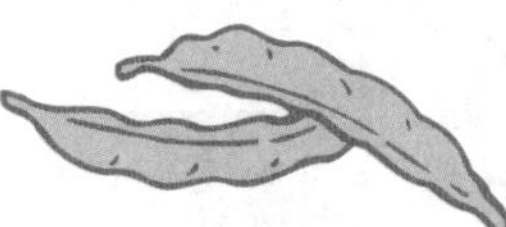

All plants with green leaves make food from the sun. They take water and nutrients from the soil, but they make their food from light.

You will measure in inches how fast a string bean plant grows. Record this information on the **Growing String Beans Bar Graph** on page 115.

You will need:
string bean seeds
potting soil
16 oz. plastic cup
12-inch ruler

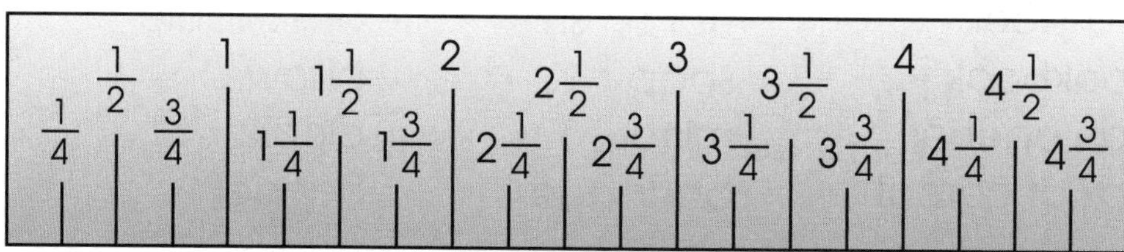

Directions:
1. Fill the cup 3/4 full with potting soil.
2. Use a pencil to make a hole 1-inch deep and drop in a bean seed. Gently cover the seed and lightly water it.
3. Water the plant regularly so that the soil does not become dried out.
4. Wait for the new plant to germinate and peek out of the soil.
5. Measure and record the plant's growth using the ruler. Record it on the bar graph at each specified interval.
6. When it has grown, enjoy the delicious string beans as a treat!

How To Measure: Place the ruler next to the plant, resting it on the soil. Measure from the top of the plant down to the soil.

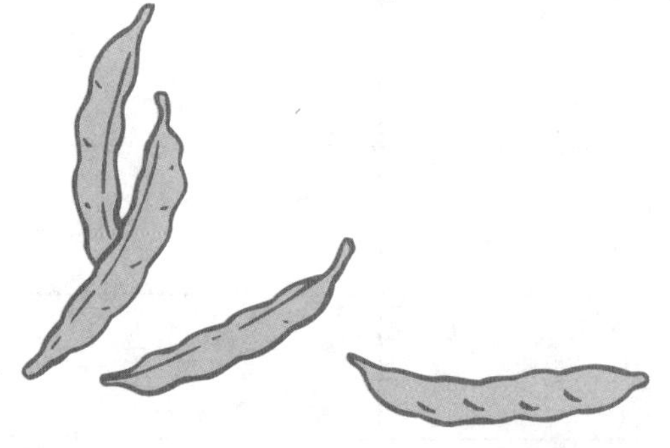

Name ____________________

Growing String Beans

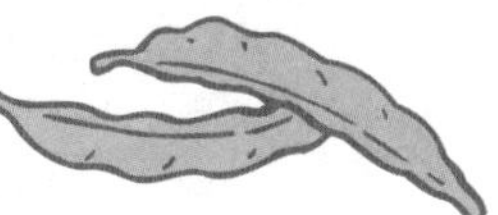

Bar Graph

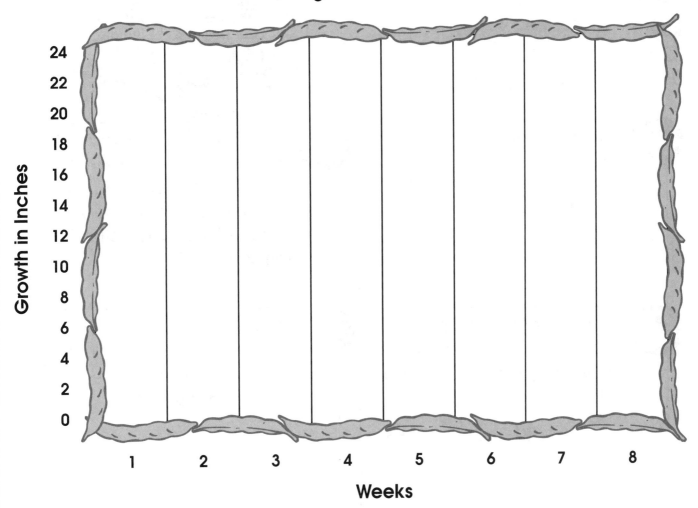

String Bean Plant Growth

Growth in Inches: 24, 22, 20, 18, 16, 14, 12, 10, 8, 6, 4, 2, 0

Weeks: 1, 2, 3, 4, 5, 6, 7, 8

Other Ideas:

Try growing a few other interesting plants like:

1. Carrot tops cut off and placed in a pie tin filled with water.
2. Plain popcorn seeds from the store (no oiled or treated). Plant them in the ground.
3. Go to your local plant nursery or hardware store and look at the selection of plant seeds available.
4. Plant a young tree in your yard and measure its growth each year.

Name ______________________________

Krab E. Krabby

Krab E. Krabby carries a yardstick with him everywhere he goes and he measures everything he can.

Key:
12 inches = 1 foot
36 inches = 3 feet = 1 yard

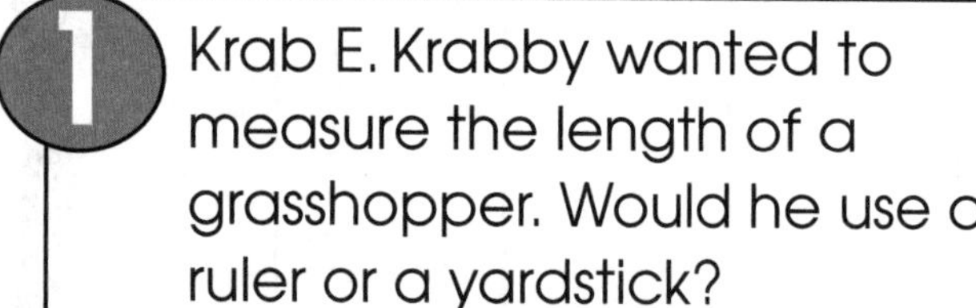

1. Krab E. Krabby wanted to measure the length of a grasshopper. Would he use a ruler or a yardstick?

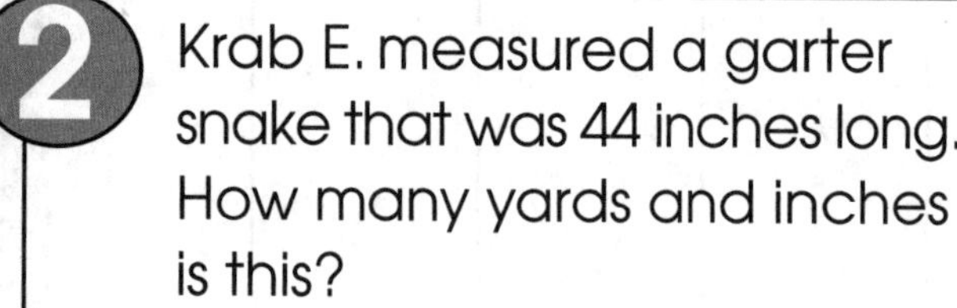

2. Krab E. measured a garter snake that was 44 inches long. How many yards and inches is this?

   ______ yard ______ inches

3. Krab E. measured a monarch butterfly that was 4 inches wide. How many inches less than a foot is the butterfly?

4. Krab E. Krabby scolded Rollo Rattlesnake because Rollo wouldn't straighten out and cooperate. Should Krab E. use a ruler or a yardstick to measure Rollo?

5. Krab E. measured a tomato hornworm that was 5 inches long. How many inches less than a foot is this?

6. Krab E. measured a lazy tuna that was 1 foot 11 inches long. How many total inches is the tuna?

Name ____________________

Calculating Lengths

Use your yardstick to **calculate** and **write** the following lengths. Remember to write feet or yards. Some lengths may not be exactly in feet or yards, so be sure to write the inches too. Have a friend or parent help you **measure** these lengths.

1. How long is the biggest step you can take? ____________
2. How far can a paper airplane fly? ____________
3. From start to finish, how much distance do you cover when you do a somersault? ____________
4. How far can you throw a feather? ____________
5. How wide is your driveway? ____________
6. How far can you walk balancing a book on your head? ____________
7. How high can you stack wooden blocks before they fall? ____________
8. How high can you jump? (Measure from where your finger touches to the floor.) ____________
9. How far can you jump? (Begin with your feet together.) ____________
10. How much distance is covered if you skip 10 times? ____________
11. What is the distance you can hit a softball with your bat before it hits the ground? ____________
12. What is the distance you can throw a baseball? ____________
13. How far away were you when you caught your friend's throw? ____________
14. How far can you spit a seed? ____________
15. How much distance do you cover when you sprint for 3 seconds? ____________

Name ______________________________

Animal Math

The chart below lists some of the body statistics of 15 endangered animals. Use these measurements to **solve** the problems below the chart.

Animal	Height	Weight	Length
Mountain gorilla	6 feet	450 pounds	
Black rhinoceros	5.5 feet	4,000 pounds	12 feet
Cheetah	2.5 feet	100 pounds	5 feet
Leopard	2 feet	150 pounds	4.5 feet
Spectacled bear	2.5 feet	300 pounds	5 feet
Giant armadillo		100 pounds	4 feet
Vicuna	2.5 feet	100 pounds	
Siberian tiger	38 inches	600 pounds	6 feet
Orangutan	4.5 feet	200 pounds	
Giant panda		300 pounds	6 feet
Polar bear		1,600 pounds	8 feet
Yak	5.5 feet	1,200 pounds	

1. What is the total height of a mountain gorilla, a vicuna and a yak? __________
2. What is the total weight of a leopard, a cheetah and a polar bear? __________
3. What is the total weight of a giant panda and a giant armadillo? __________
4. Add the lengths of a black rhinoceros, a spectacled bear and a Siberian tiger. __________
5. Add the heights of two leopards, three yaks and four orangutans. __________
6. Subtract the height of a vicuna from the height of a cheetah. __________
7. Add the weights of all the animals. __________
8. Write the lengths of the animals from longest to shortest.

____

____

____

 0-7696-8513-7

Discovering Capacity

Capacity measures how much can fit inside an object.

You will need:

measuring cup (2 cup capacity)
pie tin
1 cup of salt
bathroom sink
1 gallon plastic jug
2 liter plastic jug
tablespoon
cake pan
1 cup of ice
baking pan
1 gallon freezer bag

Complete the tasks below to discover the capacity of objects around your house.

1. How many cups of water are there in a 1-gallon plastic jug? __________

2. How many tablespoons of salt does it take to fill up 1 cup? __________

   How many tablespoons of water does it take to fill up 1/2 cup? __________

3. Plug your bathroom sink. How many cups of water will it hold? __________

   How many gallons is that? __________

5. How many cups of water does it take to fill a pie tin? __________

6. Does a gallon-size plastic freezer bag really hold a gallon of something?

   __________ Count how many cups of water you can fit inside one. ________

   __________ Is that a gallon?

7. Fill a cake pan with water. Count how many cups it takes. __________

   If 2 cups = 1 pint, how many pints does it hold? __________

   If 2 pints = 1 quart, what is the quart capacity of your cake pan? __________

Name ______________________

Comparing Temperatures

Temperatures tell how warm or cold something is.
You will need: Fahrenheit thermometer
measuring cup (1 or 2 cup capacity)

Measure and **record** the temperatures of:

_______ 1. Water from the tap

_______ 2. The dairy section at the grocery store (Call or visit store to ask.)

_______ 3. A pet's body temperature (Call or visit veterinarian.)

_______ 4. Your freezer (Have your parents help you.)

_______ 5. Bathtub water (Fill a cup from the bathtub and place the thermometer in it.)

_______ 6. A cup of water outside in the sun

- Place a cup of water in a safe place with the thermometer resting inside.
- Let it set until the temperature stops rising.
- Record the temperature.

Is it the same as the temperature outside? _______

_______ 7. A cup of ice water

_______ 8. Your body temperature

Now, **compare**.

1. How many degrees warmer is the bathtub water than the tap water?

   ____

2. How many degrees difference is a pet's body temperature than yours?

   _______ Who is warmer? ______________

3. What is the difference between your freezer's temperature and the temperature in the dairy section of your grocery store? _______

4. What is the difference in temperature between a cup of water that has set out in the sun and a cup of ice water? _______

Name ______________________________

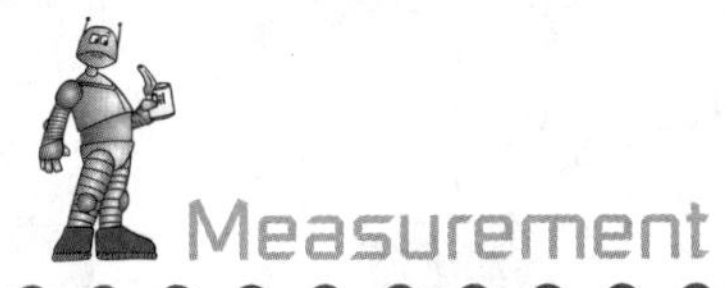

Today's Temperature

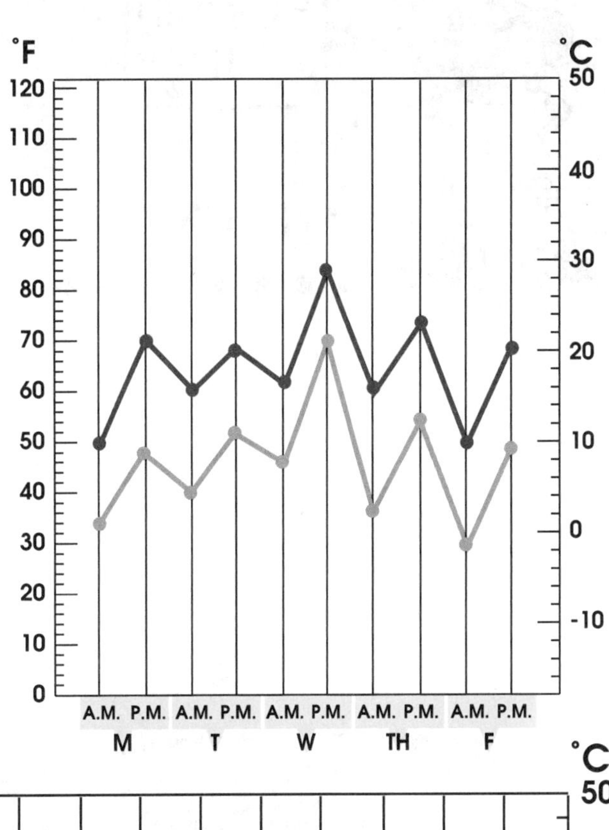

Record the indoor and outdoor temperatures in degrees Celsius and Fahrenheit. Post the daily temperature on poster paper on your refrigerator. If desired, use an almanac or newspaper to share record high and low temperatures for each day.

Indoor temperature
(8 A.M. and 3 P.M.)

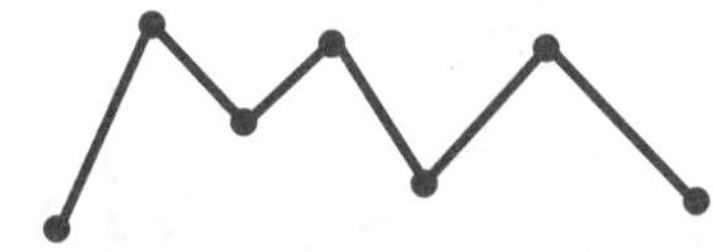

Outdoor temperature
(8 A.M. and 3 P.M.)

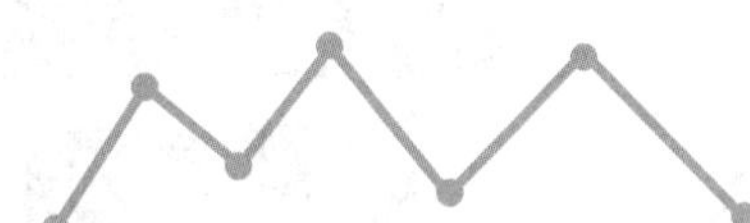

Extension: Create ongoing line graphs to show temperature differences. Each day, plot the temperatures. Display them near the daily temperature recordings.

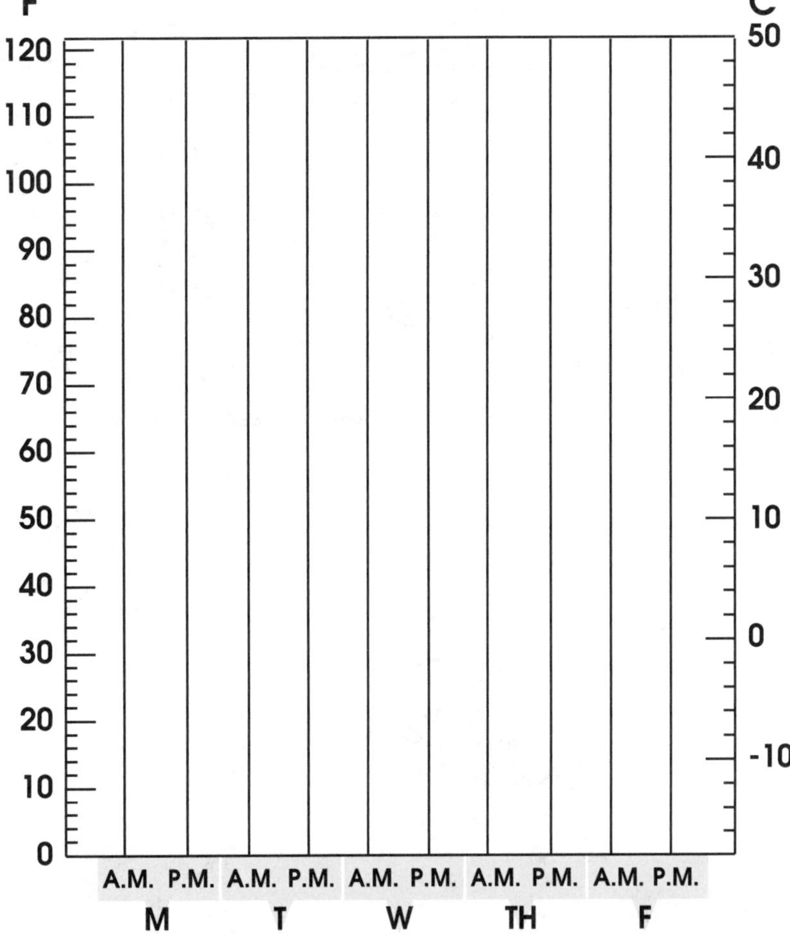

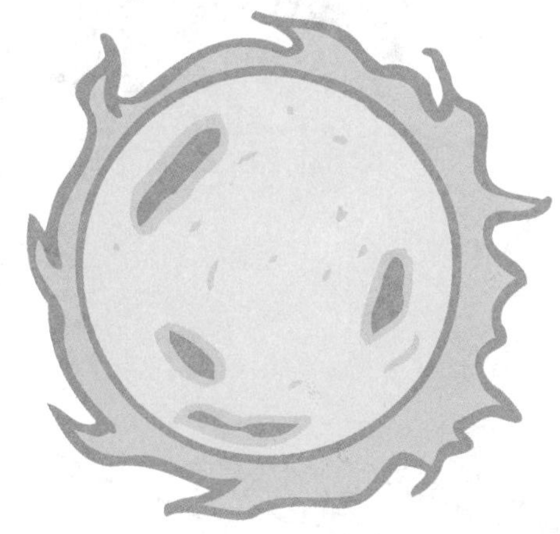

Time

Name 

My Schedule

Keep track of what you do all day for a week on several copies of this page. **Write** the day and date at the start of the day. Then, **write** what you do and the time you do it. Each time you change activities, you should **write** a new time entry. At the end of the day, **add** how much time was spent in each type of activity. Some activities can be grouped together (i.e., breakfast, lunch, dinner = eating; social studies, language, math = school subjects; etc.). Tally up your activities on Friday.

Extension: Use the information collected to plot a pie graph, bar graph, line graph or pictograph.

Day and date

Time	Activity

Totals

Name ______________________________

Time on My Hands

Draw the hour and minute hands to show each time below.

Example:

3:35

10:05

4:55

8:10

12:50

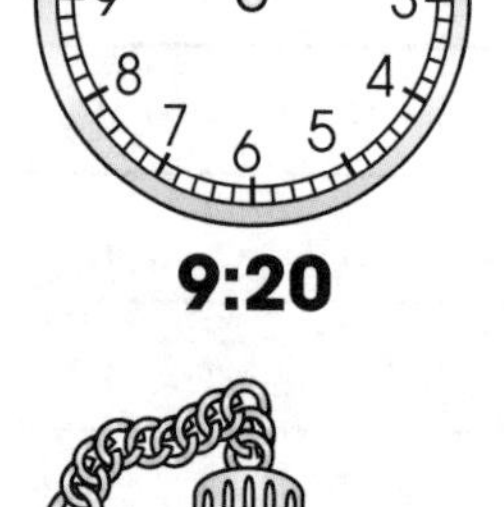

9:20

7:25

1:15

11:45

3:30

6:40

12:55

2:00

5:35

3:15

10:50

Name ____________________

Take Time for These

Write the time shown on these clocks.

Example:

6:47

Name ____________________

Time "Tables"

Draw the hands on these clocks.

10 minutes before
12:17

36 minutes after
8:19

8 minutes before
1:05

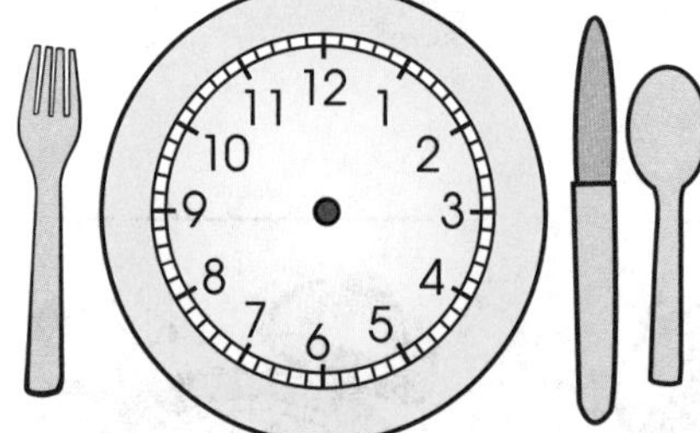

21 minutes after
8:40

16 minutes before
4:30

46 minutes after
10:11

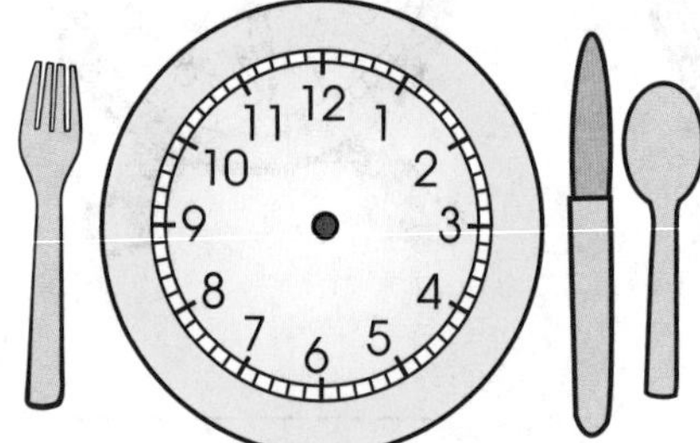

32 minutes before
5:25

11 minutes after
3:16

24 minutes before
12:30

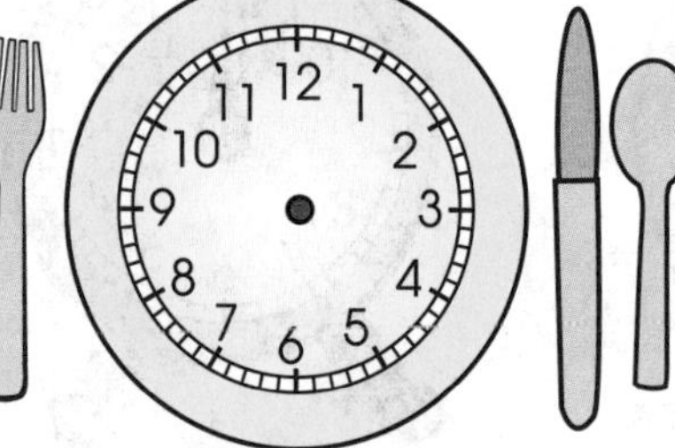

17 minutes after
1:31

43 minutes before
2:01

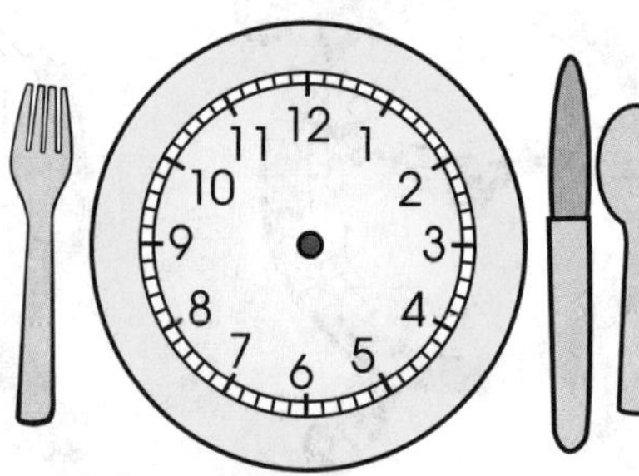

18 minutes after
6:45

Feeding Time

The abbreviations **A.M.** and **P.M.** help tell the time of day. At midnight, A.M. begins. At noon, P.M. begins. Ken and Angie enjoy watching the animals being fed at the zoo. However, when they arrived, they were a little confused by the signs. Help them figure out the feeding time for each kind of animal. Be sure to include if it's A.M. or P.M.

Zebras: Feeding time is 2 hours after the monkeys.

____

Tigers: Feeding time is 2 hours after 9:00 A.M.

____

Elephants: Feeding time is 1:00 P.M.

Giraffes: Feeding time is 1 hour before the lions.

____

Monkeys: Feeding time is 3 hours before the giraffes.

____

Lions: Feeding time is 3 hours after the elephants.

____

Now, **trace** the path in the zoo that Ken and Angie would take so that they could see all the animals being fed.

Name ______________________________

How Far Is It?

Drawing pictures can be a good problem-solving strategy. **Draw** pictures to help you **solve** the problems below. Each problem requires three answers.

1. Jimmy has to walk 12 blocks to get to the park where he likes to play ball. It takes him 3 minutes to walk one block. How many minutes will it take him to walk to the park?

   Distance ____________ Speed ____________ Time ____________

2. An airplane leaves the airport at 9:00 A.M. It flies at 200 miles per hour. When it lands at 11:00 A.M., how far will it have gone?

   Distance ____________ Speed ____________ Time ____________

3. It is 50 miles between Dakota City and Blue Falls. It takes Mr. Oliver 1 hour to make the drive. How fast does he drive?

   Distance ____________ Speed ____________ Time ____________

4. Tad rides his bike to his grandmother's house. It takes him 45 minutes to ride there. She lives 5 miles from his house. How many minutes does it take him to ride 1 mile?

   Distance ____________ Speed ____________ Time ____________

5. Rachel loves to visit her grandparents who live 150 miles from her house. When they make the trip, her dad drives. He averages 50 miles an hour. How many hours will the trip take?

   Distance ____________ Speed ____________ Time ____________

Name ______________________________

Racing Chimps

One chimpanzee in the forest always likes to brag that it can get more fruit than any other animal in the forest. So an older and wiser chimpanzee decided to challenge him to a race.

"Let us see who can bring back more bananas in 1 hour," said the older chimp. The race began.

Quickly, the younger chimp picked a bunch of five bananas and carried it back. He continued doing this every 5 minutes.

The older chimp was not quite as fast. Every 10 minutes he carried back eight bananas.

After 45 minutes, the young chimp decided to stop and eat one of his bananas before continuing. By the time he finished, the hour was over and the older chimp called out, "The race is over. Whose pile of bananas is bigger?"

Using the information above, figure out how many bananas were in each pile and which chimp won the race.

The younger chimp had ____________________ bananas in his pile.

The older chimp had ____________________ bananas in his pile.

The winner was the ____________________ chimp!

Money

Name ____________________

Garage Sale

Use the fewest number of coins possible to equal the amount shown in each box. **Write** or **draw** the coins you would use in each box.

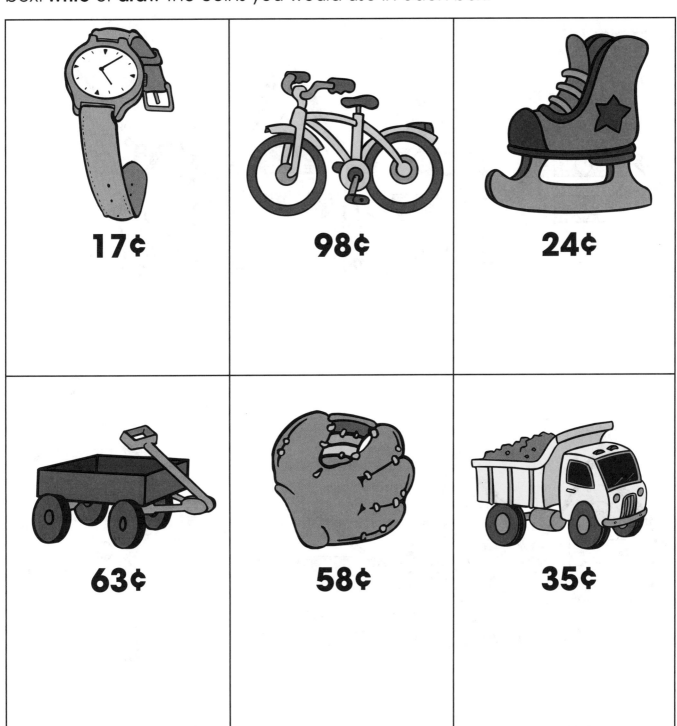

 17¢	 98¢	 24¢
 63¢	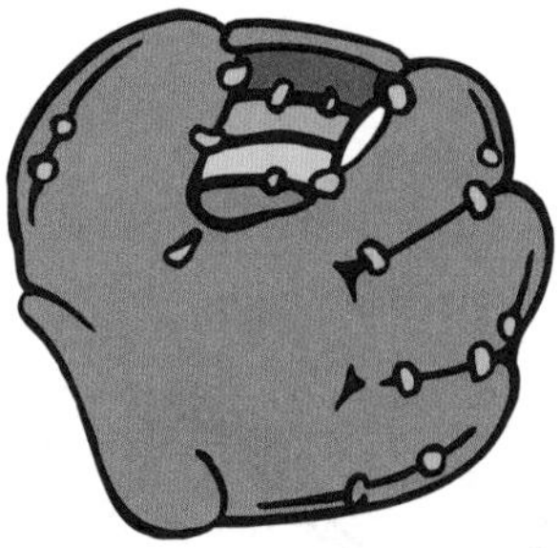 58¢	 35¢

 0-7696-8513-7

Name ____________________

Easy Street

What is each house worth? **Count** the money in each house on Easy Street. **Write** the amount on the line below it.

Example:

$2.40 ________ ________ ________ ________

________ ________ ________ ________ ________

Name ______________________

Add 'Em Up!

Write the prices, then **add**. **Regroup**, when needed.

1. ______ skateboard
+ ______ hat

7. ______ hot dog
+ ______ rocket

2. ______ dictionary
+ ______ radio

8. ______ skateboard
+ ______ goldfish

3. ______ wallet
+ ______ goldfish

9. ______ hat
+ ______ kite

4. ______ hot dog
+ ______ watch

10. ______ radio
+ ______ trumpet

5. ______ dictionary
+ ______ kite

11. ______ rocket
+ ______ goldfish

6. ______ in-line skates
+ ______ trumpet

12. ______ skateboard
+ ______ in-line skates

Name ____________________

Making Change

When you do not have the exact change to buy something at a store, the clerk must give you change. The first amount of money is what you give the clerk. The second amount is what the item costs. In the box, **list** the fewest number of coins and bills you will receive in change.

	Amount I Have	Cost of Item	Change
1	\$3.75	\$3.54	
2	\$10.00	\$5.63	
3	\$7.00	\$6.05	
4	\$7.25	\$6.50	
5	\$7.50	\$6.13	
6	\$0.75	\$0.37	
7	\$7.00	\$6.99	
8	\$15.00	\$12.75	

Name ____________________

Fast Food

Mealwormy is the latest restaurant of that famous fast food creator, Buggs I. Lyke. His Mealwormy Burger costs $1.69. An order of Roasted Roaches cost $0.59 for the regular size and $0.79 for the larger size. A Cricket Cola is $0.89.

1. You buy a Mealwormy Burger and a regular order of Roasted Roaches. What is the total?

2. Your teacher buys a Cricket Cola and a regular order of Roasted Roaches. What does it cost her?

3. Your mom goes to Mealwormy to buy your dinner. She spends $3.37. How much change does she get from a $5.00 bill?

4. Your best friend orders a Mealwormy Burger, a large order of Roasted Roaches and Cricket Cola. How much will it cost?

5. The principal is very hungry, so his bill comes to $14.37. How much change will he get from $20.00?

6. You have $1.17 in your bank. How much more do you need to pay for a Mealwormy Burger?

Name ______________________________

Spending Spree

Use the clues to figure out what each person bought. Then, **subtract** to find out how much change each had left.

		Clue:
1. David began with:	$40.25 – ______	He loves to see things zoom into the sky!
2. Mark started with:	$50.37 – ______	He likes to travel places with his hands free and a breeze in his face!
3. Eva started with:	$14.84 – ______	She loves to practice her jumping and exercise at the same time!
4. Bill brought:	$61.49 – ______	He wants to see the heavens for himself!
5. Michelle brought:	$40.29 – ______	Fuzzy companions make such great friends!
6. Cheryl started with:	$16.80 – ______	She loves to hear music that is soft and beautiful!
7. Heather arrived with:	$20.48 – ______	She loves to put it down on paper for everyone to see!

$12.49

$9.31

$21.52

$13.45

$15.29

$2.43

$3.95

$52.28

$32.51

$47.29

Name ____________________

Match the Sale

Which item did each child purchase? **Calculate** the amount. **Write** each purchase price below.

Jessica:	Tammy:	Heather:	Mark:	Eva:
$17.43	$43.21	$10.06	$52.46	$65.04
– ____	– ____	– ____	– ____	– ____
$9.14	$34.86	$1.64	$14.17	$36.94

Monica:	Katelyn:	David:	Curt:	Michele:
$6.99	$9.06	$15.25	$63.45	$32.45
– ____	– ____	– ____	– ____	– ____
$3.56	$5.24	$6.82	$46.16	$13.50

Gwen:	Thomas:
$19.24	$9.43
– ____	– ____
$6.38	$5.59

$8.29 $28.10 $38.29 $17.29 $8.43 $8.42 $3.82 $3.43 $18.95 $12.86 $3.84 $8.35

Frosted NEW OATS Cereal

ONE OF A KIND

Name ____________________

Dessert Included

Brenda and Doug really like chocolate—chocolate-covered raisins, chocolate candy, chocolate cake and hot chocolate! Most of all, they love chocolate sundaes with chocolate chip ice cream. When they find out that the Eats and Sweets Restaurant is offering a free chocolate dessert with any meal costing exactly $5.00, they decide to go there for dinner.

Menu

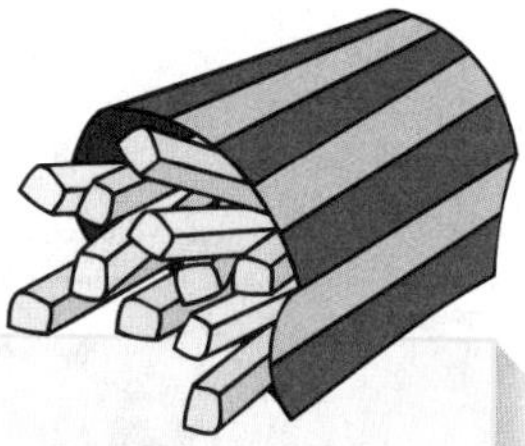

Meat		Potatoes/Vegetables	
Chicken	$1.95	Mashed Potatoes	$1.00
Roast Beef	$3.05	French Fries	$0.85
Shrimp	$3.50	Sweet Corn	$0.65
Roast Pork	$2.75	Green Beans	$0.50
Salad		**Drinks**	
Cole Slaw	$0.60	Milk	$0.40
Potato Salad	$0.95	Chocolate Milk	$0.45
Dinner Salad	$0.75	Orange Juice	$0.95
Macaroni Salad	$1.10	Soda Pop	$0.55

Choosing one item from each of the four categories, **list** four different meals Brenda and Doug could eat for exactly $5.00.

Meal # 1 ______________, ______________, ______________, ______________

Meal # 2 ______________, ______________, ______________, ______________

Meal # 3 ______________, ______________, ______________, ______________

Meal # 4 ______________, ______________, ______________, ______________

Name ____________________

Multiplying Money

Money is multiplied in the same way other numbers are. The only difference is a dollar sign and a decimal point are added to the final product.

Steps:

1. Multiply by ones.
   1. 4 x 8 = 32 (Carry the 3.)
   2. 4 x 2 = 8 + 3 = 11 (Carry the 1.)
   3. 4 x 4 = 16 + 1 = 17

$$\begin{array}{r} {\scriptstyle 1\ 3} \\ \$4.28 \\ \times\ \ 34 \\ \hline 1712 \end{array}$$

2. 1. Cross out the carried digits.
   2. Add the zero.

$$\begin{array}{r} {\scriptstyle \times\times} \\ \$4.28 \\ \times\ \ 34 \\ \hline 1712 \\ 0 \end{array}$$

3. Multiply by tens.
   1. 3 x 8 = 24 (Carry the 2.)
   2. 3 x 2 = 6 + 2 = 8
   3. 3 x 4 = 12

$$\begin{array}{r} {\scriptstyle 2} \\ \$4.28 \\ \times\ \ 34 \\ \hline 1712 \\ 12840 \end{array}$$

4. Add.
   1,712 + 12,840 = 14,552

$$\begin{array}{r} \$4.28 \\ \times\ \ 34 \\ \hline 1712 \\ +12840 \\ \hline 14,552 \end{array}$$

5. Add the dollar sign and the decimal point.

$$\begin{array}{r} \$4.28 \\ \times\ \ 34 \\ \hline 1712 \\ +12840 \\ \hline \$145.52 \end{array}$$

Multiply.

$$\begin{array}{r} \$3.42 \\ \times\ \ 25 \\ \hline \end{array} \qquad \begin{array}{r} \$5.42 \\ \times\ \ 61 \\ \hline \end{array}$$

$$\begin{array}{r} \$3.81 \\ \times\ \ 46 \\ \hline \end{array} \qquad \begin{array}{r} \$8.20 \\ \times\ \ 55 \\ \hline \end{array}$$

$$\begin{array}{r} \$9.42 \\ \times\ \ 31 \\ \hline \end{array} \qquad \begin{array}{r} \$4.23 \\ \times\ \ 96 \\ \hline \end{array}$$

Name ______________________

Science Trip

The science class is planning a field trip to Chicago to visit the Museum of Science and Industry. There are 18 students in the class and each student needs $40.00 to cover the expenses. The class decided to sell candy to raise money.

Answer the questions using the chart below.

Weekly Class Sales

	Week One	Week Two	Week Three	Week Four
Amount Raised	$282.00	$176.00	$202.00	$150.00

1. What is the weekly average of money raised during 4 weeks of candy sales?

   ____

2. What is the average amount of dollars raised per child during 4 weeks of candy sales?

   ____

3. Did the class meet its goal of $40.00 per child?

   ____

4. How much above or beneath their goal per child did the class earn?

   ____

Name ______________________

Perplexing Problems

Solve these problems.

Mark, David, Curt and Jordan rented a motorized skateboard for 1 hour. What was the cost for each of them—split equally 4 ways?

Total:
$17.36 $ ________

Five students pitched in to buy Mr. Foley a birthday gift. How much did each of them contribute?

Total:
$9.60 $ ________

Mary, Cheryl and Betty went to the skating rink. What was their individual cost?

Total:
$7.44 $ ________

Carol, Katelyn and Kimberly bought lunch at their favorite salad shop. What did each of them pay for lunch?

Total:
$12.63 $ ________

Debbie, Sarah, Michele and Kelly earned $6.56 altogether collecting cans. How much did each of them earn individually?

Total:
$6.56 $ ________

Five friends went to the Hot Spot Café for lunch. They all ordered the special. What did it cost?

Total:
$27.45 $ ________

Lee and Ricardo purchased an awesome model rocket together. What was the cost for each of them?

Total:
$9.52 $ ________

The total fee for Erik, Bill and Steve to enter the science museum was $8.76. What amount did each of them pay?

Total:
$8.76 $ ________

Name ______________________________

Let's Take a Trip!

You will plan a car trip to calculate approximately how much the trip will cost. You will calculate distances between locations and the amount of gasoline needed based upon miles per gallon of the car. Then, you will estimate the cost of the gasoline, hotel, food and entertainment.

Directions: Using graph paper, plot out your trip starting and ending at "point A." The trip should have five points of travel, including point A. Each square on the graph paper represents 10 miles. Calculate the mileage between points.

Use a copy of the **Expense Chart** on page 143 to keep track of your calculations. Use newspapers, travel brochures and menus to help you estimate the cost of food, gas, hotels, entertainment, etc. You will also want to use a calculator. When you have completed the **Expense Chart**, answer the questions below.

1. If two people go on this trip, how will the cost change? ______________
2. If a family of four goes on the trip, how will the cost change? ______________
3. Would the cost of gas change? ______________________
   Why or why not? ______________________________
4. What else could change the cost of the trip? ______________
5. Why is this just an estimate? ______________________________

____

Name ______________________

Expense Chart

Distance to travel

Miles from Point A to Point B: __________

Miles from Point B to Point C: __________

Miles from Point C to Point D: __________

Miles from Point D to Point E: __________

Miles from Point E to Point A: __________

Total miles to travel: __________

Your car gets 22 miles per gallon of gas.

Total gas needed: __________

Gas costs $1.19 per gallon.

Total amount needed for gas: __________

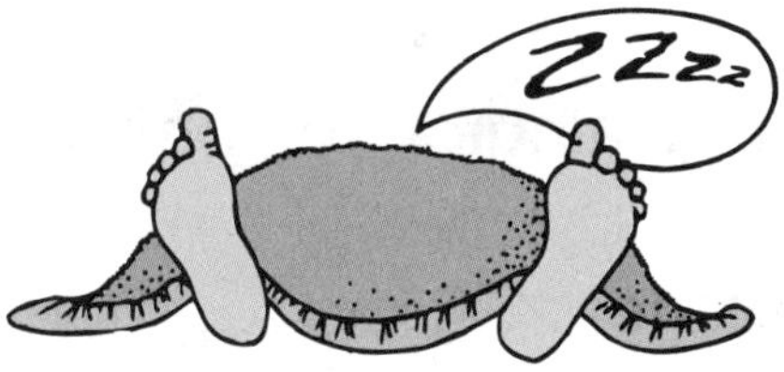

You will stay at a hotel/motel for four nights at $79.00 per night.

Total cost for four nights: __________

Estimated food cost per day (5 days)

breakfast—$2.50

lunch—$4.75

dinner—$9.25

Total per day: __________

Total for 5 days: __________

Estimated entertainment expenses

Admission to movies: __________

Admission to museums: __________

Admission to theme parks: __________

Admission to sports events: __________

Add all the entries to get a total estimate for the cost of the trip.

Total estimated cost of the trip: ______________________

0-7696-8513-7

Glossary

Acute angle: Any angle that is less than a right angle or 90°.
Angle: The part of a shape where two lines come together.
Area: The number of square units needed to cover a flat surface.
Average: A number that tells about how something is normally. Find an average by adding all the numbers together and dividing by the number of addends.
Capacity: The measure of how much can fit inside an object.
Circle: A round, closed figure.
Common denominator: One number that is a common multiple of two or more denominators.
Congruent figures: Figures that have the same shape and size.
Decimal: A dot placed between the ones place and the tenths place in a number.
Denominator: The bottom number of a fraction that numbers the total amount of equal pieces.
Diameter: A line segment with both points on the circle, which always passes through the center of the circles.
Difference: The answer in a subtraction problem.
Dividend: The number to be divided in a division problem.
Divisor: The number to divide by in a division problem.
Equivalent fractions: Two different fractions that represent the same number.
Factors: The two numbers multiplied together in a multiplication problem.
Fraction: One or more equal parts of a whole or part of a group.
Improper fractions: A fraction representing a whole and a fraction. The numerator is larger than the denominator.

Glossary

Like Fractions: Fractions with the same denominator.
Mixed number: A number made up of a whole number and a fraction.
Multiplication: A quick way to add.
Numerator: The top number of a fraction that numbers the parts.
Obtuse angle: Any angle that is more than a right angle or 90°.
Ordered pair: A set of numbers used to find a point on a grid.
Perimeter: The distance around the outside of a shape.
Pictograph: A graph using pictures to give information.
Place value: The value of a numeral determined by its place in a number.
Polygon: A closed shape with straight sides.
Probability: The chance that a given event will happen.
Product: The answer in a multiplication problem.
Quotient: The answer in a division problem.
Radius: A line segment from the center of a circle to any point on the circle.
Regrouping: Borrowing or carrying numbers between places.
Remainder: The amount left over after dividing a number.
Right angle: Any angle that measures 90°. It forms a square corner.
Rounding: Changing an exact amount to an estimate of the number.
Sum: The answer in an addition problem.
Survey: A mini-interview of many people to find out what they like or do not like.
Symmetry: A figure with two parts that match exactly.
Tally mark: A line to represent one. The fifth tally of any grouping is written diagonally over the first four marks. **Example:** 卌
Temperature: The measure of how warm or cold something is.
Unlike fractions: Fractions with different denominators.
Volume: The measure of the inside of a shape.

Answer Key

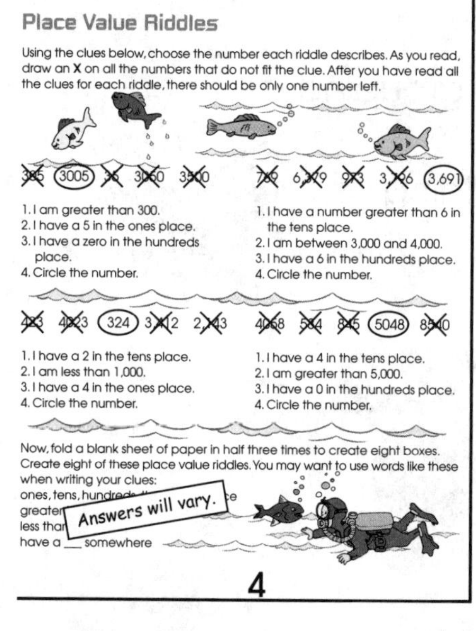

Place Value Riddles

Using the clues below, choose the number each riddle describes. As you read, draw an **X** on all the numbers that do not fit the clue. After you have read all the clues for each riddle, there should be only one number left.

~~385~~ (3005) ~~35~~ ~~3050~~ ~~3500~~

1. I am greater than 300.
2. I have a 5 in the ones place.
3. I have a zero in the hundreds place.
4. Circle the number.

~~769~~ ~~6,379~~ ~~973~~ ~~3,796~~ (3,691)

1. I have a number greater than 6 in the tens place.
2. I am between 3,000 and 4,000.
3. I have a 6 in the hundreds place.
4. Circle the number.

~~423~~ ~~4023~~ (324) ~~3,412~~ ~~2,143~~

1. I have a 2 in the tens place.
2. I am less than 1,000.
3. I have a 4 in the ones place.
4. Circle the number.

~~4068~~ ~~584~~ ~~845~~ (5048) ~~8540~~

1. I have a 4 in the tens place.
2. I am greater than 5,000.
3. I have a 0 in the hundreds place.
4. Circle the number.

Now, fold a blank sheet of paper in half three times to create eight boxes. Create eight of these place value riddles. You may want to use words like these when writing your clues:
ones, tens, hundreds ... ce
greater ...
less than ...
have a ___ somewhere

Answers will vary.

4

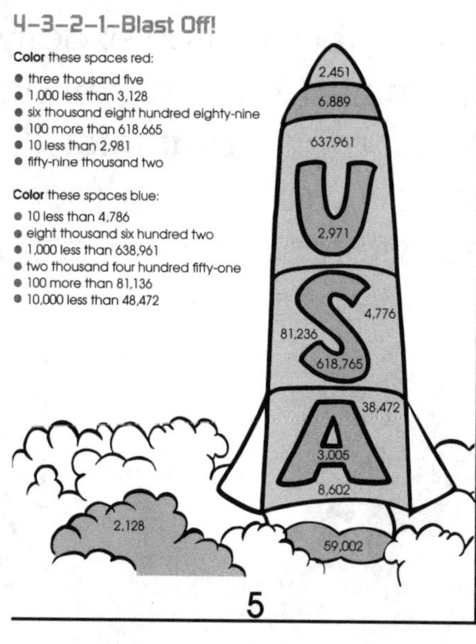

4-3-2-1-Blast Off!

Color these spaces red:

- three thousand five
- 1,000 less than 3,128
- six thousand eight hundred eighty-nine
- 100 more than 618,665
- 10 less than 2,981
- fifty-nine thousand two

Color these spaces blue:

- 10 less than 4,786
- eight thousand six hundred two
- 1,000 less than 638,961
- two thousand four hundred fifty-one
- 100 more than 81,136
- 10,000 less than 48,472

5

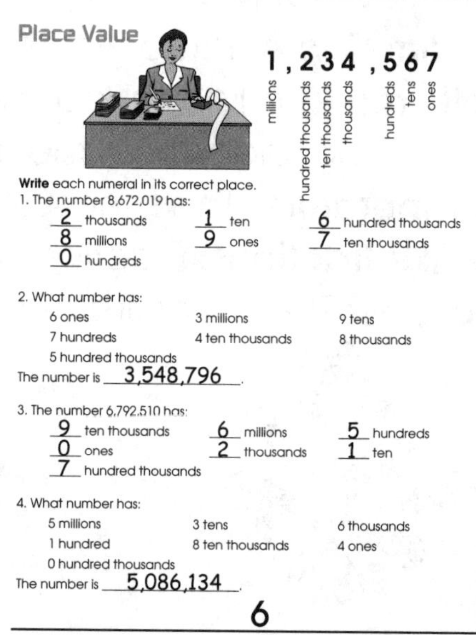

Place Value

Write each numeral in its correct place.

1. The number 8,672,019 has:
   2 thousands — 1 ten — 6 hundred thousands
   8 millions — 9 ones — 7 ten thousands
   0 hundreds

2. What number has:
   6 ones — 3 millions — 9 tens
   7 hundreds — 4 ten thousands — 8 thousands
   5 hundred thousands
   The number is 3,548,796.

3. The number 6,792,510 has:
   9 ten thousands — 6 millions — 5 hundreds
   0 ones — 2 thousands — 1 ten
   7 hundred thousands

4. What number has:
   5 millions — 3 tens — 6 thousands
   1 hundred — 8 ten thousands — 4 ones
   0 hundred thousands
   The number is 5,086,134.

6

Estimate by Rounding Numbers

Estimate by rounding numbers to different place values. Use these rules.

Example: Round 283 to the nearest hundred.

- Find the digit in the place to be rounded. — 283
- Now, look at the digit to its right. — 283
- If the digit to the right is less than 5, the digit being rounded remains the same.
- If the digit to the right is 5 or more, the digit being rounded is increased by 1. — 283 Rounds to 300
- Digits to the right of the place to be rounded become 0's. Digits to the left remain the same.

Examples: Round 4,385 . . .

to the nearest thousand	to the nearest hundred	to the nearest ten
4,385	4,385	4,385
3 is less than 5.	8 is more than 5.	5 = 5.
The 4 stays the same.	The 3 is rounded up to 4.	The 8 is rounded up to 9.
4,000	4,400	4,390

Complete the table.

NUMBERS TO BE ROUNDED	ROUND TO THE NEAREST THOUSAND	NEAREST HUNDRED	NEAREST TEN
2,725	3,000	2,700	2,730
10,942	11,000	10,900	10,940
6,816	7,000	6,800	6,820
2,309	2,000	2,300	2,310
7,237	7,000	7,200	7,240
959	1,000	1,000	960

7

The First State

What state is known as the first state? Follow the directions below to find out.

1. If 31,842 rounded to the nearest thousand is 31,000, put an **A** above number 2.
2. If 62 rounded to the nearest ten is 60, put an **E** above number 2 .
3. If 4,234 rounded to the nearest hundred is 4,200, put an **R** above number 7.
4. If 677 rounded to the nearest hundred is 600, put an **L** above number 3.
5. If 344 rounded to the nearest ten is 350, put an **E** above number 5.
6. If 5,599 rounded to the nearest thousand is 6,000, put an **A** above number 4.
7. If 1,549 rounded to the nearest hundred is 1,500, put an **A** above number 6.
8. If 885 rounded to the nearest hundred is 800, put a **W** above number 2.
9. If 521 rounded to the nearest ten is 520, put an **E** above number 8.
10. If 74 rounded to the nearest ten is 80, put an **R** above number 6.
11. If 3,291 rounded to the nearest thousand is 3,000, put an **L** above number 3.
12. If 248 rounded to the nearest hundred is 300, put an **R** above number 4.
13. If 615 rounded to the nearest ten is 620, put a **D** above number 1.
14. If 188 rounded to the nearest ten is 200, put a **W** above number 1.
15. If 6,817 rounded to the nearest thousand is 7,000, put a **W** above number 5.

Peach Blossom State Flower

Blue Hen Chicken State Bird

Fort Christina—site of the first state's first permanent settlement. Built by the Swedes and Finns.

D	E	L	A	W	A	R	E
1	2	3	4	5	6	7	8

8

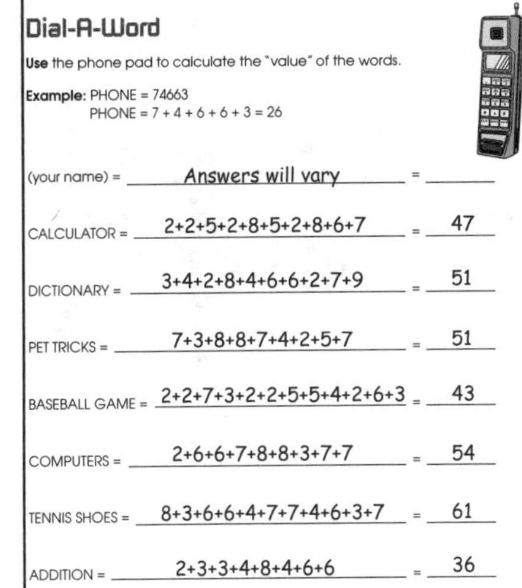

Dial-A-Word
Use the phone pad to calculate the "value" of the words.
Example: PHONE = 74663
PHONE = 7 + 4 + 6 + 6 + 3 = 26
(your name) = Answers will vary =
CALCULATOR = 2+2+5+2+8+5+2+8+6+7 = 47
DICTIONARY = 3+4+2+8+4+6+6+2+7+9 = 51
PET TRICKS = 7+3+8+8+7+4+2+5+7 = 51
BASEBALL GAME = 2+2+7+3+2+2+5+5+4+2+6+3 = 43
COMPUTERS = 2+6+6+7+8+8+3+7+7 = 54
TENNIS SHOES = 8+3+6+6+4+7+7+4+6+3+7 = 61
ADDITION = 2+3+3+4+8+4+6+6 = 36
MENTAL MATH = 6+3+6+8+2+5+6+2+8+4 = 50
10

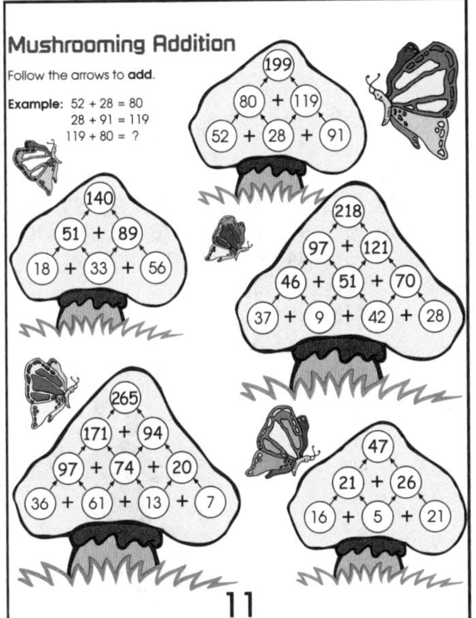

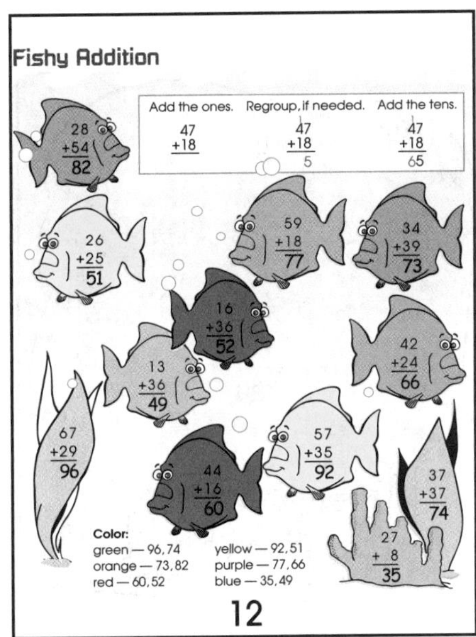

Fishy Addition
Add the ones. Regroup, if needed. Add the tens.
47 +18
47 +18 5
47 +18 65
28 +54 82
26 +25 51
59 +18 77
34 +39 73
16 +36 52
13 +36 49
42 +24 66
67 +29 96
57 +35 92
44 +16 60
37 +37 74
27 + 8 35
Color:
green — 96, 74
orange — 73, 82
red — 60, 52
yellow — 92, 51
purple — 77, 66
blue — 35, 49
12

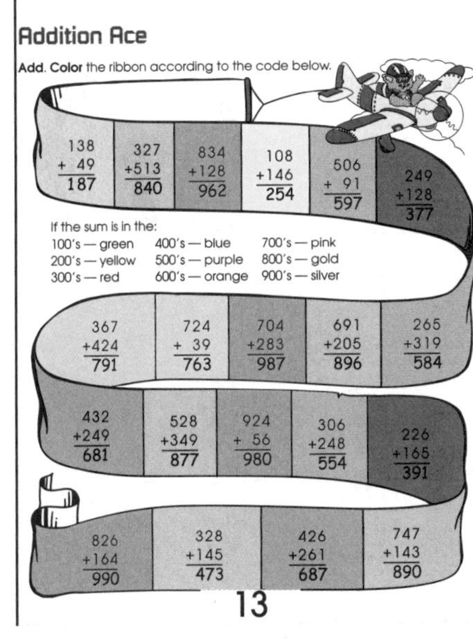

Addition Ace
Add. Color the ribbon according to the code below.
138 + 49 187
327 +513 840
834 +128 962
108 +146 254
506 + 91 597
249 +128 377
If the sum is in the:
100's — green
200's — yellow
300's — red
400's — blue
500's — purple
600's — orange
700's — pink
800's — gold
900's — silver
367 +424 791
724 + 39 763
704 +283 987
691 +205 896
265 +319 584
432 +249 681
528 +349 877
924 + 56 980
306 +248 554
226 +165 391
826 +164 990
328 +145 473
426 +261 687
747 +143 890
13

Cotton Pickin' Math

Solve the problems.

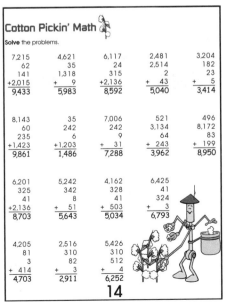

7,215 + 62 + 141 + 2,015 = 9,433	4,621 + 35 + 1,318 + 9 = 5,983	6,117 + 24 + 315 + 2,136 = 8,592	2,481 + 2,514 + 2 + 43 = 5,040	3,204 + 182 + 23 + 5 = 3,414
8,143 + 60 + 235 + 1,423 = 9,861	35 + 242 + 6 + 1,203 = 1,486	7,006 + 242 + 9 + 31 = 7,288	521 + 3,134 + 64 + 243 = 3,962	496 + 8,172 + 83 + 199 = 8,950
6,201 + 325 + 41 + 2,136 = 8,703	5,242 + 342 + 8 + 51 = 5,643	4,162 + 328 + 41 + 503 = 5,034	6,425 + 41 + 324 + 3 = 6,793	
4,205 + 81 + 3 + 414 = 4,703	2,516 + 310 + 82 + 3 = 2,911	5,426 + 310 + 512 + 4 = 6,252		

14

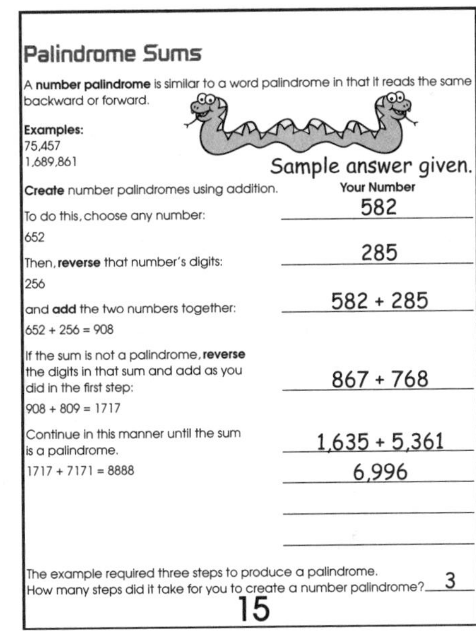

Palindrome Sums
A number palindrome is similar to a word palindrome in that it reads the same backward or forward.
Examples:
75,457
1,689,861
Sample answer given.
Create number palindromes using addition.
Your Number
582
To do this, choose any number:
652
285
Then, reverse that number's digits:
256
582 + 285
and add the two numbers together:
652 + 256 = 908
867 + 768
If the sum is not a palindrome, reverse the digits in that sum and add as you did in the first step:
908 + 809 = 1717
1,635 + 5,361
Continue in this manner until the sum is a palindrome.
1717 + 7171 = 8888
6,996
The example required three steps to produce a palindrome.
How many steps did it take for you to create a number palindrome? 3
15

Stay on Track
Add or subtract. Write each answer in the puzzle.
Across
1. 413 +312 725
3. 102 +415 517
4. 223 +103 326
6. 131 +253 384
8. 324 +321 645
10. 207 +222 429
12. 105 +214 319
14. 315 +400 715
16. 121 +503 624
18. 451 +421 872
20. 312 +281 593
Down
1. 859 −112 747
2. 985 −402 583
3. 887 −344 543
5. 789 −583 206
7. 699 −240 459
9. 589 −100 489
11. 767 −512 255
13. 497 −321 176
15. 259 −151 108
17. 974 −511 463
19. 689 −450 239
20. 797 −236 561
17

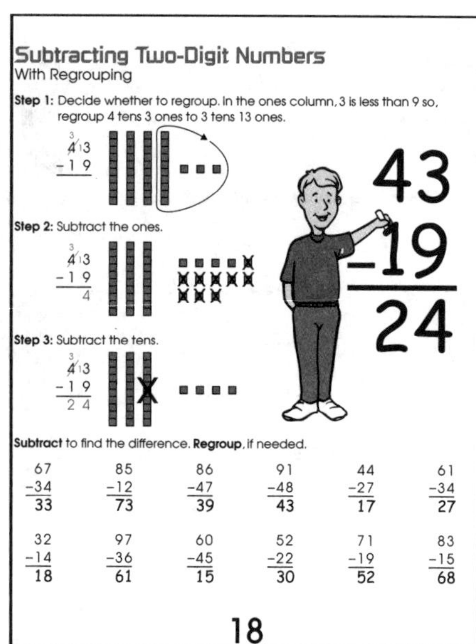

Subtracting Two-Digit Numbers
With Regrouping

Step 1: Decide whether to regroup. In the ones column, 3 is less than 9 so, regroup 4 tens 3 ones to 3 tens 13 ones.

Step 2: Subtract the ones.

Step 3: Subtract the tens.

43 − 19 = 24

Subtract to find the difference. **Regroup**, if needed.

67 − 34 = 33	85 − 12 = 73	86 − 47 = 39	91 − 48 = 43	44 − 27 = 17	61 − 34 = 27
32 − 14 = 18	97 − 36 = 61	60 − 45 = 15	52 − 22 = 30	71 − 19 = 52	83 − 15 = 68

18

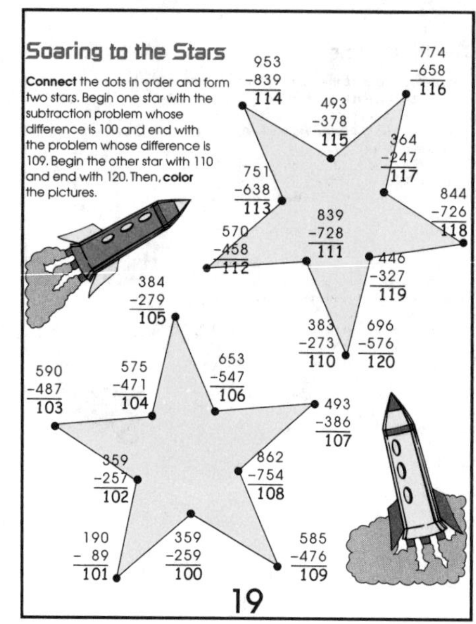

Soaring to the Stars

Connect the dots in order and form two stars. Begin one star with the subtraction problem whose difference is 100 and end with the problem whose difference is 109. Begin the other star with 110 and end with 120. Then, **color** the pictures.

953 − 839 = 114; 774 − 658 = 116; 493 − 378 = 115; 364 − 247 = 117; 751 − 638 = 113; 844 − 726 = 118; 839 − 728 = 111; 570 − 458 = 112; 446 − 327 = 119; 384 − 279 = 105; 383 − 273 = 110; 696 − 576 = 120; 590 − 487 = 103; 575 − 471 = 104; 653 − 547 = 106; 493 − 386 = 107; 359 − 257 = 102; 862 − 754 = 108; 190 − 89 = 101; 359 − 259 = 100; 585 − 476 = 109

19

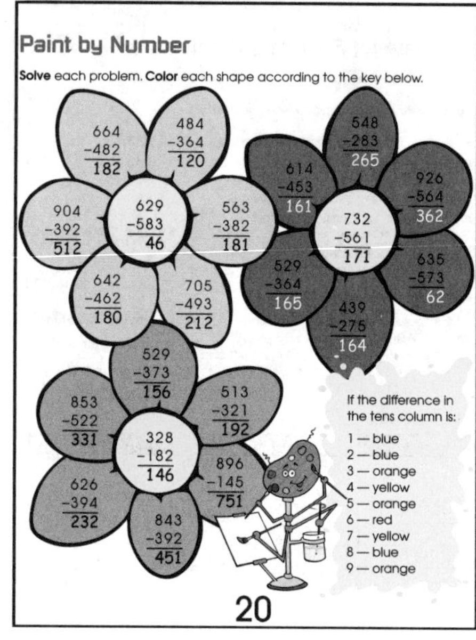

Paint by Number

Solve each problem. **Color** each shape according to the key below.

664 − 482 = 182; 484 − 364 = 120; 548 − 283 = 265; 614 − 453 = 161; 926 − 564 = 362; 904 − 392 = 512; 629 − 583 = 46; 563 − 382 = 181; 732 − 561 = 171; 635 − 573 = 62; 642 − 462 = 180; 705 − 493 = 212; 529 − 364 = 165; 439 − 275 = 164; 529 − 373 = 156; 853 − 522 = 331; 513 − 321 = 192; 328 − 182 = 146; 896 − 145 = 751; 626 − 394 = 232; 843 − 392 = 451

If the difference in the tens column is:
1 — blue
2 — blue
3 — orange
4 — yellow
5 — orange
6 — red
7 — yellow
8 — blue
9 — orange

20

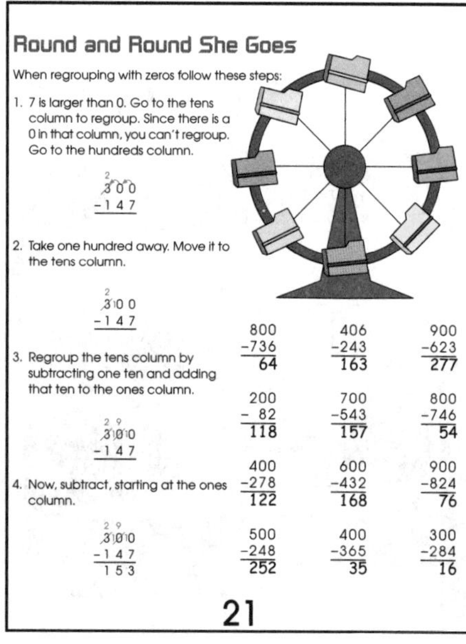

Round and Round She Goes

When regrouping with zeros follow these steps:

1. 7 is larger than 0. Go to the tens column to regroup. Since there is a 0 in that column, you can't regroup. Go to the hundreds column.
   300 − 147
2. Take one hundred away. Move it to the tens column.
3. Regroup the tens column by subtracting one ten and adding that ten to the ones column.
4. Now, subtract, starting at the ones column.
   300 − 147 = 153

800 − 736 = 64	406 − 243 = 163	900 − 623 = 277
200 − 82 = 118	700 − 543 = 157	800 − 746 = 54
400 − 278 = 122	600 − 432 = 168	900 − 824 = 76
500 − 248 = 252	400 − 365 = 35	300 − 284 = 16

21

High Class Math

Solve these problems.

3,270 − 1,529 = 1,741; 8,248 − 1,513 = 6,735

7,648 − 3,291 = 4,357; 4,321 − 1,809 = 2,512; 8,241 − 3,516 = 4,725; 3,002 − 1,231 = 1,771; 9,200 − 3,146 = 6,054

5,017 − 2,408 = 2,609; 8,254 − 3,187 = 5,067; 7,265 − 2,134 = 5,131; 3,846 − 1,359 = 2,487; 8,006 − 3,084 = 4,922

3,084 − 1,926 = 1,158; 6,265 − 4,189 = 2,076; 4,824 − 1,913 = 2,911; 6,205 − 1,054 = 5,151; 5,253 − 4,428 = 825

9,205 − 3,187 = 6,018; 5,809 − 3,913 = 1,896; 5,642 − 2,408 = 3,234

22

Skipping Through the Tens

Skip count by tens. Begin with the number on the first line. **Write** each number that follows.

0, 10	20	30	40	50	60	70	80	90	100
3, 13	23	33	43	53	63	73	83	93	103
1, 11	21	31	41	51	61	71	81	91	101
8, 18	28	38	48	58	68	78	88	98	108
6, 16	26	36	46	56	66	76	86	96	106
4, 14	24	34	44	54	64	74	84	94	104
2, 12	22	32	42	52	62	72	82	92	102
5, 15	25	35	45	55	65	75	85	95	105
7, 17	27	37	47	57	67	77	87	97	107
9, 19	29	39	49	59	69	79	89	99	109

What is ten more than . . . ?

26 36	29 39
44 54	77 87
53 63	91 101
24 34	49 59
66 76	35 45
54 64	82 92

24

Count the Legs!

Multiplication is a quick way to add. For example, count the legs of the horses below. They each have 4 legs. You could add 4 + 4 + 4. But it is quicker to say that there are 3 groups of 4 legs. In multiplication, that is 3 x 4.
Multiply to find the number of legs. **Write** each problem twice.

3 horses x 4 legs = 12; 3 x 4 = 12
3 ostriches x 2 legs = 6; 3 x 2 = 6
2 insects x 6 legs = 12; 2 x 6 = 12
3 stools x 3 legs = 9; 3 x 3 = 9
6 cows x 4 legs = 24; 6 x 4 = 24
3 birds x 2 legs = 6; 3 x 2 = 6

25

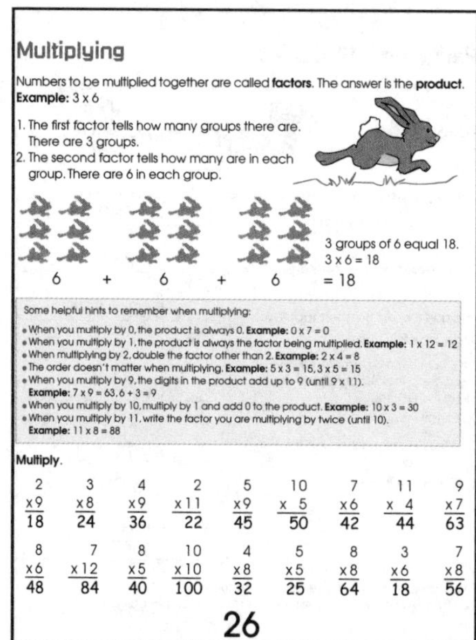

Multiplying

Numbers to be multiplied together are called **factors**. The answer is the **product**.
Example: 3 x 6

1. The first factor tells how many groups there are. There are 3 groups.
2. The second factor tells how many are in each group. There are 6 in each group.

6 + 6 + 6 = 18
3 groups of 6 equal 18.
3 x 6 = 18

Some helpful hints to remember when multiplying:
- When you multiply by 0, the product is always 0. **Example:** 0 x 7 = 0
- When you multiply by 1, the product is always the factor being multiplied. **Example:** 1 x 12 = 12
- When multiplying by 2, double the factor other than 2. **Example:** 2 x 4 = 8
- The order doesn't matter when multiplying. **Example:** 5 x 3 = 15, 3 x 5 = 15
- When you multiply by 9, the digits in the product add up to 9 (until 9 x 11). **Example:** 7 x 9 = 63, 6 + 3 = 9
- When you multiply by 10, multiply by 1 and add 0 to the product. **Example:** 10 x 3 = 30
- When you multiply by 11, write the factor you are multiplying by twice (until 10). **Example:** 11 x 8 = 88

Multiply.

2 x 9 = 18; 3 x 8 = 24; 4 x 9 = 36; 2 x 11 = 22; 5 x 9 = 45; 10 x 5 = 50; 7 x 6 = 42; 11 x 4 = 44; 9 x 7 = 63

8 x 6 = 48; 7 x 12 = 84; 8 x 5 = 40; 10 x 10 = 100; 4 x 8 = 32; 5 x 5 = 25; 8 x 8 = 64; 3 x 6 = 18; 7 x 8 = 56

26

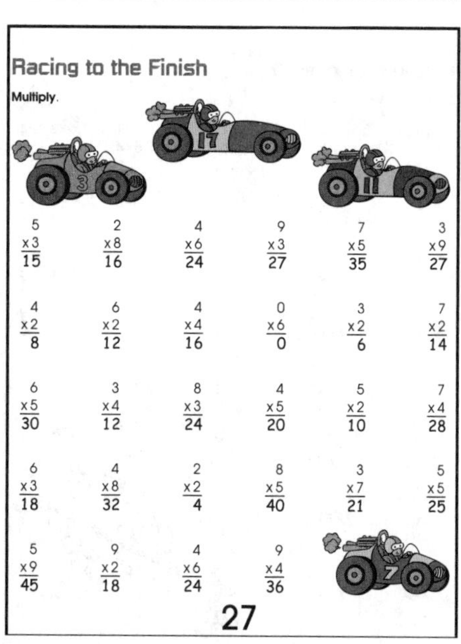

Racing to the Finish

Multiply.

5 x 3 = 15	2 x 8 = 16	4 x 6 = 24	9 x 3 = 27	7 x 5 = 35	3 x 9 = 27
4 x 2 = 8	6 x 2 = 12	4 x 4 = 16	0 x 6 = 0	3 x 2 = 6	7 x 2 = 14
6 x 5 = 30	3 x 4 = 12	8 x 3 = 24	4 x 5 = 20	5 x 2 = 10	7 x 4 = 28
6 x 3 = 18	4 x 8 = 32	2 x 2 = 4	8 x 5 = 40	3 x 7 = 21	5 x 5 = 25
5 x 9 = 45	9 x 2 = 18	4 x 6 = 24	9 x 4 = 36		

27

Double Trouble

Solve each multiplication problem. Below each answer, **write** the letter from the code that matches the answer. **Read** the coded question and **write** the answer in the space provided.

1	4	9	16	25	36	49	64	81	100	121	144
E	G	H	I	N	O	S	T	U	W	X	Y

10 x10	3 x3	6 x6
100	9	36
W	H	O

4 x4	7 x7
16	49
I	S

7 x7	4 x4	8 x8	8 x8	4 x4	5 x5	2 x2
49	16	64	64	16	25	4
S	I	T	T	I	N	G

5 x5	1 x1	11 x11	8 x8
25	1	121	64
N	E	X	T

8 x8	6 x6
64	36
T	O

12 x12	6 x6	9 x9
144	36	81
Y	O	U ?

Answer: Answers will vary.

28

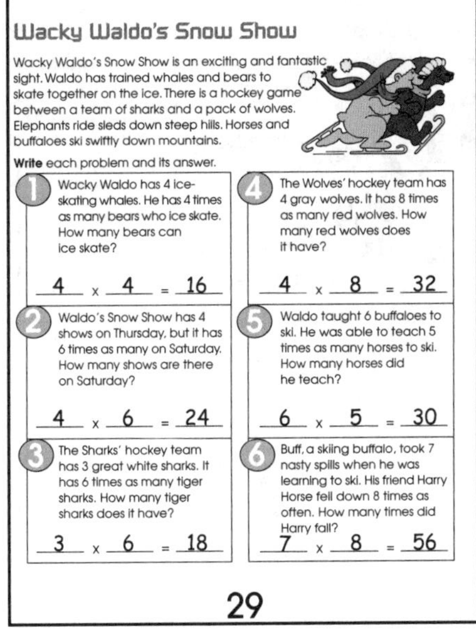

Wacky Waldo's Snow Show

Wacky Waldo's Snow Show is an exciting and fantastic sight. Waldo has trained whales and bears to skate together on the ice. There is a hockey game between a team of sharks and a pack of wolves. Elephants ride sleds down steep hills. Horses and buffaloes ski swiftly down mountains.

Write each problem and its answer.

1. Wacky Waldo has 4 ice-skating whales. He has 4 times as many bears who ice skate. How many bears can ice skate? 4 x 4 = 16
2. Waldo's Snow Show has 4 shows on Thursday, but it has 6 times as many on Saturday. How many shows are there on Saturday? 4 x 6 = 24
3. The Sharks' hockey team has 3 great white sharks. It has 6 times as many tiger sharks. How many tiger sharks does it have? 3 x 6 = 18
4. The Wolves' hockey team has 4 gray wolves. It has 8 times as many red wolves. How many red wolves does it have? 4 x 8 = 32
5. Waldo taught 6 buffaloes to ski. He was able to teach 5 times as many horses to ski. How many horses did he teach? 6 x 5 = 30
6. Buff, a skiing buffalo, took 7 nasty spills when he was learning to ski. His friend Harry Horse fell down 8 times as often. How many times did Harry fall? 7 x 8 = 56

29

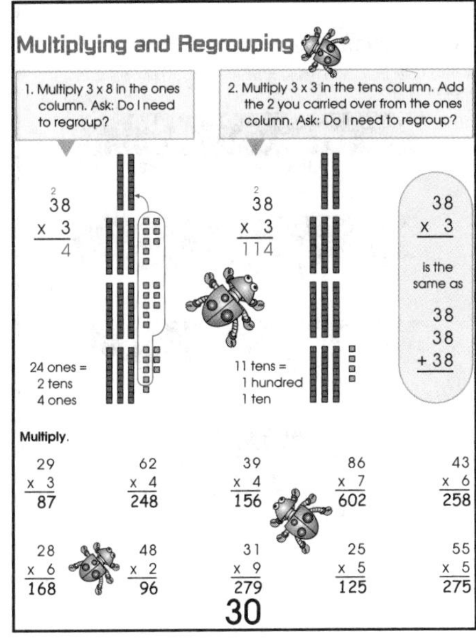

Multiplying and Regrouping

1. Multiply 3 x 8 in the ones column. Ask: Do I need to regroup?

38 x 3 = 4 (carry 2)

24 ones = 2 tens 4 ones

2. Multiply 3 x 3 in the tens column. Add the 2 you carried over from the ones column. Ask: Do I need to regroup?

38 x 3 = 114

11 tens = 1 hundred 1 ten

38 x 3 is the same as 38 + 38 + 38

Multiply.

29 x 3 = 87; 62 x 4 = 248; 39 x 4 = 156; 86 x 7 = 602; 43 x 6 = 258

28 x 6 = 168; 48 x 2 = 96; 31 x 9 = 279; 25 x 5 = 125; 55 x 5 = 275

30

Under the Big Top!

Complete this crossnumber puzzle.

43 x 4 = 172

x

2 x 58 = 116

= x

86 x 7 = 602

=

406

65 x 4 = 260

x x

5 x 77 = 385

= =

325 308

31

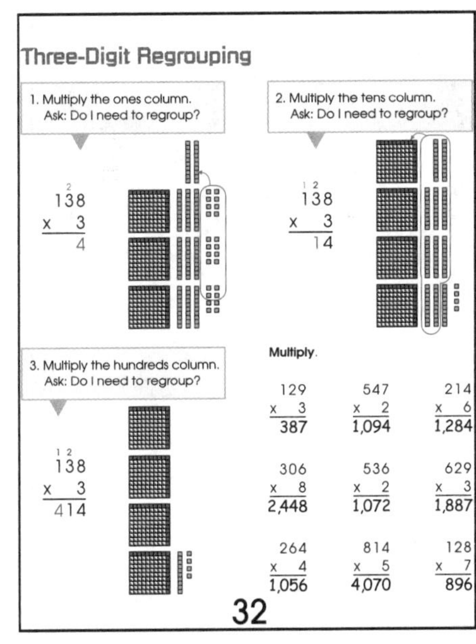

Three-Digit Regrouping

1. Multiply the ones column. Ask: Do I need to regroup?

138 x 3 = 4 (carry 2)

2. Multiply the tens column. Ask: Do I need to regroup?

138 x 3 = 14 (carry 1, 2)

3. Multiply the hundreds column. Ask: Do I need to regroup?

138 x 3 = 414

Multiply.

129 x 3 = 387; 547 x 2 = 1,094; 214 x 6 = 1,284

306 x 8 = 2,448; 536 x 2 = 1,072; 629 x 3 = 1,887

264 x 4 = 1,056; 814 x 5 = 4,070; 128 x 7 = 896

32

Solve It!

What set of ridges and loops are different on every person? To find out, **solve** the following problems and **write** the matching letter above each answer at the bottom of the page.

I. 303 x 3 = 909; 303 x 3 = 09; 303 x 3 = 909 (worked steps); R. 214 x 2 = 428; N. 413 x 2 = 826

N. 142 x 2 = 284; R. 211 x 4 = 844; F. 104 x 2 = 208

T. 131 x 2 = 262; P. 232 x 3 = 696; E. 301 x 2 = 602; I. 134 x 1 = 134

G. 244 x 2 = 488; S. 334 x 2 = 668

F	I	N	G	E	R	P	R	I	N	T	S
208	909	826	488	602	844	696	428	134	284	262	668

33

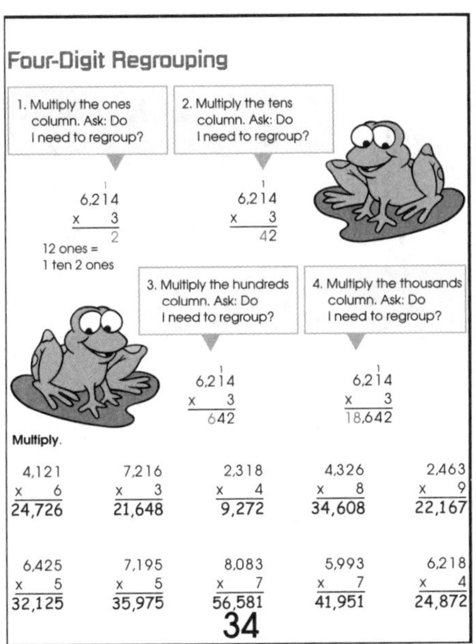

Four-Digit Regrouping

1. Multiply the ones column. Ask: Do I need to regroup?

6,214 x 3 = 2 (carry 1)

12 ones = 1 ten 2 ones

2. Multiply the tens column. Ask: Do I need to regroup?

6,214 x 3 = 42

3. Multiply the hundreds column. Ask: Do I need to regroup?

6,214 x 3 = 642

4. Multiply the thousands column. Ask: Do I need to regroup?

6,214 x 3 = 18,642

Multiply.

4,121 x 6 = 24,726; 7,216 x 3 = 21,648; 2,318 x 4 = 9,272; 4,326 x 8 = 34,608; 2,463 x 9 = 22,167

6,425 x 5 = 32,125; 7,195 x 5 = 35,975; 8,083 x 7 = 56,581; 5,993 x 7 = 41,951; 6,218 x 4 = 24,872

34

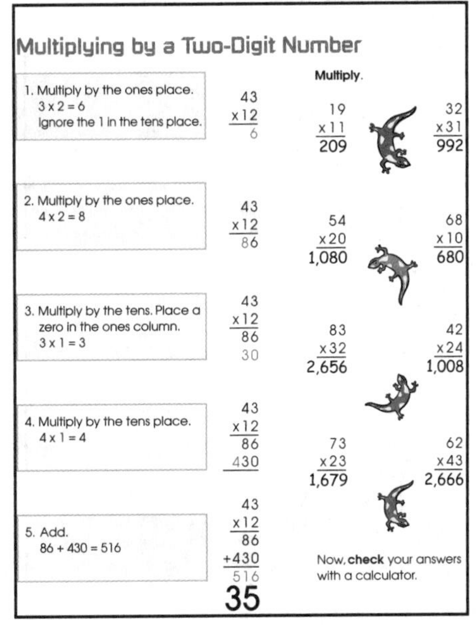

Multiplying by a Two-Digit Number

1. Multiply by the ones place. 3 x 2 = 6. Ignore the 1 in the tens place. (43 x 12 → 6)
2. Multiply by the ones place. 4 x 2 = 8 (43 x 12 → 86)
3. Multiply by the tens. Place a zero in the ones column. 3 x 1 = 3 (43 x 12 → 86, 30)
4. Multiply by the tens place. 4 x 1 = 4 (43 x 12 → 86, 430)
5. Add. 86 + 430 = 516

Multiply.

19 x 11 = 209; 32 x 31 = 992

54 x 20 = 1,080; 68 x 10 = 680

83 x 32 = 2,656; 42 x 24 = 1,008

73 x 23 = 1,679; 62 x 43 = 2,666

Now, **check** your answers with a calculator.

35

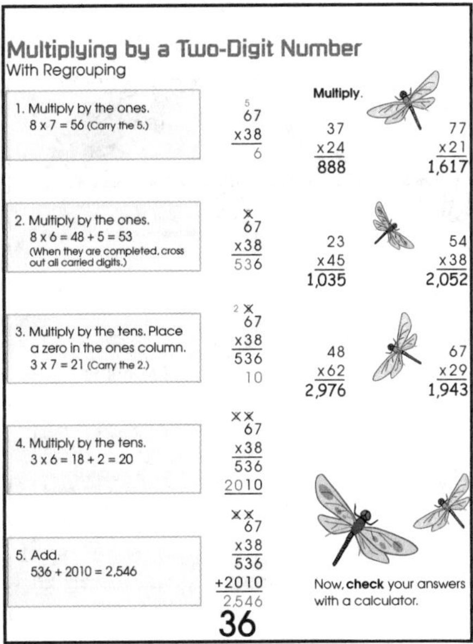

Multiplying by a Two-Digit Number

With Regrouping

1. Multiply by the ones. 8 x 7 = 56 (Carry the 5.) (67 x 38 → 6)
2. Multiply by the ones. 8 x 6 = 48 + 5 = 53 (When they are completed, cross out all carried digits.) (67 x 38 → 536)
3. Multiply by the tens. Place a zero in the ones column. 3 x 7 = 21 (Carry the 2.) (67 x 38 → 536, 10)
4. Multiply by the tens. 3 x 6 = 18 + 2 = 20 (67 x 38 → 536, 2010)
5. Add. 536 + 2010 = 2,546

Multiply.

37 x 24 = 888; 77 x 21 = 1,617

23 x 45 = 1,035; 54 x 38 = 2,052

48 x 62 = 2,976; 67 x 29 = 1,943

Now, **check** your answers with a calculator.

36

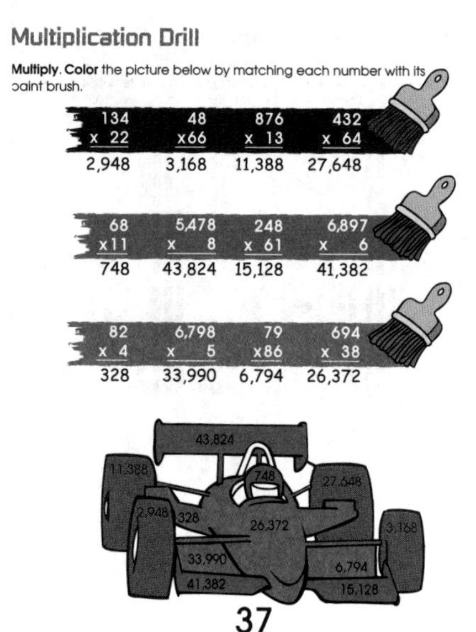

Multiplication Drill

Multiply. Color the picture below by matching each number with its paint brush.

134 × 22	48 × 66	876 × 13	432 × 64
2,948	3,168	11,388	27,648

68 × 11	5,478 × 8	248 × 61	6,897 × 6
748	43,824	15,128	41,382

82 × 4	6,798 × 5	79 × 86	694 × 38
328	33,990	6,794	26,372

37

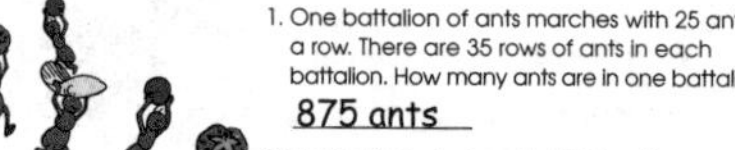

Step by Step

Read the problems below. **Write** each answer in the space provided.

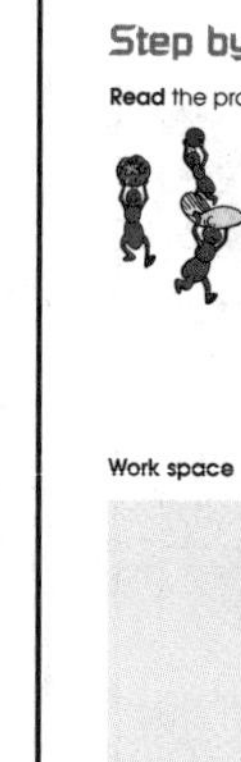

1. One battalion of ants marches with 25 ants in a row. There are 35 rows of ants in each battalion. How many ants are in one battalion?
   875 ants
2. The Ant Army finds a picnic! Now, they need to figure out how many ants should carry each piece of food. A team of 137 ants moves a celery stick. They need 150 ants to carry a carrot stick. A troop of 121 ants carries a very large radish. How many ants in all are needed to move the vegetables?
   408 ants
3. Now, the real work begins—the big pieces of food that would feed their whole colony. It takes 1,259 ants to haul a peanut butter and jelly sandwich. It takes a whole battalion of 2,067 ants to lug the lemonade back, and it takes 1,099 ants to steal the pickle jar. How many soldiers carry these big items?
   4,425 ants
4. Look-outs are posted all around the picnic blanket. It takes 53 soldiers to watch in front of the picnic basket. Another group of 69 ants watch out by the grill. Three groups of 77 watch the different trails in the park. How many ant-soldiers are on the look-out?
   353 ants

Work space

38

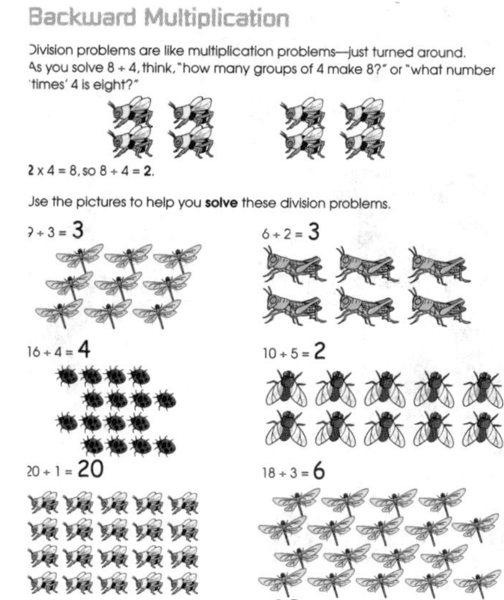

Backward Multiplication

Division problems are like multiplication problems—just turned around. As you solve 8 ÷ 4, think, "how many groups of 4 make 8?" or "what number 'times' 4 is eight?"

2 × 4 = 8, so 8 ÷ 4 = **2**.

Use the pictures to help you **solve** these division problems.

9 ÷ 3 = 3
6 ÷ 2 = 3
16 ÷ 4 = 4
10 ÷ 5 = 2
20 ÷ 1 = 20
18 ÷ 3 = 6

40

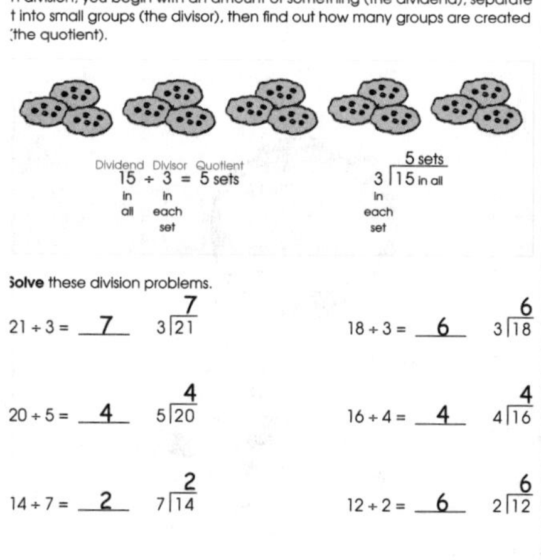

What Exactly Is Division?

In division, you begin with an amount of something (the dividend), separate it into small groups (the divisor), then find out how many groups are created (the quotient).

Solve these division problems.

21 ÷ 3 = 7   3)21 = 7
18 ÷ 3 = 6   3)18 = 6
20 ÷ 5 = 4   5)20 = 4
16 ÷ 4 = 4   4)16 = 4
14 ÷ 7 = 2   7)14 = 2
12 ÷ 2 = 6   2)12 = 6
18 ÷ 2 = 9   2)18 = 9
24 ÷ 6 = 4   6)24 = 4

41

Blastoff!

Divide.

1)6 = 6
20)0 = 0
2)12 = 6
2)14 = 7
2)16 = 8
9)0 = 0
9)0 = 0
2)8 = 4
15)0 = 0
1)19 = 19
2)18 = 9
7)0 = 0
2)10 = 5
1)35 = 35
1)23 = 23
1)17 = 17
1)7 = 7
2)4 = 2
12)0 = 0
2)6 = 3
1)11 = 11
1)5 = 5

42

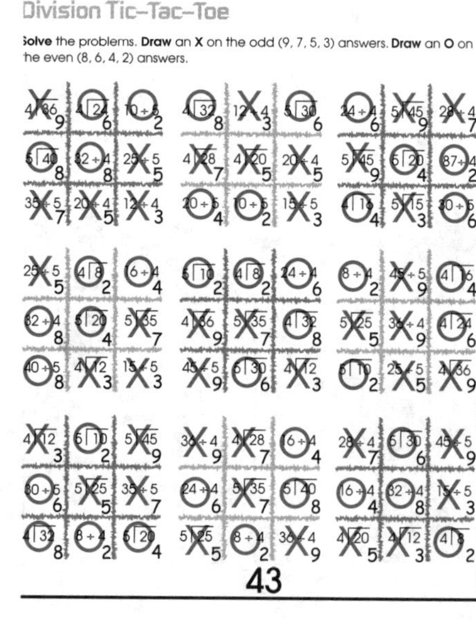

Division Tic-Tac-Toe

Solve the problems. **Draw** an **X** on the odd (9, 7, 5, 3) answers. **Draw** an **O** on the even (8, 6, 4, 2) answers.

43

Lizzy the Lizard Bags Her Bugs

Lizzy the Lizard separates her bugs into separate bags so that her lunch is ready for the week. Help her decide how to divide the bugs.

1. Lizzy caught 45 cockroaches. She put 5 into each bag. How many bags did she use?
   45 ÷ 5 = 9 bags
2. Lizzy found 32 termites. She put 4 into each bag. How many bags did she need?
   32 ÷ 4 = 8 bags
3. Lizzy captured 49 stinkbugs. She put them into 7 bags. How many stinkbugs were in each bag?
   49 ÷ 7 = 7 stinkbugs
4. Lizzy bagged 27 horn beetles. She used 3 bags. How many beetles went into each bag?
   27 ÷ 3 = 9 beetles
5. Lizzy lassoed 36 butterflies. She put 9 into each bag. How many bags did she need?
   36 ÷ 9 = 4 bags
6. Lizzy went fishing and caught 48 water beetles. She used 6 bags for her catch. How many beetles went into each bag?
   48 ÷ 6 = 8 beetles

44

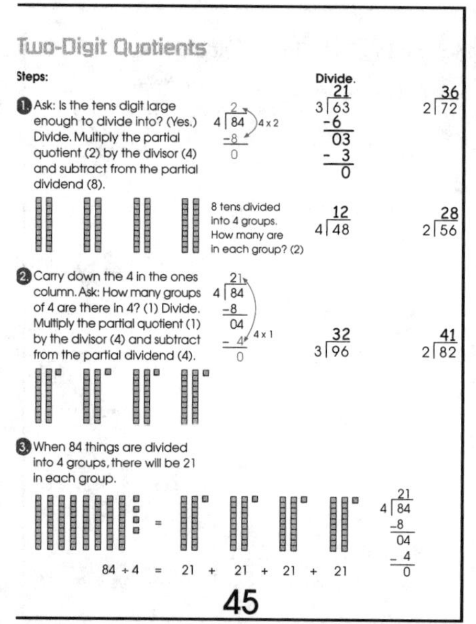

Two-Digit Quotients

Steps:

1. Ask: Is the tens digit large enough to divide into? (Yes.) Divide. Multiply the partial quotient (2) by the divisor (4) and subtract from the partial dividend (8).
   8 tens divided into 4 groups. How many are in each group? (2)
2. Carry down the 4 in the ones column. Ask: How many groups of 4 are there in 4? (1) Divide. Multiply the partial quotient (1) by the divisor (4) and subtract from the partial dividend (4).
3. When 84 things are divided into 4 groups, there will be 21 in each group.
   84 ÷ 4 = 21 + 21 + 21 + 21

Divide.

3)63 = 21
2)72 = 36
4)48 = 12
2)56 = 28
3)96 = 32
2)82 = 41

45

Snowball Bash

Divide this mound of giant snowballs!

7)84 = 12
5)75 = 15
3)45 = 15
9)99 = 11
4)88 = 22
5)80 = 16
4)64 = 16
3)57 = 19
3)78 = 26
3)72 = 24
8)96 = 12
2)86 = 43
2)38 = 19
6)66 = 11
5)65 = 13
4)52 = 13
4)68 = 17
6)78 = 13
7)91 = 13
2)42 = 21
6)72 = 12

46

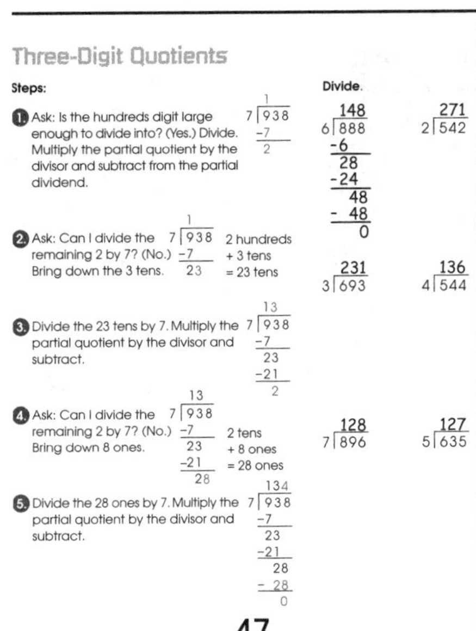

Three-Digit Quotients

Steps:

1. Ask: Is the hundreds digit large enough to divide into? (Yes.) Divide. Multiply the partial quotient by the divisor and subtract from the partial dividend.
2. Ask: Can I divide the remaining 2 by 7? (No.) Bring down the 3 tens. (2 hundreds + 3 tens = 23 tens)
3. Divide the 23 tens by 7. Multiply the partial quotient by the divisor and subtract.
4. Ask: Can I divide the remaining 2 by 7? (No.) Bring down 8 ones. (2 tens + 8 ones = 28 ones)
5. Divide the 28 ones by 7. Multiply the partial quotient by the divisor and subtract.

7)938 134

Divide.

6)888 148; 2)542 271; 3)693 231; 4)544 136; 7)896 128; 5)635 127

47

On-Stage Division

Divide.

6)888 148; 2)956 478; 2)712 356; 4)860 215; 5)845 169

6)750 125; 9)999 111; 8)968 121; 3)774 258; 5)735 147; 8)920 115

8)984 123; 4)500 125; 2)846 423; 4)712 178

48

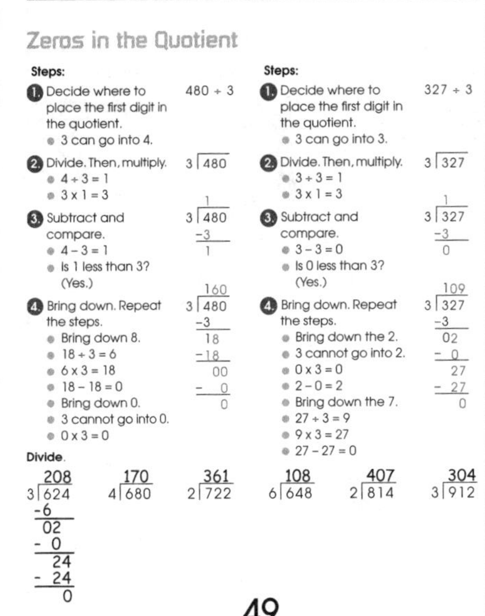

Zeros in the Quotient

Steps:

1. Decide where to place the first digit in the quotient. (480 ÷ 3)
   - 3 can go into 4.
2. Divide. Then, multiply.
   - 4 ÷ 3 = 1
   - 3 x 1 = 3
3. Subtract and compare.
   - 4 − 3 = 1
   - Is 1 less than 3? (Yes.)
4. Bring down. Repeat the steps.
   - Bring down 8.
   - 18 ÷ 3 = 6
   - 6 x 3 = 18
   - 18 − 18 = 0
   - Bring down 0.
   - 3 cannot go into 0.
   - 0 x 3 = 0

3)480 160

Steps:

1. Decide where to place the first digit in the quotient. (327 ÷ 3)
   - 3 can go into 3.
2. Divide. Then, multiply.
   - 3 ÷ 3 = 1
   - 3 x 1 = 3
3. Subtract and compare.
   - 3 − 3 = 0
   - Is 0 less than 3? (Yes.)
4. Bring down. Repeat the steps.
   - Bring down the 2.
   - 3 cannot go into 2.
   - 0 x 3 = 0
   - 2 − 0 = 2
   - Bring down the 7.
   - 27 ÷ 3 = 9
   - 9 x 3 = 27
   - 27 − 27 = 0

3)327 109

Divide.

3)624 208; 4)680 170; 2)722 361; 6)648 108; 2)814 407; 3)912 304

49

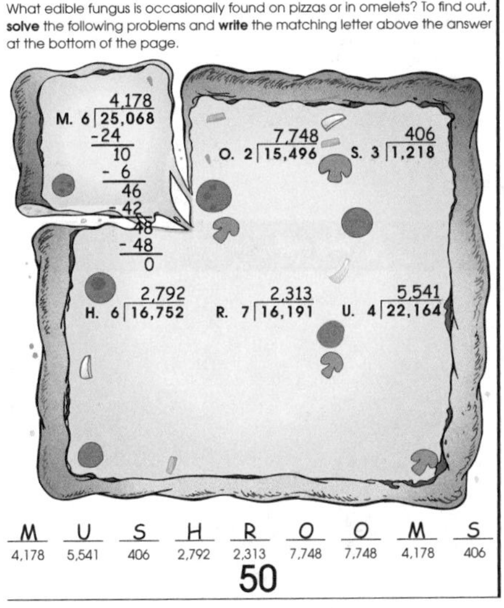

Yum! Yum!

What edible fungus is occasionally found on pizzas or in omelets? To find out, **solve** the following problems and **write** the matching letter above the answer at the bottom of the page.

M. 6)25,068 4,178; O. 2)15,496 7,748; S. 3)1,218 406; H. 6)16,752 2,792; R. 7)16,191 2,313; U. 4)22,164 5,541

M	U	S	H	R	O	O	M	S
4,178	5,541	406	2,792	2,313	7,748	7,748	4,178	406

50

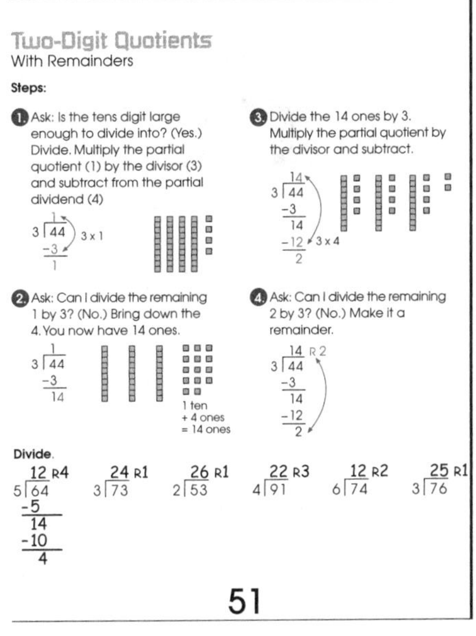

Two-Digit Quotients
With Remainders

Steps:

1. Ask: Is the tens digit large enough to divide into? (Yes.) Divide. Multiply the partial quotient (1) by the divisor (3) and subtract from the partial dividend (4).
2. Ask: Can I divide the remaining 1 by 3? (No.) Bring down the 4. You now have 14 ones. (1 ten + 4 ones = 14 ones)
3. Divide the 14 ones by 3. Multiply the partial quotient by the divisor and subtract.
4. Ask: Can I divide the remaining 2 by 3? (No.) Make it a remainder.

3)44 14 R2

Divide.

5)64 12 R4; 3)73 24 R1; 2)53 26 R1; 4)91 22 R3; 6)74 12 R2; 3)76 25 R1

51

Looking to the Stars

Solve the problems. To find the path to the top, your answers should match the problem number. **Color** the path.

27. 3)63 21; 28. 3)84 28; 29. 4)97 24 R1; 30. 6)74 12 R2

22. 4)74 18 R2; 23. 2)46 23; 24. 2)48 24; 25. 3)75 25; 26. 6)96 16

15. 5)92 18 R2; 16. 3)41 13 R2; 17. 3)57 19; 18. 4)84 21; 19. 4)76 19; 20. 7)86 12 R2; 21. 5)72 14 R2

8. 5)57 11 R2; 9. 3)65 21 R2; 10. 2)87 43 R1; 11. 5)55 11; 12. 7)84 12; 13. 3)87 29; 14. 7)93 13 R2

1. 3)96 32; 2. 6)94 15 R4; 3. 5)93 18 R3; 4. 9)36 4; 5. 2)97 48 R1; 6. 6)84 14; 7. 3)68 22 R2

52

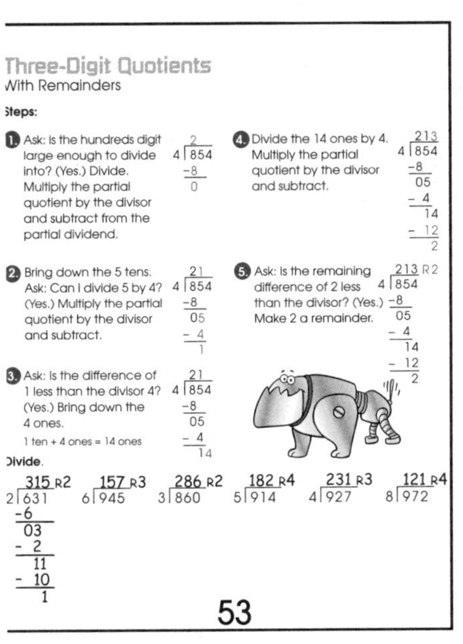

Three-Digit Quotients
With Remainders

Steps:

1. Ask: Is the hundreds digit large enough to divide into? (Yes.) Divide. Multiply the partial quotient by the divisor and subtract from the partial dividend.
2. Bring down the 5 tens. Ask: Can I divide 5 by 4? (Yes.) Multiply the partial quotient by the divisor and subtract.
3. Ask: Is the difference of 1 less than the divisor 4? (Yes.) Bring down the 4 ones. (1 ten + 4 ones = 14 ones)
4. Divide the 14 ones by 4. Multiply the partial quotient by the divisor and subtract.
5. Ask: Is the remaining difference of 2 less than the divisor? (Yes.) Make 2 a remainder.

4)854 213 R2

Divide.

2)631 315 R2; 6)945 157 R3; 3)860 286 R2; 5)914 182 R4; 4)927 231 R3; 8)972 121 R4

53

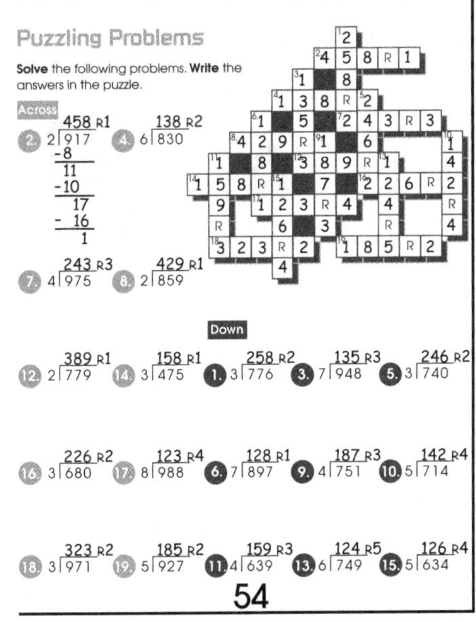

Puzzling Problems

Solve the following problems. **Write** the answers in the puzzle.

Across

2. 2)917 458 R1; 4. 6)830 138 R2; 7. 4)975 243 R3; 8. 2)859 429 R1

Down

12. 2)779 389 R1; 14. 3)475 158 R1; 1. 3)776 258 R2; 3. 7)948 135 R3; 5. 3)740 246 R2

16. 3)680 226 R2; 17. 8)988 123 R4; 6. 7)897 128 R1; 9. 4)751 187 R3; 10. 5)714 142 R4

18. 3)971 323 R2; 19. 5)927 185 R2; 11. 4)639 159 R3; 13. 6)749 124 R5; 15. 5)634 126 R4

54

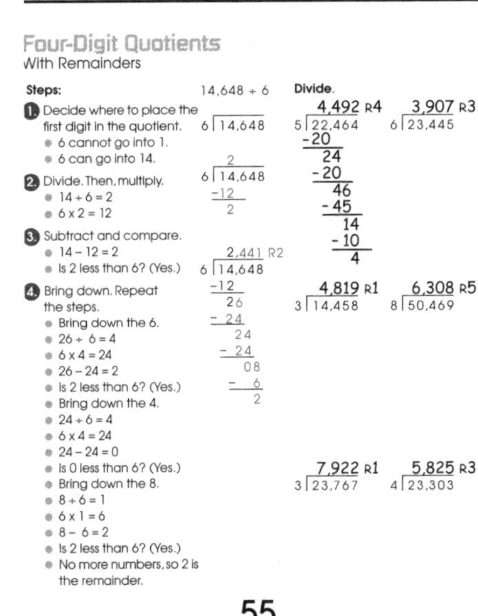

Four-Digit Quotients
With Remainders

Steps:

1. Decide where to place the first digit in the quotient. (14,648 ÷ 6)
   - 6 cannot go into 1.
   - 6 can go into 14.
2. Divide. Then, multiply.
   - 14 ÷ 6 = 2
   - 6 x 2 = 12
3. Subtract and compare.
   - 14 − 12 = 2
   - Is 2 less than 6? (Yes.)
4. Bring down. Repeat the steps.
   - Bring down the 6.
   - 26 ÷ 6 = 4
   - 6 x 4 = 24
   - 26 − 24 = 2
   - Is 2 less than 6? (Yes.)
   - Bring down the 4.
   - 24 ÷ 6 = 4
   - 6 x 4 = 24
   - 24 − 24 = 0
   - Is 0 less than 6? (Yes.)
   - Bring down the 8.
   - 8 ÷ 6 = 1
   - 6 x 1 = 6
   - 8 − 6 = 2
   - Is 2 less than 6? (Yes.)
   - No more numbers, so 2 is the remainder.

6)14,648 2,441 R2

Divide.

5)22,464 4,492 R4; 6)23,445 3,907 R3; 3)14,458 4,819 R1; 8)50,469 6,308 R5; 3)23,767 7,922 R1; 4)23,303 5,825 R3

55

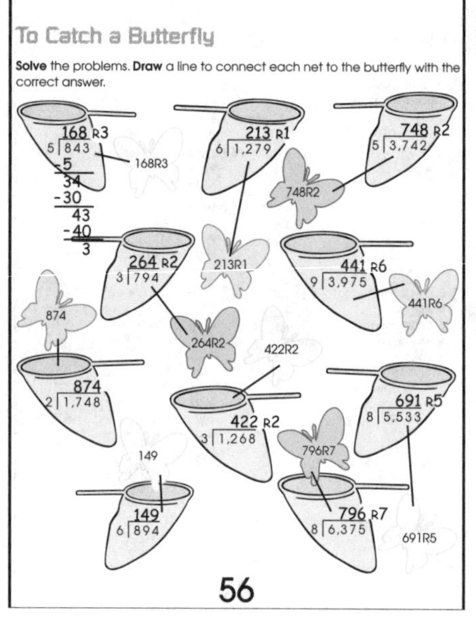

To Catch a Butterfly

Solve the problems. **Draw** a line to connect each net to the butterfly with the correct answer.

56

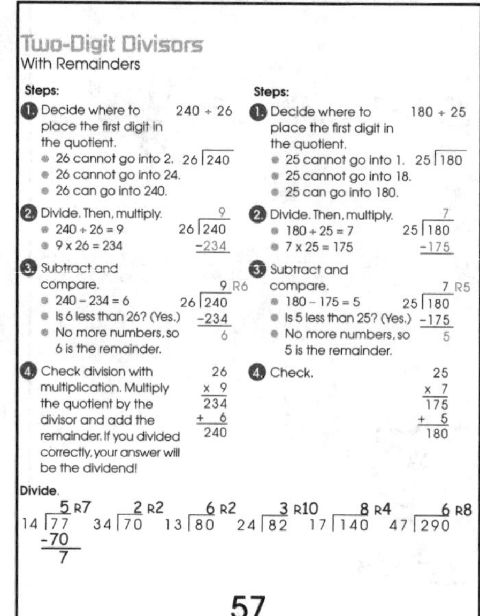

Two-Digit Divisors

With Remainders

Steps: 240 ÷ 26

1. Decide where to place the first digit in the quotient.
   - 26 cannot go into 2.
   - 26 cannot go into 24.
   - 26 can go into 240.

   26 | 240
2. Divide. Then, multiply.
   - 240 ÷ 26 = 9
   - 9 x 26 = 234

   9 / 26 | 240 / -234
3. Subtract and compare.
   - 240 – 234 = 6
   - Is 6 less than 26? (Yes.)
   - No more numbers, so 6 is the remainder.

   9 R6 / 26 | 240 / -234 / 6
4. Check division with multiplication. Multiply the quotient by the divisor and add the remainder. If you divided correctly, your answer will be the dividend!

   26 / x 9 / 234 / + 6 / 240

Steps: 180 ÷ 25

1. Decide where to place the first digit in the quotient.
   - 25 cannot go into 1.
   - 25 cannot go into 18.
   - 25 can go into 180.

   25 | 180
2. Divide. Then, multiply.
   - 180 ÷ 25 = 7
   - 7 x 25 = 175

   7 / 25 | 180 / -175
3. Subtract and compare.
   - 180 – 175 = 5
   - Is 5 less than 25? (Yes.)
   - No more numbers, so 5 is the remainder.

   7 R5 / 25 | 180 / -175 / 5
4. Check.

   25 / x 7 / 175 / + 5 / 180

Divide.

14 | 77 = 5 R7 (-70, 7) 34 | 70 = 2 R2 13 | 80 = 6 R2 24 | 82 = 3 R10 17 | 140 = 8 R4 47 | 290 = 6 R8

57

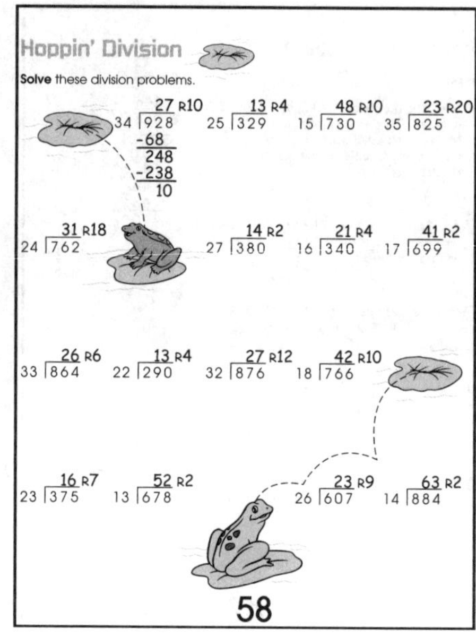

Hoppin' Division

Solve these division problems.

34 | 928 = 27 R10 (-68, 248, -238, 10) 25 | 329 = 13 R4 15 | 730 = 48 R10 35 | 825 = 23 R20

24 | 762 = 31 R18 27 | 380 = 14 R2 16 | 340 = 21 R4 17 | 699 = 41 R2

33 | 864 = 26 R6 22 | 290 = 13 R4 32 | 876 = 27 R12 18 | 766 = 42 R10

23 | 375 = 16 R7 13 | 678 = 52 R2 26 | 607 = 23 R9 14 | 884 = 63 R2

58

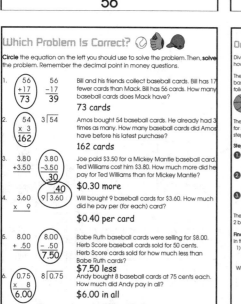

Which Problem Is Correct?

Circle the equation on the left you should use to solve the problem. Then, **solve** the problem. Remember the decimal point in money questions.

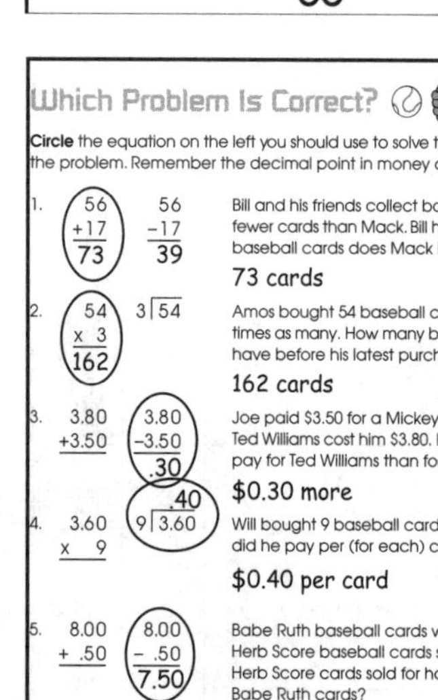

1. 56 +17 = 73 (circled) 56 −17 = 39
   Bill and his friends collect baseball cards. Bill has 17 fewer cards than Mack. Bill has 56 cards. How many baseball cards does Mack have?
   73 cards
2. 54 x 3 = 162 (circled) 3 | 54
   Amos bought 54 baseball cards. He already had 3 times as many. How many baseball cards did Amos have before his latest purchase?
   162 cards
3. 3.80 +3.50 3.80 −3.50 = .30 (circled)
   Joe paid $3.50 for a Mickey Mantle baseball card. Ted Williams cost him $3.80. How much more did he pay for Ted Williams than for Mickey Mantle?
   $0.30 more
4. 3.60 x 9 9 | 3.60 = .40 (circled)
   Will bought 9 baseball cards for $3.60. How much did he pay per (for each) card?
   $0.40 per card
5. 8.00 + .50 8.00 − .50 = 7.50 (circled)
   Babe Ruth baseball cards were selling for $8.00. Herb Score baseball cards sold for 50 cents. Herb Score cards sold for how much less than Babe Ruth cards?
   $7.50 less
6. 0.75 x 8 = 6.00 (circled) 8 | 0.75
   Andy bought 8 baseball cards at 75 cents each. How much did Andy pay in all?
   $6.00 in all

59

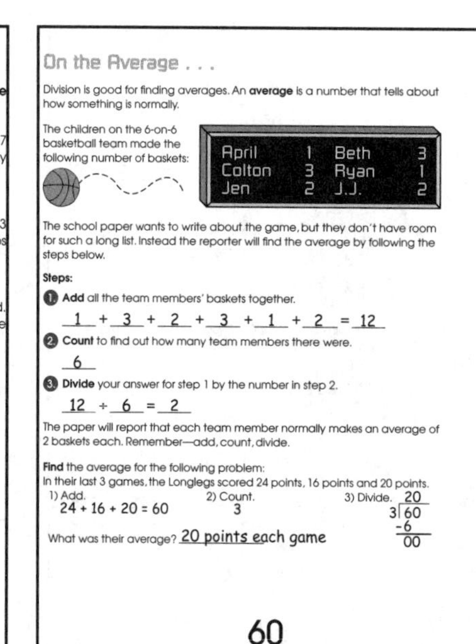

On the Average . . .

Division is good for finding averages. An **average** is a number that tells about how something is normally.

The children on the 6-on-6 basketball team made the following number of baskets:

The school paper wants to write about the game, but they don't have room for such a long list. Instead the reporter will find the average by following the steps below.

Steps:

1. **Add** all the team members' baskets together.
   1 + 3 + 2 + 3 + 1 + 2 = 12
2. **Count** to find out how many team members there were.
   6
3. **Divide** your answer for step 1 by the number in step 2.
   12 ÷ 6 = 2

The paper will report that each team member normally makes an average of 2 baskets each. Remember—add, count, divide.

Find the average for the following problem:
In their last 3 games, the Longlegs scored 24 points, 16 points and 20 points.
1) Add. 24 + 16 + 20 = 60 2) Count. 3 3) Divide. 3 | 60 = 20 (-6, 00)

What was their average? 20 points each game

60

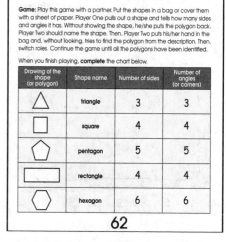

Geometry Match-Ups

A **polygon** is a closed shape with straight sides.

Directions: Cut out each polygon on the next page. To make them more durable, glue them onto cardboard or oaktag. Use the shapes to fill out the table below. (Keep the shapes for other activities as well.)

Game: Play this game with a partner. Put the shapes in a bag or cover them with a sheet of paper. Player One pulls out a shape and tells how many sides and angles it has. Without showing the shape, he/she puts the polygon back. Player Two should name the shape. Then, Player Two puts his/her hand in the bag and, without looking, tries to find the polygon from the description. Then, switch roles. Continue the game until all the polygons have been identified.

When you finish playing, **complete** the chart below.

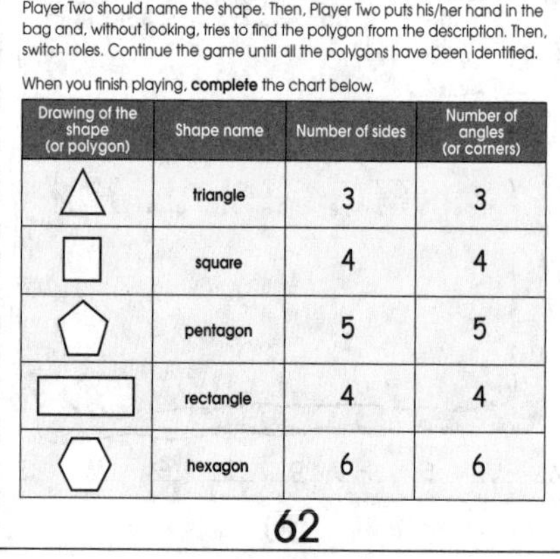

Drawing of the shape (or polygon)	Shape name	Number of sides	Number of angles (or corners)
△	triangle	3	3
□	square	4	4
⬠	pentagon	5	5
▭	rectangle	4	4
⬡	hexagon	6	6

62

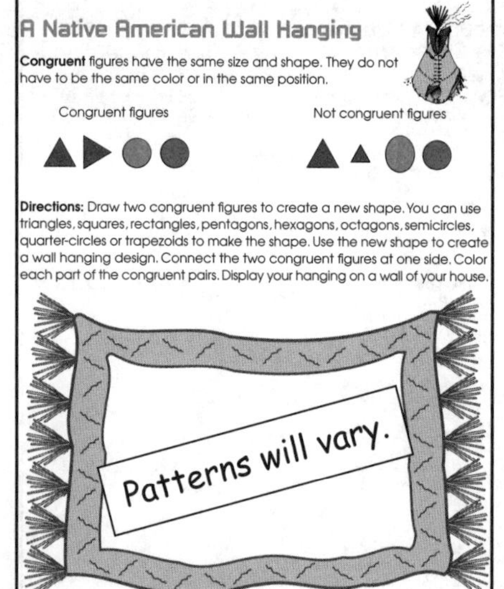

A Native American Wall Hanging

Congruent figures have the same size and shape. They do not have to be the same color or in the same position.

Congruent figures — Not congruent figures

Directions: Draw two congruent figures to create a new shape. You can use triangles, squares, rectangles, pentagons, hexagons, octagons, semicircles, quarter-circles or trapezoids to make the shape. Use the new shape to create a wall hanging design. Connect the two congruent figures at one side. Color each part of the congruent pairs. Display your hanging on a wall of your house.

65

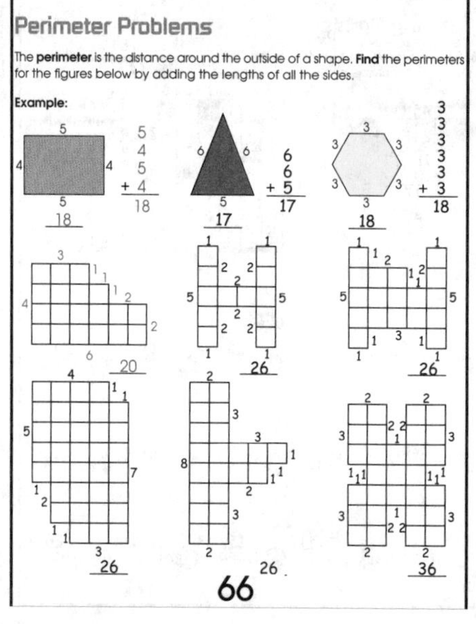

Perimeter Problems

The **perimeter** is the distance around the outside of a shape. **Find** the perimeters for the figures below by adding the lengths of all the sides.

Example:

5 + 4 + 5 + 4 = 18 6 + 6 + 5 = 17 3 + 3 + 3 + 3 + 3 + 3 = 18

66

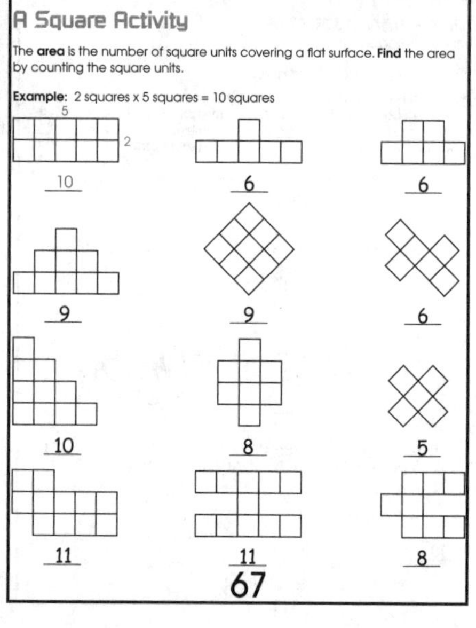

A Square Activity

The **area** is the number of square units covering a flat surface. **Find** the area by counting the square units.

Example: 2 squares x 5 squares = 10 squares

67

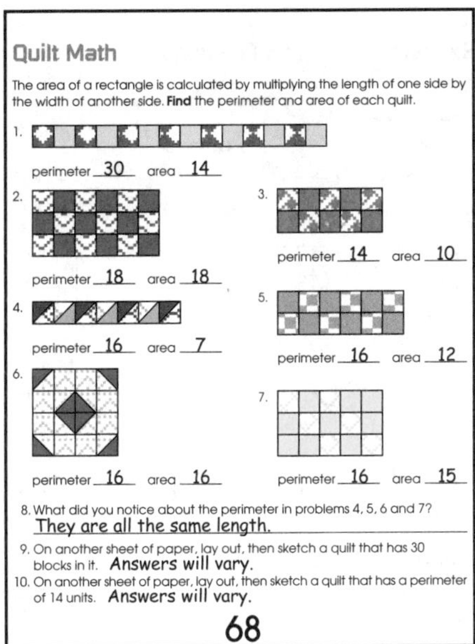

Quilt Math

The area of a rectangle is calculated by multiplying the length of one side by the width of another side. **Find** the perimeter and area of each quilt.

1. perimeter 30 area 14
2. perimeter 18 area 18
3. perimeter 14 area 10
4. perimeter 16 area 7
5. perimeter 16 area 12
6. perimeter 16 area 16
7. perimeter 16 area 15
8. What did you notice about the perimeter in problems 4, 5, 6 and 7? They are all the same length.
9. On another sheet of paper, lay out, then sketch a quilt that has 30 blocks in it. Answers will vary.
10. On another sheet of paper, lay out, then sketch a quilt that has a perimeter of 14 units. Answers will vary.

68

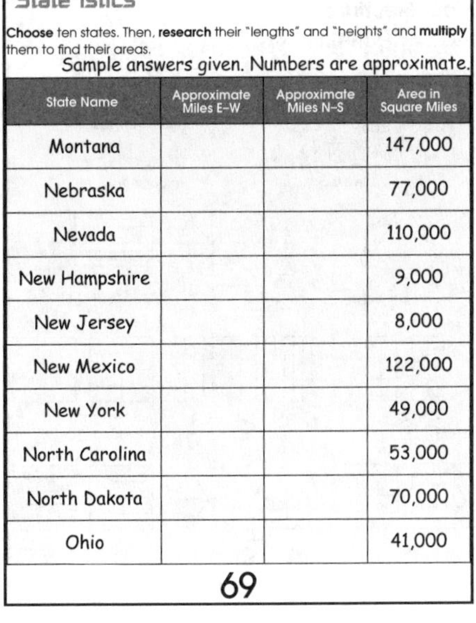

"State"istics

Choose ten states. Then, **research** their "lengths" and "heights" and **multiply** them to find their areas.

Sample answers given. Numbers are approximate.

State Name	Approximate Miles E–W	Approximate Miles N–S	Area in Square Miles
Montana			147,000
Nebraska			77,000
Nevada			110,000
New Hampshire			9,000
New Jersey			8,000
New Mexico			122,000
New York			49,000
North Carolina			53,000
North Dakota			70,000
Ohio			41,000

69

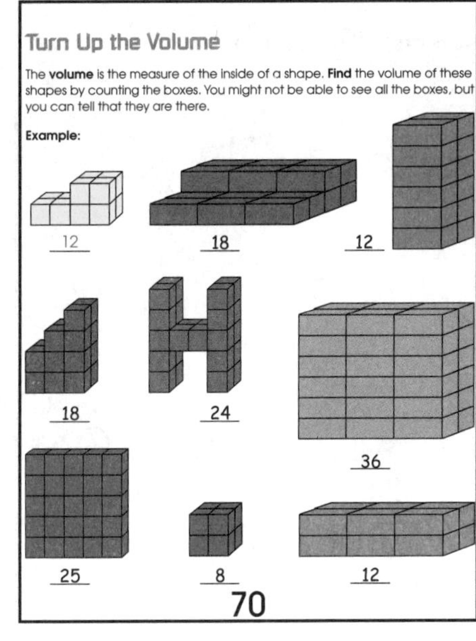

Turn Up the Volume

The **volume** is the measure of the inside of a shape. **Find** the volume of these shapes by counting the boxes. You might not be able to see all the boxes, but you can tell that they are there.

Example: 12

18 12 18 24 36 25 8 12

70

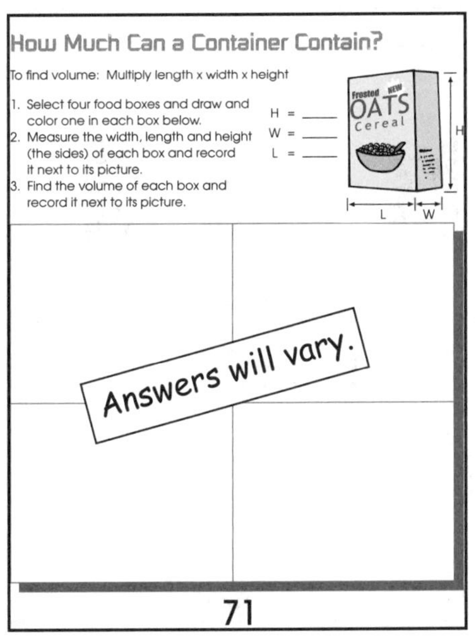

How Much Can a Container Contain?

To find volume: Multiply length x width x height

1. Select four food boxes and draw and color one in each box below.
2. Measure the width, length and height (the sides) of each box and record it next to its picture.
3. Find the volume of each box and record it next to its picture.

Answers will vary.

71

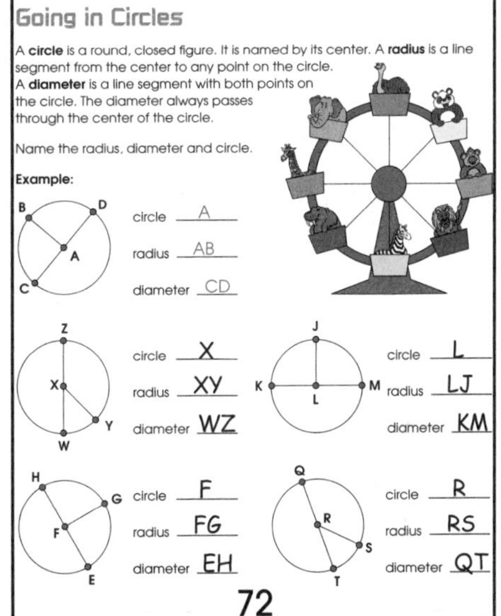

Going in Circles

A **circle** is a round, closed figure. It is named by its center. A **radius** is a line segment from the center to any point on the circle.

A **diameter** is a line segment with both points on the circle. The diameter always passes through the center of the circle.

Name the radius, diameter and circle.

Example: circle A, radius AB, diameter CD

circle X, radius XY, diameter WZ

circle L, radius LJ, diameter KM

circle F, radius FG, diameter EH

circle R, radius RS, diameter QT

72

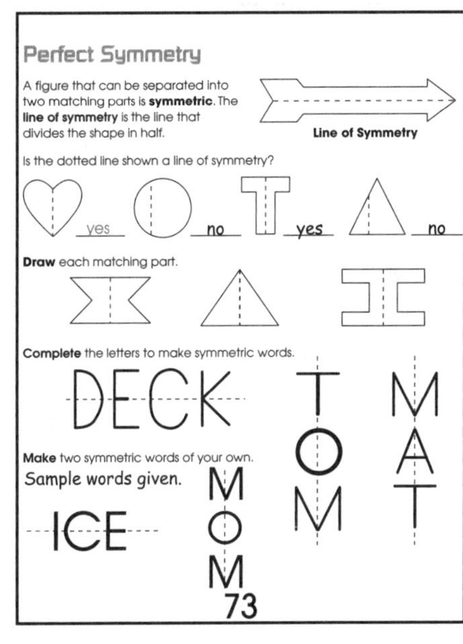

Perfect Symmetry

A figure that can be separated into two matching parts is **symmetric**. The **line of symmetry** is the line that divides the shape in half.

Line of Symmetry

Is the dotted line shown a line of symmetry?

yes no yes no

Draw each matching part.

Complete the letters to make symmetric words.

DECK TOT MAT

Make two symmetric words of your own.

Sample words given.

ICE MOM

73

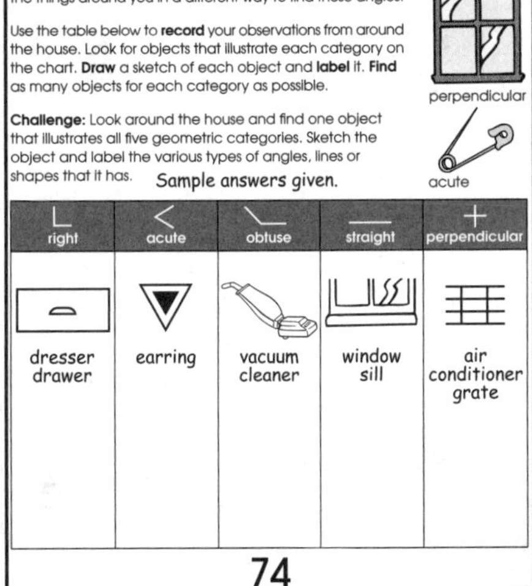

Look at the World From a Different Angle

Lines come together in many different ways. The point where two lines meet is called an **angle**. You may have to look at the things around you in a different way to find these angles.

Use the table below to **record** your observations from around the house. Look for objects that illustrate each category on the chart. **Draw** a sketch of each object and **label** it. **Find** as many objects for each category as possible.

Challenge: Look around the house and find one object that illustrates all five geometric categories. Sketch the object and label the various types of angles, lines or shapes that it has.

Sample answers given.

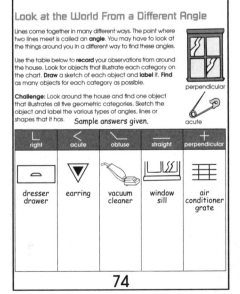

right	acute	obtuse	straight	perpendicular
dresser drawer	earring	vacuum cleaner	window sill	air conditioner grate

74

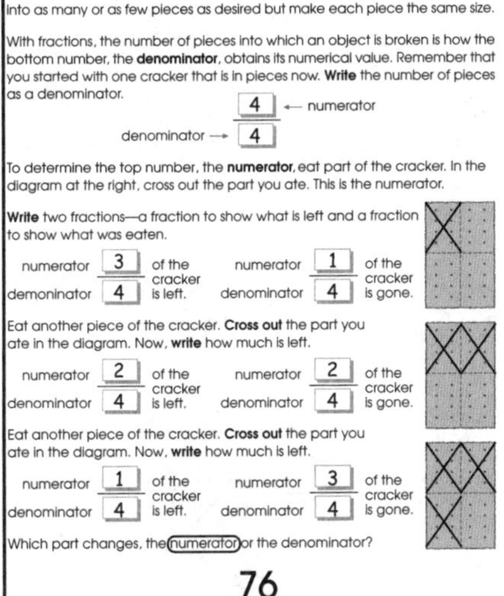

Graham Cracker Denominator

Find a cracker. If possible, use one that has four pieces. Break your crackers into as many or as few pieces as desired but make each piece the same size.

With fractions, the number of pieces into which an object is broken is how the bottom number, the **denominator**, obtains its numerical value. Remember that you started with one cracker that is in pieces now. **Write** the number of pieces as a denominator.

numerator 4 / denominator 4

To determine the top number, the **numerator**, eat part of the cracker. In the diagram at the right, cross out the part you ate. This is the numerator.

Write two fractions—a fraction to show what is left and a fraction to show what was eaten.

numerator 3 / denominator 4 of the cracker is left. numerator 1 / denominator 4 of the cracker is gone.

Eat another piece of the cracker. **Cross out** the part you ate in the diagram. Now, **write** how much is left.

numerator 2 / denominator 4 of the cracker is left. numerator 2 / denominator 4 of the cracker is gone.

Eat another piece of the cracker. **Cross out** the part you ate in the diagram. Now, **write** how much is left.

numerator 1 / denominator 4 of the cracker is left. numerator 3 / denominator 4 of the cracker is gone.

Which part changes, the numerator or the denominator? (numerator circled)

76

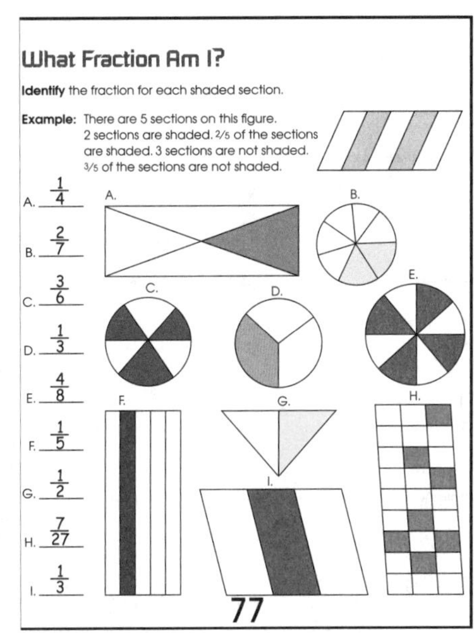

What Fraction Am I?

Identify the fraction for each shaded section.

Example: There are 5 sections on this figure. 2 sections are shaded. 2/5 of the sections are shaded. 3 sections are not shaded. 3/5 of the sections are not shaded.

A. $\frac{1}{4}$

B. $\frac{2}{7}$

C. $\frac{3}{6}$

D. $\frac{1}{3}$

E. $\frac{4}{8}$

F. $\frac{1}{5}$

G. $\frac{1}{2}$

H. $\frac{7}{27}$

I. $\frac{1}{3}$

77

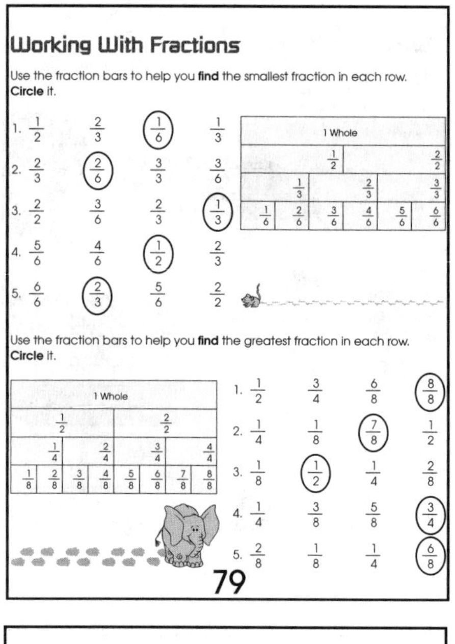

Working With Fractions

Use the fraction bars to help you **find** the smallest fraction in each row. **Circle** it.

1. $\frac{1}{2}$ $\frac{2}{3}$ ($\frac{1}{6}$) $\frac{1}{3}$
2. $\frac{2}{3}$ ($\frac{2}{6}$) $\frac{3}{3}$ $\frac{3}{6}$
3. $\frac{2}{2}$ $\frac{3}{6}$ $\frac{2}{3}$ ($\frac{1}{3}$)
4. $\frac{5}{6}$ $\frac{4}{6}$ ($\frac{1}{2}$) $\frac{2}{3}$
5. $\frac{6}{6}$ ($\frac{2}{3}$) $\frac{5}{6}$ $\frac{2}{2}$

Use the fraction bars to help you **find** the greatest fraction in each row. **Circle** it.

1. $\frac{1}{2}$ $\frac{3}{4}$ $\frac{6}{8}$ ($\frac{8}{8}$)
2. $\frac{1}{4}$ $\frac{1}{8}$ ($\frac{7}{8}$) $\frac{1}{2}$
3. $\frac{1}{8}$ ($\frac{1}{2}$) $\frac{1}{4}$ $\frac{2}{8}$
4. $\frac{1}{4}$ $\frac{3}{8}$ $\frac{5}{8}$ ($\frac{3}{4}$)
5. $\frac{2}{8}$ $\frac{1}{8}$ $\frac{1}{4}$ ($\frac{6}{8}$)

79

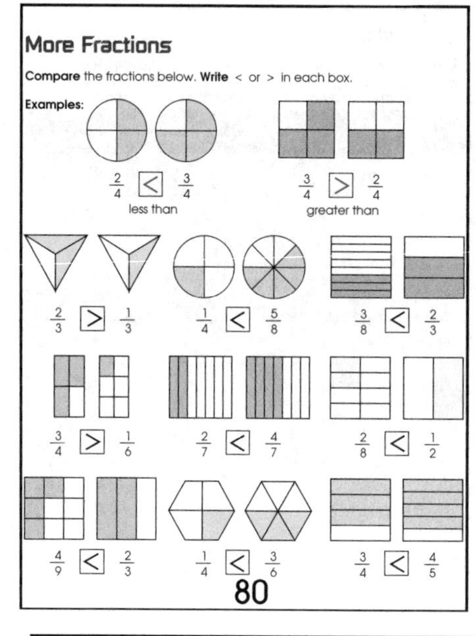

More Fractions

Compare the fractions below. **Write** < or > in each box.

Examples:

$\frac{2}{4} < \frac{3}{4}$ less than

$\frac{3}{4} > \frac{2}{4}$ greater than

$\frac{2}{3} > \frac{1}{3}$ $\frac{1}{4} < \frac{5}{8}$ $\frac{3}{8} < \frac{2}{3}$

$\frac{3}{4} > \frac{1}{6}$ $\frac{2}{7} < \frac{4}{7}$ $\frac{2}{8} < \frac{1}{2}$

$\frac{4}{9} < \frac{2}{3}$ $\frac{1}{4} < \frac{3}{6}$ $\frac{3}{4} < \frac{4}{5}$

80

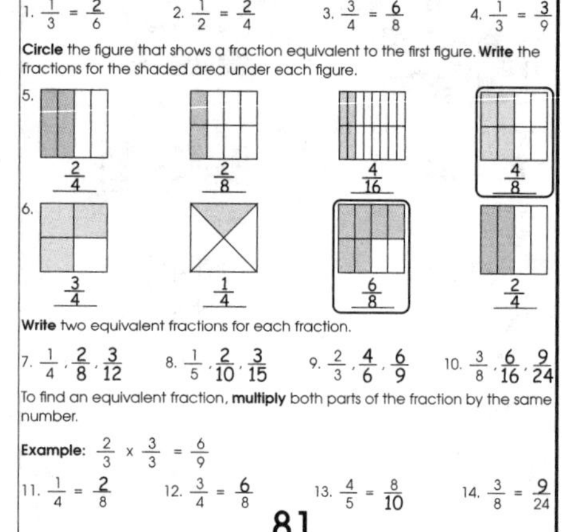

Exploring Equivalent Fractions

Equivalent fractions are two different fractions which represent the same number. For example, on page 172, the picture shows that ½ and 3/6 are the same or equivalent fractions.

Complete these equivalent fractions. **Use** your fraction bars.

1. $\frac{1}{3} = \frac{2}{6}$ 2. $\frac{1}{2} = \frac{2}{4}$ 3. $\frac{3}{4} = \frac{6}{8}$ 4. $\frac{1}{3} = \frac{3}{9}$

Circle the figure that shows a fraction equivalent to the first figure. **Write** the fractions for the shaded area under each figure.

5. $\frac{2}{4}$ $\frac{2}{8}$ $\frac{4}{16}$ ($\frac{4}{8}$)

6. $\frac{3}{4}$ $\frac{1}{4}$ ($\frac{6}{8}$) $\frac{2}{4}$

Write two equivalent fractions for each fraction.

7. $\frac{1}{4}, \frac{2}{8}, \frac{3}{12}$ 8. $\frac{1}{5}, \frac{2}{10}, \frac{3}{15}$ 9. $\frac{2}{3}, \frac{4}{6}, \frac{6}{9}$ 10. $\frac{3}{8}, \frac{6}{16}, \frac{9}{24}$

To find an equivalent fraction, **multiply** both parts of the fraction by the same number.

Example: $\frac{2}{3} \times \frac{3}{3} = \frac{6}{9}$

11. $\frac{1}{4} = \frac{2}{8}$ 12. $\frac{3}{4} = \frac{6}{8}$ 13. $\frac{4}{5} = \frac{8}{10}$ 14. $\frac{3}{8} = \frac{9}{24}$

81

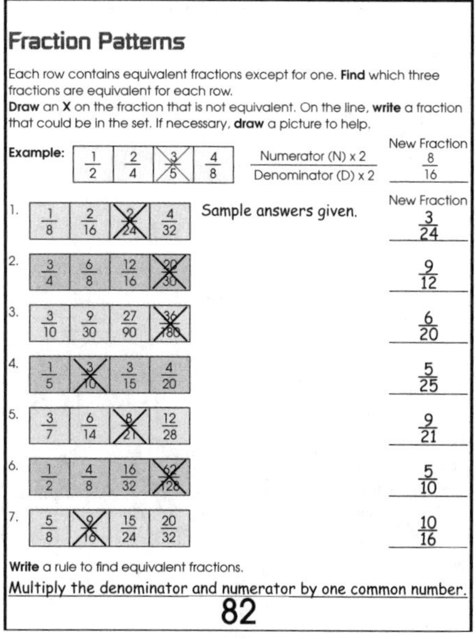

Fraction Patterns

Each row contains equivalent fractions except for one. **Find** which three fractions are equivalent for each row.

Draw an **X** on the fraction that is not equivalent. On the line, **write** a fraction that could be in the set. If necessary, **draw** a picture to help.

Example: $\frac{1}{2}$ $\frac{2}{4}$ X $\frac{3}{5}$ $\frac{4}{8}$ Numerator (N) x 2 / Denominator (D) x 2 New Fraction $\frac{8}{16}$

Sample answers given.

					New Fraction
1.	$\frac{1}{8}$	$\frac{2}{16}$	X $\frac{2}{24}$	$\frac{4}{32}$	$\frac{3}{24}$
2.	$\frac{3}{4}$	$\frac{6}{8}$	$\frac{12}{16}$	X $\frac{20}{30}$	$\frac{9}{12}$
3.	$\frac{3}{10}$	$\frac{9}{30}$	$\frac{27}{90}$	X $\frac{36}{180}$	$\frac{6}{20}$
4.	$\frac{1}{5}$	X $\frac{3}{10}$	$\frac{3}{15}$	$\frac{4}{20}$	$\frac{5}{25}$
5.	$\frac{3}{7}$	$\frac{6}{14}$	X $\frac{8}{21}$	$\frac{12}{28}$	$\frac{9}{21}$
6.	$\frac{1}{2}$	$\frac{4}{8}$	$\frac{16}{32}$	X $\frac{62}{128}$	$\frac{5}{10}$
7.	$\frac{5}{8}$	X $\frac{9}{16}$	$\frac{15}{24}$	$\frac{20}{32}$	$\frac{10}{16}$

Write a rule to find equivalent fractions.

Multiply the denominator and numerator by one common number.

82

More Than Peanuts

Write <, >, or = to compare the fractions below. **Draw** pictures or **write** equivalent fractions, if needed.

$\frac{3}{8} > \frac{2}{8}$ $\frac{2}{3} > \frac{3}{6}$ $\frac{3}{6} = \frac{1}{2}$

$\frac{4}{7} > \frac{4}{14}$ $\frac{1}{3} < \frac{6}{9}$ $\frac{7}{10} > \frac{2}{5}$

$\frac{8}{12} > \frac{3}{6}$ $\frac{7}{14} = \frac{1}{2}$ $\frac{4}{7} > \frac{3}{7}$ $\frac{4}{8} = \frac{8}{16}$

$\frac{1}{3} = \frac{2}{6}$ $\frac{2}{8} < \frac{1}{2}$ $\frac{1}{5} < \frac{3}{10}$ $\frac{6}{11} > \frac{5}{11}$

$\frac{6}{12} = \frac{1}{2}$ $\frac{2}{3} > \frac{2}{6}$ $\frac{7}{12} > \frac{2}{4}$ $\frac{5}{6} > \frac{1}{3}$

$\frac{7}{10} > \frac{3}{10}$ $\frac{1}{2} < \frac{8}{12}$ $\frac{1}{5} < \frac{8}{10}$ $\frac{7}{8} > \frac{2}{4}$

$\frac{3}{8} > \frac{1}{4}$ $\frac{2}{5} < \frac{5}{10}$

$\frac{5}{6} > \frac{2}{3}$ $\frac{6}{10} > \frac{2}{5}$

$\frac{6}{10} > \frac{3}{10}$ $\frac{3}{6} = \frac{6}{12}$

$\frac{1}{8} < \frac{1}{4}$ $\frac{1}{2} > \frac{1}{4}$

83

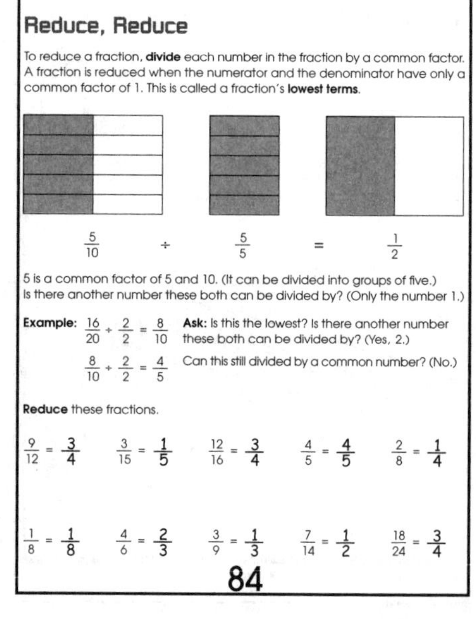

Reduce, Reduce

To reduce a fraction, **divide** each number in the fraction by a common factor. A fraction is reduced when the numerator and the denominator have only a common factor of 1. This is called a fraction's **lowest terms**.

$\frac{5}{10} \div \frac{5}{5} = \frac{1}{2}$

5 is a common factor of 5 and 10. (It can be divided into groups of five.) Is there another number these both can be divided by? (Only the number 1.)

Example: $\frac{16}{20} \div \frac{2}{2} = \frac{8}{10}$ **Ask:** Is this the lowest? Is there another number these both can be divided by? (Yes, 2.)

$\frac{8}{10} \div \frac{2}{2} = \frac{4}{5}$ Can this still divided by a common number? (No.)

Reduce these fractions.

$\frac{9}{12} = \frac{3}{4}$ $\frac{3}{15} = \frac{1}{5}$ $\frac{12}{16} = \frac{3}{4}$ $\frac{4}{5} = \frac{4}{5}$ $\frac{2}{8} = \frac{1}{4}$

$\frac{1}{8} = \frac{1}{8}$ $\frac{4}{6} = \frac{2}{3}$ $\frac{3}{9} = \frac{1}{3}$ $\frac{7}{14} = \frac{1}{2}$ $\frac{18}{24} = \frac{3}{4}$

84

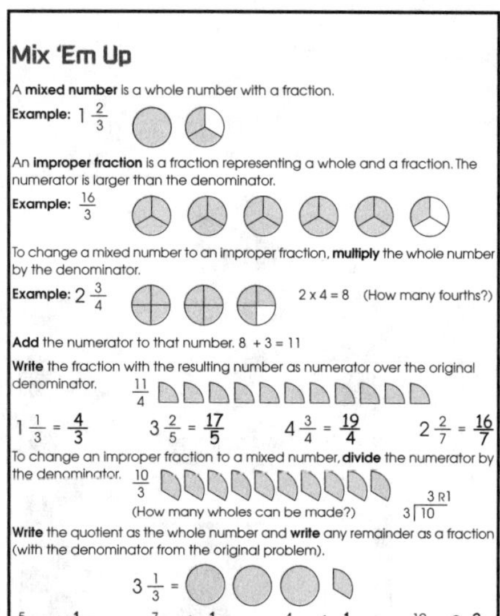

Mix 'Em Up

A **mixed number** is a whole number with a fraction.

Example: $1\frac{2}{3}$

An **improper fraction** is a fraction representing a whole and a fraction. The numerator is larger than the denominator.

Example: $\frac{16}{3}$

To change a mixed number to an improper fraction, **multiply** the whole number by the denominator.

Example: $2\frac{3}{4}$ 2 x 4 = 8 (How many fourths?)

Add the numerator to that number. 8 + 3 = 11

Write the fraction with the resulting number as numerator over the original denominator. $\frac{11}{4}$

$1\frac{1}{3} = \frac{4}{3}$ $3\frac{2}{5} = \frac{17}{5}$ $4\frac{3}{4} = \frac{19}{4}$ $2\frac{2}{7} = \frac{16}{7}$

To change an improper fraction to a mixed number, **divide** the numerator by the denominator. $\frac{10}{3}$

(How many wholes can be made?) 3 R1 / 3)10

Write the quotient as the whole number and **write** any remainder as a fraction (with the denominator from the original problem).

$3\frac{1}{3} =$

$\frac{5}{2} = 2\frac{1}{2}$ $\frac{7}{6} = 1\frac{1}{6}$ $\frac{4}{3} = 1\frac{1}{3}$ $\frac{10}{4} = 2\frac{2}{4}$

85

Oh, My!

When the numerator is greater than the denominator (an improper fraction), write a mixed number or divide to write a whole number. A mixed number is made up of a whole number and a fraction. **Example:** $2\frac{1}{2}$

Draw the correct mouths on the animals by finding the whole or mixed number for each.

Example:

$\frac{11}{2} =$ 11 ÷ 2 = 5 R1 = $5\frac{1}{2}$

$\frac{20}{3} = 6\frac{2}{3}$ $\frac{21}{7} = 3$ $\frac{24}{2} = 12$

$\frac{16}{2} = 8$ $\frac{49}{7} = 7$ $\frac{16}{16} = 1$ $\frac{16}{6} = 2\frac{4}{6}$

86

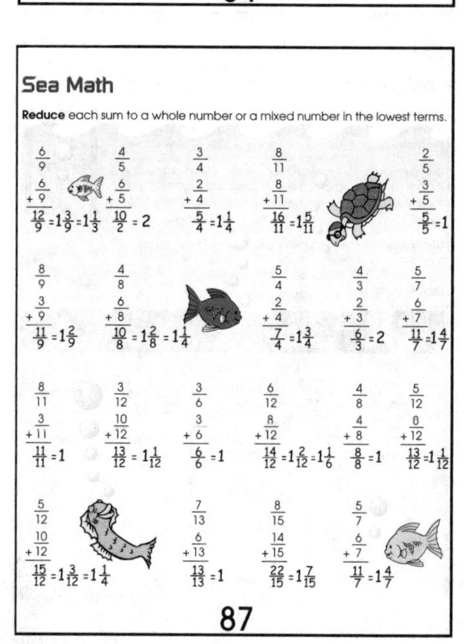

Sea Math

Reduce each sum to a whole number or a mixed number in the lowest terms.

$\frac{6}{9} + \frac{6}{9} = \frac{12}{9} = 1\frac{3}{9} = 1\frac{1}{3}$ $\frac{4}{5} + \frac{6}{5} = \frac{10}{5} = 2$ $\frac{3}{4} + \frac{2}{4} = \frac{5}{4} = 1\frac{1}{4}$ $\frac{8}{11} + \frac{8}{11} = \frac{16}{11} = 1\frac{5}{11}$ $\frac{2}{5} + \frac{3}{5} = \frac{5}{5} = 1$

$\frac{8}{9} + \frac{3}{9} = \frac{11}{9} = 1\frac{2}{9}$ $\frac{4}{8} + \frac{6}{8} = \frac{10}{8} = 1\frac{2}{8} = 1\frac{1}{4}$ $\frac{5}{4} + \frac{2}{4} = \frac{7}{4} = 1\frac{3}{4}$ $\frac{4}{3} + \frac{2}{3} = \frac{6}{3} = 2$ $\frac{5}{7} + \frac{6}{7} = \frac{11}{7} = 1\frac{4}{7}$

$\frac{8}{11} + \frac{3}{11} = \frac{11}{11} = 1$ $\frac{3}{12} + \frac{10}{12} = \frac{13}{12} = 1\frac{1}{12}$ $\frac{3}{6} + \frac{3}{6} = \frac{6}{6} = 1$ $\frac{6}{12} + \frac{8}{12} = \frac{14}{12} = 1\frac{2}{12} = 1\frac{1}{6}$ $\frac{4}{8} + \frac{4}{8} = \frac{8}{8} = 1$ $\frac{5}{12} + \frac{8}{12} = \frac{13}{12} = 1\frac{1}{12}$

$\frac{5}{12} + \frac{10}{12} = \frac{15}{12} = 1\frac{3}{12} = 1\frac{1}{4}$ $\frac{7}{13} + \frac{6}{13} = \frac{13}{13} = 1$ $\frac{8}{15} + \frac{14}{15} = \frac{22}{15} = 1\frac{7}{15}$ $\frac{5}{7} + \frac{6}{7} = \frac{11}{7} = 1\frac{4}{7}$

87

Finding a Common Denominator

When adding or subtracting fractions with different denominators, find a common denominator first. A **common denominator** is a common multiple of two or more denominators.

Cut a paper plate in half. **Cut** another paper plate into eighths. Use these models to help **solve** the following addition and subtraction problems.

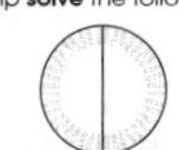 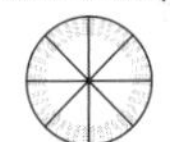

$\frac{1}{2} + \frac{2}{8}$ = The common denominator is 8 because 2 x 4 = 8; 8 x 1 = 8.

$\frac{1}{2} \times \frac{4}{4} = \frac{4}{8}$ $\qquad \frac{4}{8} + \frac{2}{8} = \frac{6}{8}$

$\frac{7}{8} - \frac{1}{2}$ = The common denominator is 8 because 1 x 4 = 8; 2 x 4 = 8.

$\frac{7}{8} - \frac{4}{8} = \frac{3}{8}$

To find a common denominator of two or more fractions, follow these steps:

1. Write equivalent fractions so that the fractions have the same denominator.
2. Write the fractions with the same denominator.

Example: Step 1 Step 2

$\frac{1}{2} + \frac{2}{6} =$ $\qquad \frac{1}{2} \times \frac{3}{3} = \frac{3}{6}$ $\qquad \frac{3}{6} + \frac{2}{6} = \frac{5}{6}$

Follow the steps above. Then, **add**. **Reduce** the answer to its lowest terms.

$\frac{5}{9} + \frac{1}{3} = \frac{8}{9}$ $\qquad \frac{3}{8} - \frac{1}{4} = \frac{1}{8}$

$\frac{1}{3} + \frac{5}{12} = \frac{9}{12} = \frac{3}{4}$ $\qquad \frac{5}{12} - \frac{1}{6} = \frac{3}{12} = \frac{1}{4}$

88

Make a Wish

Solve these problems.

Example: $\frac{2}{9}$ of 27 = $(27 \div 9) \times 2 = 6$

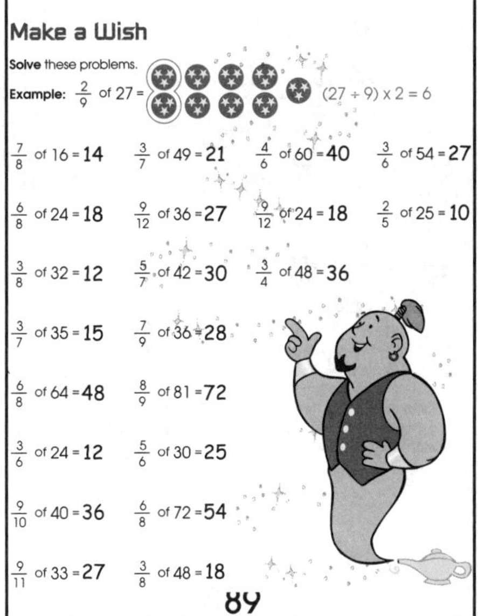

$\frac{7}{8}$ of 16 = 14	$\frac{3}{7}$ of 49 = 21	$\frac{4}{6}$ of 60 = 40	$\frac{3}{6}$ of 54 = 27
$\frac{6}{8}$ of 24 = 18	$\frac{9}{12}$ of 36 = 27	$\frac{9}{12}$ of 24 = 18	$\frac{2}{5}$ of 25 = 10
$\frac{3}{8}$ of 32 = 12	$\frac{5}{7}$ of 42 = 30	$\frac{3}{4}$ of 48 = 36	
$\frac{3}{7}$ of 35 = 15	$\frac{7}{9}$ of 36 = 28		
$\frac{6}{8}$ of 64 = 48	$\frac{8}{9}$ of 81 = 72		
$\frac{3}{6}$ of 24 = 12	$\frac{5}{6}$ of 30 = 25		
$\frac{9}{10}$ of 40 = 36	$\frac{6}{8}$ of 72 = 54		
$\frac{9}{11}$ of 33 = 27	$\frac{3}{8}$ of 48 = 18		

89

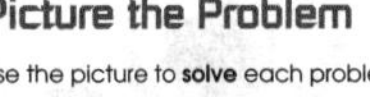

Picture the Problem

Use the picture to **solve** each problem.

1. Andy had two ropes of the same length. He cut one rope into 2 equal parts and gave the 2 halves to Bill. The other rope he cut into fourths and gave 2 of the fourths to Sue. Circle who got the most rope.

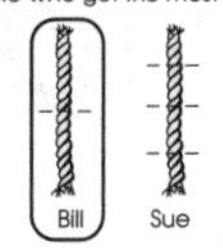

2. Mr. Johns built an office building with an aisle down the middle. He divided one side into 6 equal spaces. He divided the other side into 9 equal spaces. The Ace Company rented 5 of the ninths. The Best Company rented 4 of the sixths. Circle which company rented the larger space.

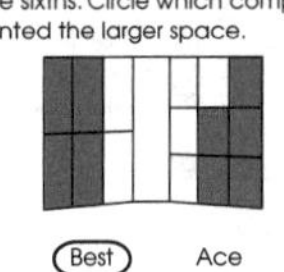

3. Hannah cut an 8-foot log into 4 equal pieces and burned 2 of them in the fireplace. Joseph cut an 8-foot log into 8 equal pieces and put 3 of them in the fireplace. Circle who put the most wood in the fireplace.

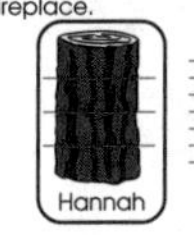
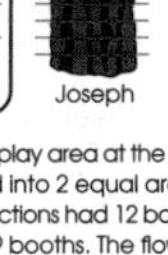

4. The 4-H Club display area at the state fair was divided into 2 equal areas. One of these sections had 12 booths, the other had 9 booths. The flower display covered 2 of the ninths, and the melon display covered 4 of the twelfths. Circle which display had the most room.

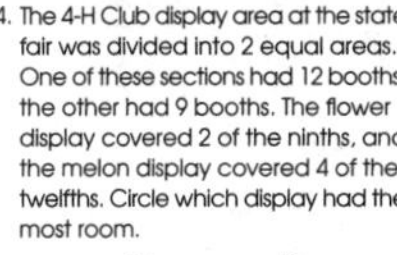
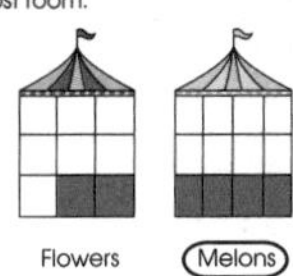
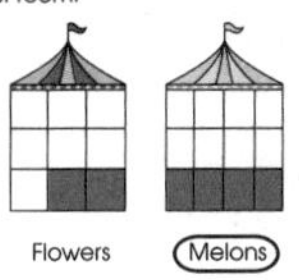
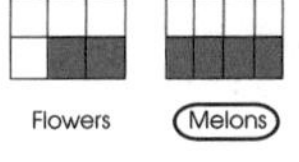

90

Doing Decimals

Just as a fraction stands for part of a whole number, a decimal also shows part of a whole number. And with decimals, the number is always broken into ten or a power of ten (hundred, thousand, etc.) parts. These place values are named tenths, hundredths, thousandths, etc.

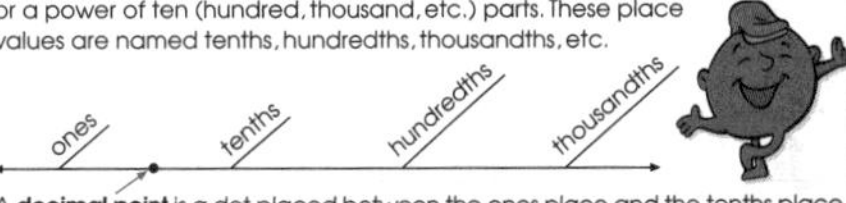

A **decimal point** is a dot placed between the ones place and the tenths place.

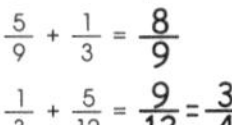 0.2 is read as "two tenths." 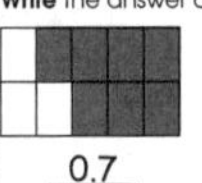 0.4 is four tenths.

Write the answer as a decimal for the shaded parts.

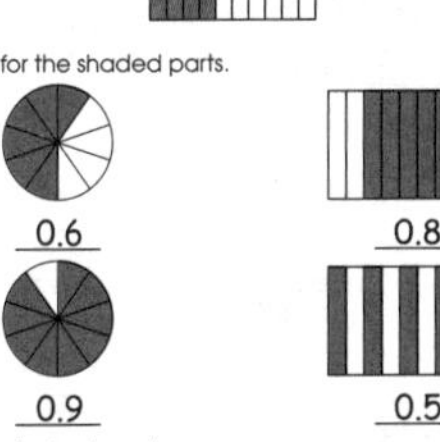
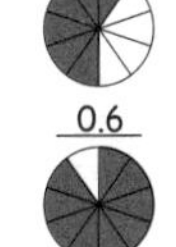
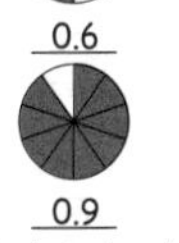

0.7 0.6 0.8

0.1 0.9 0.5

Color the parts that match the decimal numbers.

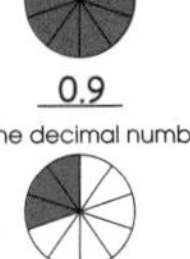
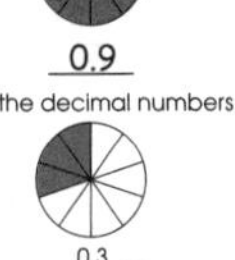
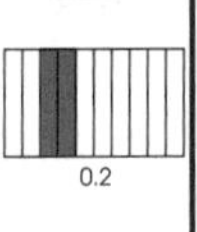

0.4 0.3 0.2

92

Hundredth Picture Grid

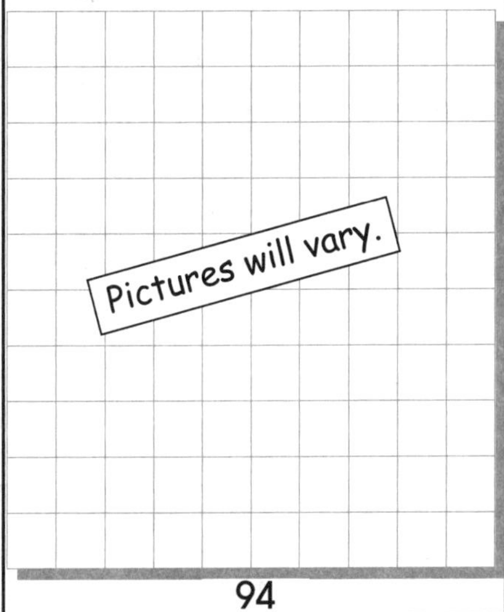

94

Decimal Divisions

Decimals are often used with whole numbers.

Examples: 2.8 3.5

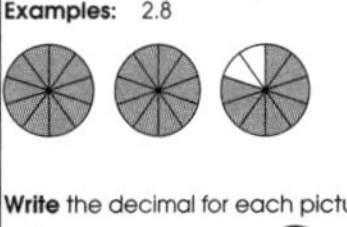

Write the decimal for each picture.

1.2 5.7 2.4

Shade in the picture to show the decimal number.

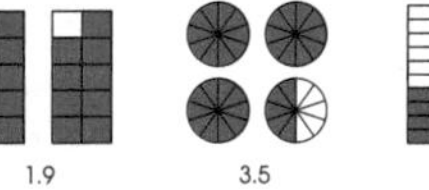

1.9 3.5 0.4 4.1

When reading decimals with whole numbers, say "point" or "and" for the decimal point.

Write the word names for each decimal from above.

1.9 one and nine tenths

0.4 four tenths or point four

3.5 three and five tenths

4.1 four and one tenth or four point one

95

Order in the Line

Look at the number lines below. **Cut out** the decimal number squares on the next page. First, **find** the number line on which each number is located. **Glue** the decimals in their correct positions on the correct number line.

Hint: Pay careful attention to the place value indicated on each line. A number which goes to the hundredths place will be on a number line showing hundredths place values.

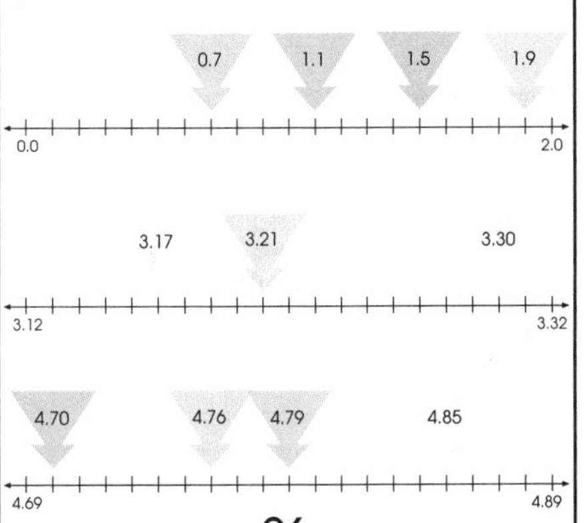

96

Order in the Line

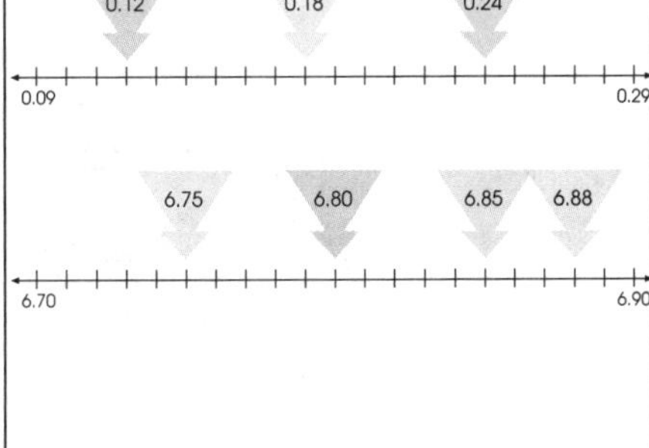

97

Get the Point

When you add or subtract decimals, remember to include the decimal point.

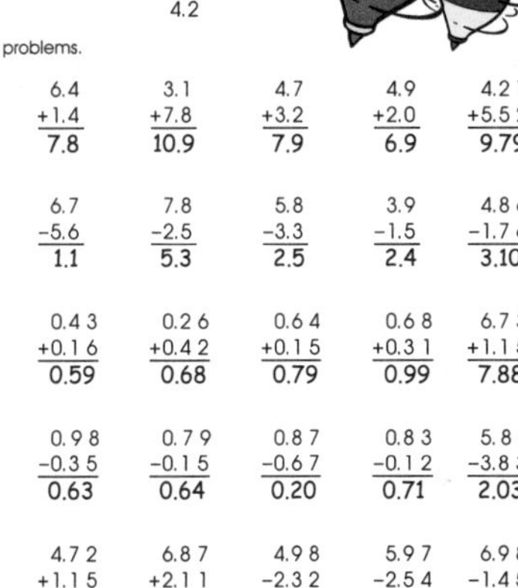

Add.

$$\begin{array}{r} 3.6 \\ +3.3 \\ \hline 6.9 \end{array}$$

Subtract.

$$\begin{array}{r} 6.8 \\ -2.6 \\ \hline 4.2 \end{array}$$

Solve these problems.

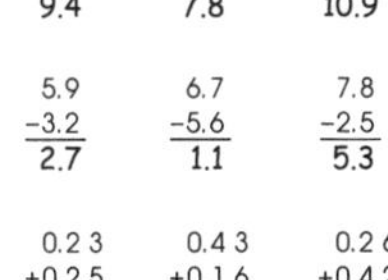
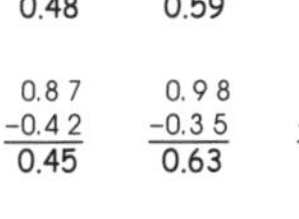
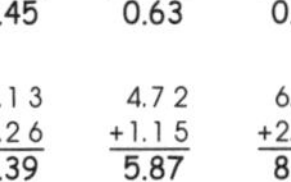
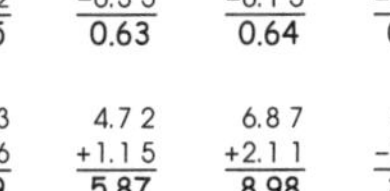
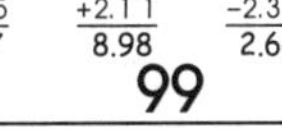

4.2 + 5.2 = 9.4	6.4 + 1.4 = 7.8	3.1 + 7.8 = 10.9	4.7 + 3.2 = 7.9	4.9 + 2.0 = 6.9	4.27 + 5.52 = 9.79
5.9 − 3.2 = 2.7	6.7 − 5.6 = 1.1	7.8 − 2.5 = 5.3	5.8 − 3.3 = 2.5	3.9 − 1.5 = 2.4	4.86 − 1.76 = 3.10
0.23 + 0.25 = 0.48	0.43 + 0.16 = 0.59	0.26 + 0.42 = 0.68	0.64 + 0.15 = 0.79	0.68 + 0.31 = 0.99	6.73 + 1.15 = 7.88
0.87 − 0.42 = 0.45	0.98 − 0.35 = 0.63	0.79 − 0.15 = 0.64	0.87 − 0.67 = 0.20	0.83 − 0.12 = 0.71	5.86 − 3.83 = 2.03
3.13 + 2.26 = 5.39	4.72 + 1.15 = 5.87	6.87 + 2.11 = 8.98	4.98 − 2.32 = 2.66	5.97 − 2.54 = 3.43	6.98 − 1.45 = 5.53

99

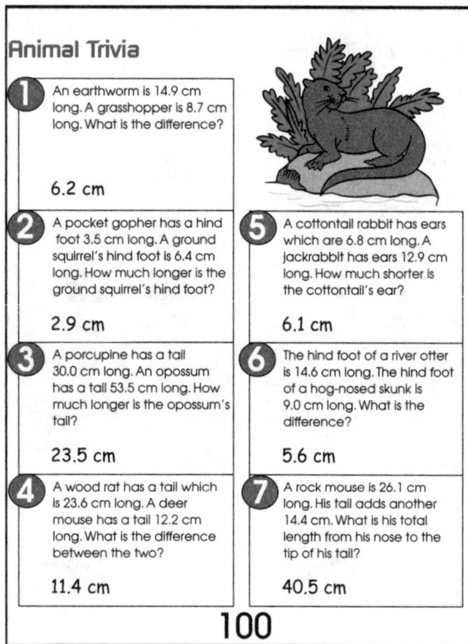
Animal Trivia

1. An earthworm is 14.9 cm long. A grasshopper is 8.7 cm long. What is the difference? 6.2 cm
2. A pocket gopher has a hind foot 3.5 cm long. A ground squirrel's hind foot is 6.4 cm long. How much longer is the ground squirrel's hind foot? 2.9 cm
3. A porcupine has a tail 30.0 cm long. An opossum has a tail 53.5 cm long. How much longer is the opossum's tail? 23.5 cm
4. A wood rat has a tail which is 23.6 cm long. A deer mouse has a tail 12.2 cm long. What is the difference between the two? 11.4 cm
5. A cottontail rabbit has ears which are 6.8 cm long. A jackrabbit has ears 12.9 cm long. How much shorter is the cottontail's ear? 6.1 cm
6. The hind foot of a river otter is 14.6 cm long. The hind foot of a hog-nosed skunk is 9.0 cm long. What is the difference? 5.6 cm
7. A rock mouse is 26.1 cm long. His tail adds another 14.4 cm. What is his total length from his nose to the tip of his tail? 40.5 cm

100

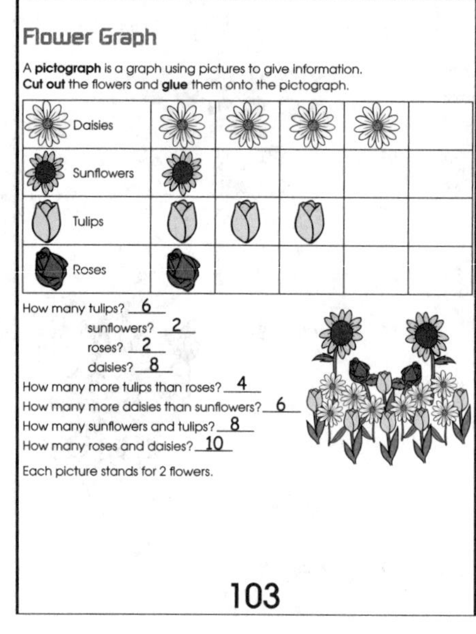
Flower Graph

A **pictograph** is a graph using pictures to give information.
Cut out the flowers and **glue** them onto the pictograph.

Daisies	✿	✿	✿	✿	
Sunflowers	✿				
Tulips	✿	✿	✿		
Roses	✿				

How many tulips? 6
sunflowers? 2
roses? 2
daisies? 8
How many more tulips than roses? 4
How many more daisies than sunflowers? 6
How many sunflowers and tulips? 8
How many roses and daisies? 10

Each picture stands for 2 flowers.

103

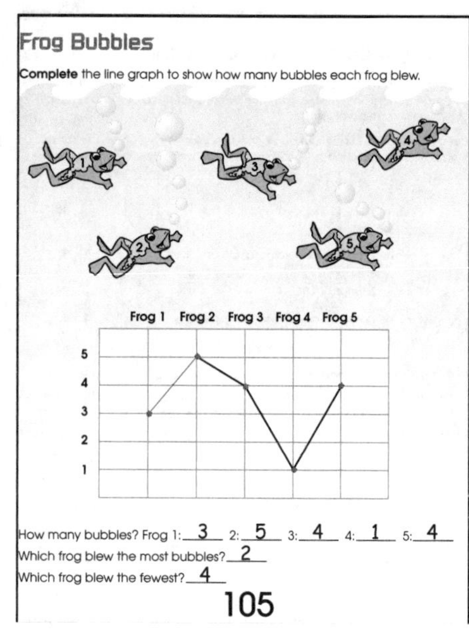
Frog Bubbles

Complete the line graph to show how many bubbles each frog blew.

How many bubbles? Frog 1: 3 2: 5 3: 4 4: 1 5: 4
Which frog blew the most bubbles? 2
Which frog blew the fewest? 4

105

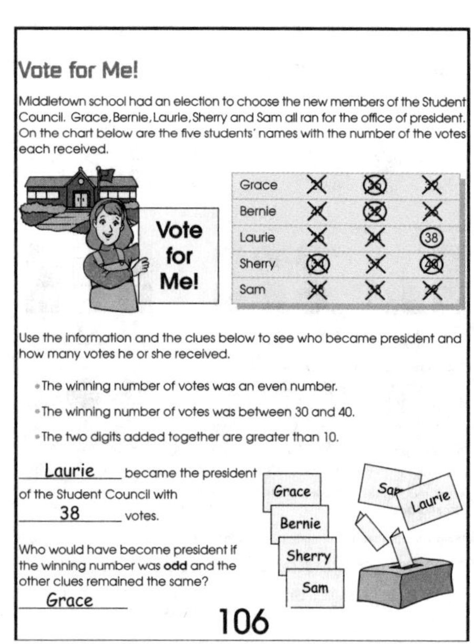
Vote for Me!

Middletown school had an election to choose the new members of the Student Council. Grace, Bernie, Laurie, Sherry and Sam all ran for the office of president. On the chart below are the five students' names with the number of the votes each received.

Use the information and the clues below to see who became president and how many votes he or she received.

- The winning number of votes was an even number.
- The winning number of votes was between 30 and 40.
- The two digits added together are greater than 10.

Laurie became the president of the Student Council with 38 votes.

Who would have become president if the winning number was **odd** and the other clues remained the same? Grace

106

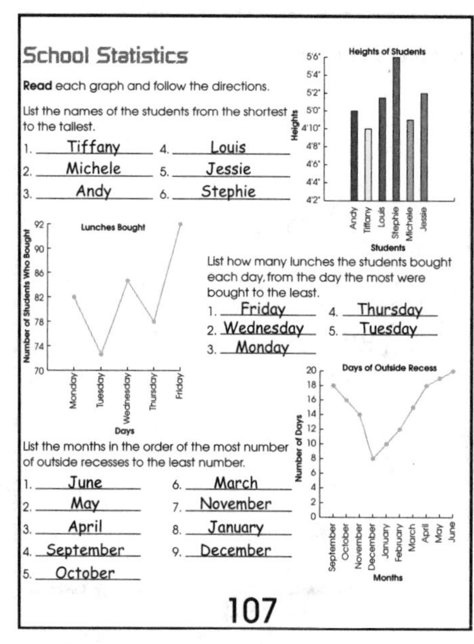
School Statistics

Read each graph and follow the directions.

List the names of the students from the shortest to the tallest.

1. Tiffany
2. Michele
3. Andy
4. Louis
5. Jessie
6. Stephie

List how many lunches the students bought each day, from the day the most were bought to the least.

1. Friday
2. Wednesday
3. Monday
4. Thursday
5. Tuesday

List the months in the order of the most number of outside recesses to the least number.

1. June
2. May
3. April
4. September
5. October
6. March
7. November
8. January
9. December

107

Hot Lunch Favorites

The cooks in the cafeteria asked each third- and fourth-grade class to rate the hot lunches. They wanted to know which food the children liked the best.

The table shows how the students rated the lunches.
Key: Each 웃 equals 2 students.

Food	Number of students who liked it best
hamburgers	12
hot dogs	14
tacos	10
chili	0
soup and sandwiches	2
spaghetti	4
fried chicken	8
fish sticks	6

Color the bar graph to show the information on the table. Remember that each 웃 equals 2 people. The first one is done for you.

Write the food in order starting with the one that students liked most.

1. hot dogs
2. hamburgers
3. tacos
4. fried chicken
5. fish sticks
6. spaghetti
7. soup and sandwiches
8. chili

108

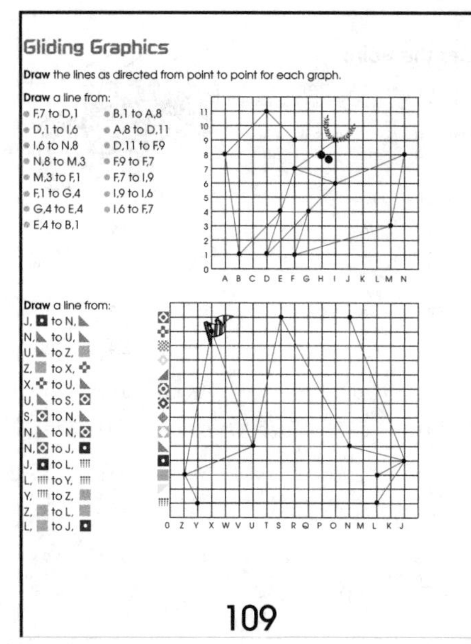
Gliding Graphics

Draw the lines as directed from point to point for each graph.

Draw a line from:

- F,7 to D,1
- D,1 to I,6
- I,6 to N,8
- N,8 to M,3
- M,3 to F,1
- F,1 to G,4
- G,4 to E,4
- E,4 to B,1
- B,1 to A,8
- A,8 to D,11
- D,11 to F,9
- F,9 to F,7
- F,7 to I,9
- I,9 to I,6
- I,6 to F,7

Draw a line from:

- J, ■ to N, ◣
- N, ◣ to U, ◣
- U, ◣ to Z, ▦
- Z, ▦ to X, ✥
- X, ✥ to U, ◣
- U, ◣ to S, ⊠
- S, ⊠ to N, ◣
- N, ◣ to N, ⊠
- N, ⊠ to J, ■
- J, ■ to L, ▥
- L, ▥ to Y, ▥
- Y, ▥ to Z, ▦
- Z, ▦ to L, ▦
- L, ▦ to J, ■

109

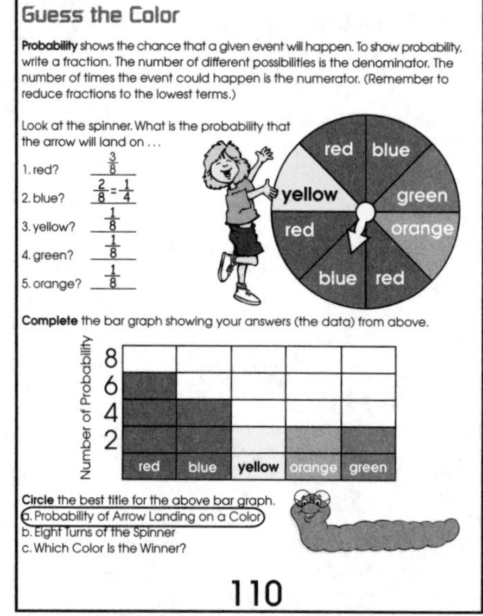
Guess the Color

Probability shows the chance that a given event will happen. To show probability, write a fraction. The number of different possibilities is the denominator. The number of times the event could happen is the numerator. (Remember to reduce fractions to the lowest terms.)

Look at the spinner. What is the probability that the arrow will land on . . .

1. red? $\frac{3}{8}$
2. blue? $\frac{2}{8} = \frac{1}{4}$
3. yellow? $\frac{1}{8}$
4. green? $\frac{1}{8}$
5. orange? $\frac{1}{8}$

Complete the bar graph showing your answers (the data) from above.

Circle the best title for the above bar graph.
a. Probability of Arrow Landing on a Color
b. Eight Turns of the Spinner
c. Which Color Is the Winner?

110

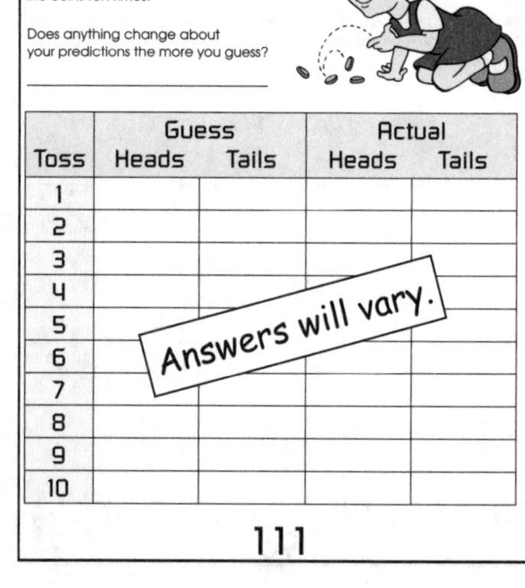
Keep Your Heads Up!

Collect 21 pennies. **Predict** the numbers of heads and tails that will turn up before you toss the pennies. Then, **toss** the coins ten times.

Does anything change about your predictions the more you guess?

Toss	Guess Heads	Guess Tails	Actual Heads	Actual Tails
1				
2				
3				
4				
5				
6				
7				
8				
9				
10				

Answers will vary.

111

How Does Your Home Measure Up?

Directions: Take a "measuring journey" through your house. To begin, brainstorm a list of various destinations around your house. Then, **list** five objects found in each room and **write** them on the left-hand side of a sheet of paper.

Example:

Kitchen	Bathroom	Bedroom
stove	toothbrush	books
teaspoon	hairbrush	desk/table
cookbook	soap	pillow
can opener	mirror	clock
box of cereal	bandage	hanger

Read through the objects on the list and **write** estimations of their measurements. Decide on a unit of measurement to use and whether to measure length, width or both. Then, **measure** the objects. (A tape measure or string may be used to measure the size or circumference of any oddly shaped objects.) Finally, compare your estimations with the actual measurements.

Sample answers given.

Object	Estimate	Actual
box of cereal	12 in. by 6 in.	11 in. by 8 in.
soap	2 in. by 3 in.	3 in. by 4 in.
pillow	24 in. by 18 in.	26 in. by 20 in.
foot stool	24 in. by 18 in.	27 in. by 24 in.
table top	40 in. by 28 in.	42 in. by 30 in.

113

Growing String Beans

Bar Graph

Sample graph given.

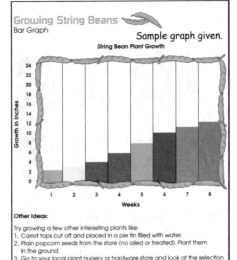

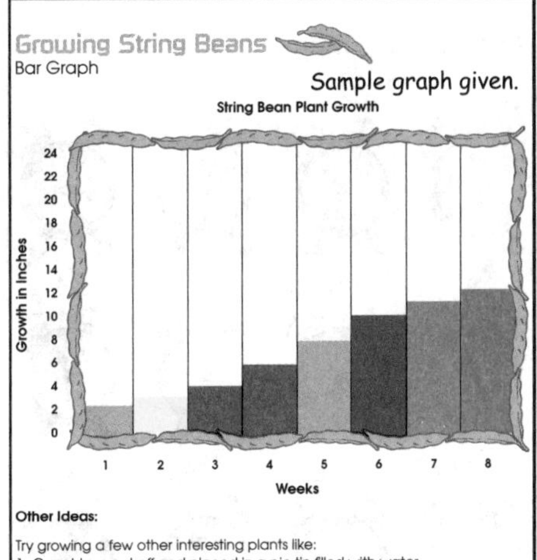

Other Ideas:

Try growing a few other interesting plants like:

1. Carrot tops cut off and placed in a pie tin filled with water.
2. Plain popcorn seeds from the store (no oiled or treated). Plant them in the ground.
3. Go to your local plant nursery or hardware store and look at the selection of plant seeds available.
4. Plant a young tree in your yard and measure its growth each year.

115

Krab E. Krabby

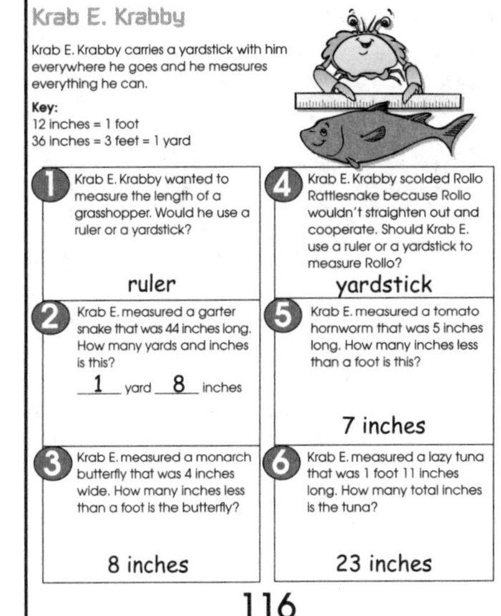

Krab E. Krabby carries a yardstick with him everywhere he goes and he measures everything he can.

Key:
12 inches = 1 foot
36 inches = 3 feet = 1 yard

1. Krab E. Krabby wanted to measure the length of a grasshopper. Would he use a ruler or a yardstick? ruler
2. Krab E. measured a garter snake that was 44 inches long. How many yards and inches is this? 1 yard 8 inches
3. Krab E. measured a monarch butterfly that was 4 inches wide. How many inches less than a foot is the butterfly? 8 inches
4. Krab E. Krabby scolded Rollo Rattlesnake because Rollo wouldn't straighten out and cooperate. Should Krab E. use a ruler or a yardstick to measure Rollo? yardstick
5. Krab E. measured a tomato hornworm that was 5 inches long. How many inches less than a foot is this? 7 inches
6. Krab E. measured a lazy tuna that was 1 foot 11 inches long. How many total inches is the tuna? 23 inches

116

Calculating Lengths

Use your yardstick to **calculate** and **write** the following lengths. Remember to write feet or yards. Some lengths may not be exactly in feet or yards, so be sure to write the inches too. Have a friend or parent help you **measure** these lengths.

Sample answers given. Answers will vary.

1. How long is the biggest step you can take? 1 yd. 2 in.
2. How far can a paper airplane fly? 100 ft.
3. From start to finish, how much distance do you cover when you do a somersault? 5 ft.
4. How far can you throw a feather? 6 in.
5. How wide is your driveway? 6 ft.
6. How far can you walk balancing a book on your head? 7 ft.
7. How high can you stack wooden blocks before they fall? 2 ft.
8. How high can you jump? (Measure from where your finger touches to the floor.) 9 in.
9. How far can you jump? (Begin with your feet together.) 12 in.
10. How much distance is covered if you skip 10 times? 10 ft.
11. What is the distance you can hit a softball with your bat before it hits the ground? 40 ft.
12. What is the distance you can throw a baseball? 30 ft.
13. How far away were you when you caught your friend's throw? 20 ft.
14. How far can you spit a seed? 8 ft.
15. How much distance do you cover when you sprint for 3 seconds? 30 ft.

117

Animal Math

The chart below lists some of the body statistics of 15 endangered animals. Use these measurements to **solve** the problems below the chart.

Animal	Height	Weight	Length
Mountain gorilla	6 feet	450 pounds	
Black rhinoceros	5.5 feet	4,000 pounds	12 feet
Cheetah	2.5 feet	100 pounds	5 feet
Leopard	2 feet	150 pounds	4.5 feet
Spectacled bear	2.5 feet	300 pounds	5 feet
Giant armadillo		100 pounds	4 feet
Vicuna	2.5 feet	100 pounds	
Siberian tiger	38 inches	600 pounds	6 feet
Orangutan	4.5 feet	200 pounds	
Giant panda		300 pounds	6 feet
Polar bear		1,600 pounds	8 feet
Yak	5.5 feet	1,200 pounds	

1. What is the total height of a mountain gorilla, a vicuna and a yak? 14 ft.
2. What is the total weight of a leopard, a cheetah and a polar bear? 1,850 lbs.
3. What is the total weight of a giant panda and a giant armadillo? 400 lbs.
4. Add the lengths of a black rhinoceros, a spectacled bear and a Siberian tiger. 23 ft.
5. Add the heights of two leopards, three yaks and four orangutans. 38.5 ft.
6. Subtract the height of a vicuna from the height of a cheetah. 0
7. Add the weights of all the animals. 9,100 lbs.
8. Write the lengths of the animals from longest to shortest.
12 ft. (black rhino) 8 ft. (polar bear) 6 ft. (panda & tiger)
5 ft. (cheetah & spectacled bear) 4.5 ft. (leopard)
4 ft. (armadillo)

118

Discovering Capacity

Sample answers given.

Capacity measures how much can fit inside an object.

You will need:

- measuring cup (2 cup capacity)
- pie tin
- 1 cup of salt
- bathroom sink
- 1 gallon plastic jug
- 2 liter plastic jug
- tablespoon
- cake pan
- 1 cup of ice
- baking pan
- 1 gallon freezer bag

Complete the tasks below to discover the capacity of objects around your house.

1. How many cups of water are there in a 1-gallon plastic jug? 16 cups
2. How many tablespoons of salt does it take to fill up 1 cup? 16 T
How many tablespoons of water does it take to fill up 1/2 cup? 8 T
3. Plug your bathroom sink. How many cups of water will it hold? 18 cups
How many gallons is that? $1\frac{1}{2}$ gal.
5. How many cups of water does it take to fill a pie tin? 4 cups
6. Does a gallon-size plastic freezer bag really hold a gallon of something?
No Count how many cups of water you can fit inside one. 14 cups
No Is that a gallon?
7. Fill a cake pan with water. Count how many cups it takes. 6 cups
If 2 cups = 1 pint, how many pints does it hold? 3 pints
If 2 pints = 1 quart, what is the quart capacity of your cake pan? $1\frac{1}{2}$ qt.

119

Comparing Temperatures

Sample answers vary.

Temperatures tell how warm or cold something is.

You will need: Fahrenheit thermometer
measuring cup (1 or 2 cup capacity)

Measure and **record** the temperatures of:

70° 1. Water from the tap
40° 2. The dairy section at the grocery store (Call or visit store to ask.)
102° 3. A pet's body temperature (Call or visit veterinarian.)
0° 4. Your freezer (Have your parents help you.)
100° 5. Bathtub water (Fill a cup from the bathtub and place the thermometer in it.)
85° 6. A cup of water outside in the sun
- Place a cup of water in a safe place with the thermometer resting inside.
- Let it set until the temperature stops rising.
- Record the temperature.

Is it the same as the temperature outside? NO

32° 7. A cup of ice water
98.6° 8. Your body temperature

Now, **compare**.

1. How many degrees warmer is the bathtub water than the tap water? 30°
2. How many degrees difference is a pet's body temperature than yours? 2.2° Who is warmer? pet
3. What is the difference between your freezer's temperature and the temperature in the dairy section of your grocery store? 40°
4. What is the difference in temperature between a cup of water that has set out in the sun and a cup of ice water? 22°

120

Today's Temperature

Record the indoor and outdoor temperatures in degrees Celsius and Fahrenheit. Post the daily temperature on poster paper on your refrigerator. If desired, use an almanac or newspaper to share record high and low temperatures for each day.

Indoor temperature
(8 A.M. and 3 P.M.)

Outdoor temperature
(8 A.M. and 3 P.M.)

Extension: Create ongoing line graphs to show temperature differences. Each day, plot the temperatures. Display them near the daily temperature recordings.

Answers will vary.

121

My Schedule

Keep track of what you do all day for a week on several copies of this page. **Write** the day and date at the start of the day. Then, **write** what you do and the time you do it. Each time you change activities, you should **write** a new time entry. At the end of the day, **add** how much time was spent in each type of activity. Some activities can be grouped together (i.e., breakfast, lunch, dinner = eating; social studies, language, math = school subjects; etc.). Tally up your activities on Friday.

Extension: Use the information collected to plot a pie graph, bar graph, line graph or pictograph.

Day and date

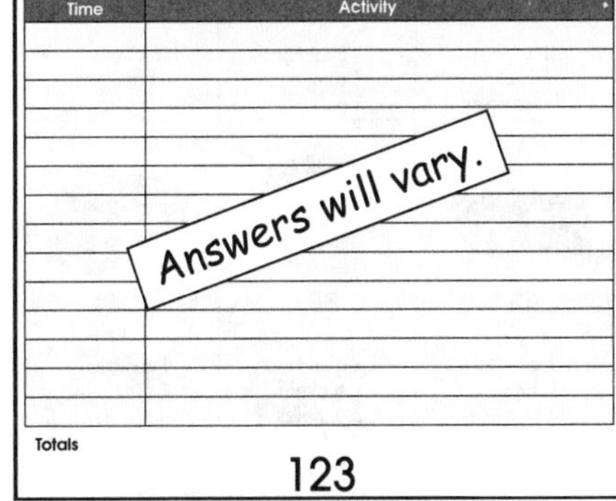

Time	Activity
Totals	

Answers will vary.

123

Time on My Hands

Draw the hour and minute hands to show each time below.

Example:

124

Take Time for These

Write the time shown on these clocks.

Example:

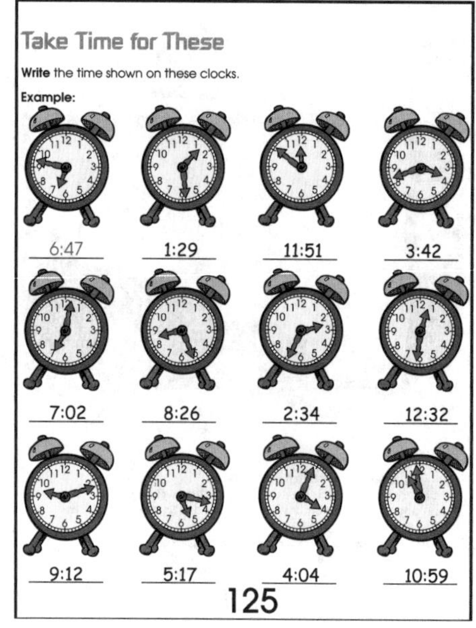

125

Time "Tables"

Draw the hands on these clocks.

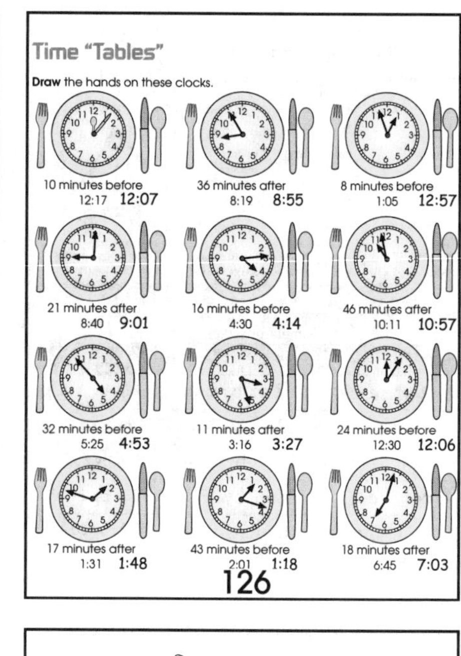

126

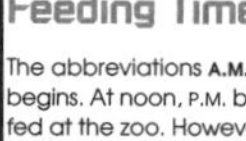

Feeding Time

The abbreviations **A.M.** and **P.M.** help tell the time of day. At midnight, A.M. begins. At noon, P.M. begins. Ken and Angie enjoy watching the animals being fed at the zoo. However, when they arrived, they were a little confused by the signs. Help them figure out the feeding time for each kind of animal. Be sure to include if it's A.M. or P.M.

Zebras: Feeding time is 2 hours after the monkeys. 2:00 P.M.

Tigers: Feeding time is 2 hours after 9:00 A.M. 11:00 A.M.

Elephants: Feeding time is 1:00 P.M.

Giraffes: Feeding time is 1 hour before the lions. 3:00 P.M.

Monkeys: Feeding time is 3 hours before the giraffes. 12:00 P.M.

Lions: Feeding time is 3 hours after the elephants. 4:00 P.M.

Now, **trace** the path in the zoo that Ken and Angie would take so that they could see all the animals being fed.

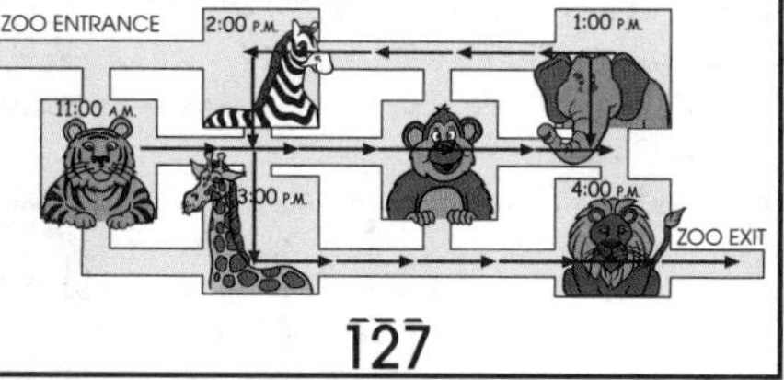

127

How Far Is It?

Drawing pictures can be a good problem-solving strategy. **Draw** pictures to help you **solve** the problems below. Each problem requires three answers.

1. Jimmy has to walk 12 blocks to get to the park where he likes to play ball. It takes him 3 minutes to walk one block. How many minutes will it take him to walk to the park? Sample diagram: J ..3..6..9..12..15..18..21..24..27..30..33..36 P

   Distance 12 blocks Speed 3 min. per block Time 36 min.

2. An airplane leaves the airport at 9:00 A.M. It flies at 200 miles per hour. When it lands at 11:00 A.M., how far will it have gone?

   Distance 400 miles Speed 200 mph. Time 2 hrs.

3. It is 50 miles between Dakota City and Blue Falls. It takes Mr. Oliver 1 hour to make the drive. How fast does he drive?

   Distance 50 miles Speed 50 mph. Time 1 hr.

4. Tad rides his bike to his grandmother's house. It takes him 45 minutes to ride there. She lives 5 miles from his house. How many minutes does it take him to ride 1 mile?

   Distance 1 mile Speed 6.7 mph. Time 9 min.

5. Rachel loves to visit her grandparents who live 150 miles from her house. When they make the trip, her dad drives. He averages 50 miles an hour. How many hours will the trip take?

   Distance 150 miles Speed 50 mph. Time 3 hrs.

128

Racing Chimps

One chimpanzee in the forest always likes to brag that it can get more fruit than any other animal in the forest. So an older and wiser chimpanzee decided to challenge him to a race.

"Let us see who can bring back more bananas in 1 hour," said the older chimp. The race began.

Quickly, the younger chimp picked a bunch of five bananas and carried it back. He continued doing this every 5 minutes.

The older chimp was not quite as fast. Every 10 minutes he carried back eight bananas.

After 45 minutes, the young chimp decided to stop and eat one of his bananas before continuing. By the time he finished, the hour was over and the older chimp called out, "The race is over. Whose pile of bananas is bigger?"

Using the information above, figure out how many bananas were in each pile and which chimp won the race.

The younger chimp had 44 bananas in his pile.

The older chimp had 48 bananas in his pile.

The winner was the older chimp!

129

Garage Sale

Use the fewest number of coins possible to equal the amount shown in each box. **Write** or **draw** the coins you would use in each box.

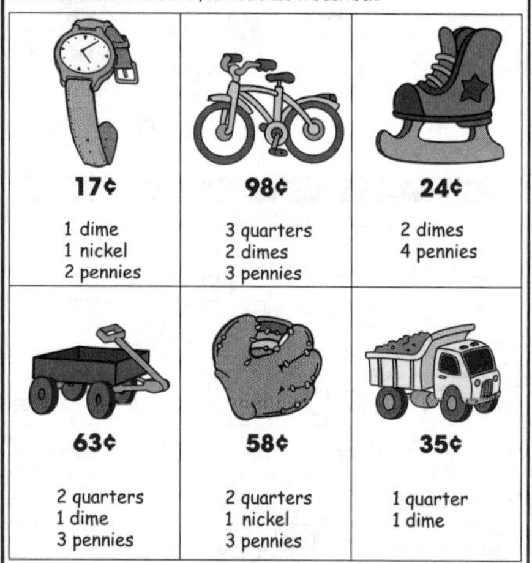

131

Easy Street

What is each house worth? **Count** the money in each house on Easy Street. **Write** the amount on the line below it.

Example:

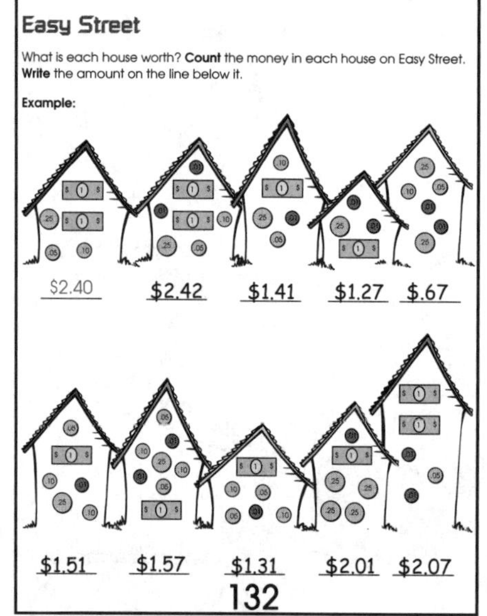

132

Add 'Em Up!

Write the prices, then **add**. **Regroup**, when needed.

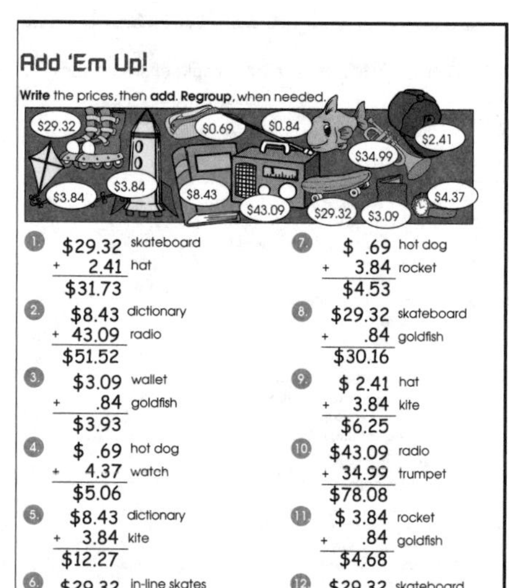

1. $29.32 skateboard + 2.41 hat = $31.73
2. $8.43 dictionary + 43.09 radio = $51.52
3. $3.09 wallet + .84 goldfish = $3.93
4. $ .69 hot dog + 4.37 watch = $5.06
5. $8.43 dictionary + 3.84 kite = $12.27
6. $29.32 in-line skates + 34.99 trumpet = $64.31
7. $ .69 hot dog + 3.84 rocket = $4.53
8. $29.32 skateboard + .84 goldfish = $30.16
9. $ 2.41 hat + 3.84 kite = $6.25
10. $43.09 radio + 34.99 trumpet = $78.08
11. $ 3.84 rocket + .84 goldfish = $4.68
12. $29.32 skateboard + 29.32 in-line skates = $58.64

133

Making Change

When you do not have the exact change to buy something at a store, the clerk must give you change. The first amount of money is what you give the clerk. The second amount is what the item costs. In the box, **list** the fewest number of coins and bills you will receive in change.

	Amount I Have	Cost of Item	Change
1	$3.75	$3.54	2 dimes, 1 penny
2	$10.00	$5.63	four 1 dollar bills, 1 quarter, 1 dime, 2 pennies
3	$7.00	$6.05	3 quarters, 2 dimes
4	$7.25	$6.50	3 quarters
5	$7.50	$6.13	1 dollar bill, 1 quarter, 1 dime, 2 pennies
6	$0.75	$0.37	1 quarter, 1 dime, 2 pennies
7	$7.00	$6.99	1 penny
8	$15.00	$12.75	two 1 dollar bills, 1 quarter

134

Fast Food

Mealwormy is the latest restaurant of that famous fast food creator, Buggs I. Lyke. His Mealwormy Burger costs $1.69. An order of Roasted Roaches cost $0.59 for the regular size and $0.79 for the larger size. A Cricket Cola is $0.89.

1. You buy a Mealwormy Burger and a regular order of Roasted Roaches. What is the total? $1.69 + .59 = $2.28
2. Your teacher buys a Cricket Cola and a regular order of Roasted Roaches. What does it cost her? $ .89 + .59 = $1.48
3. Your mom goes to Mealwormy to buy your dinner. She spends $3.37. How much change does she get from a $5.00 bill? $5.00 - 3.37 = $1.63
4. Your best friend orders a Mealwormy Burger, a large order of Roasted Roaches and Cricket Cola. How much will it cost? $1.69 + .79 + .89 = $3.37
5. The principal is very hungry, so his bill comes to $14.37. How much change will he get from $20.00? $20.00 - 14.37 = $ 5.63
6. You have $1.17 in your bank. How much more do you need to pay for a Mealwormy Burger? $1.69 - 1.17 = $ .52

135

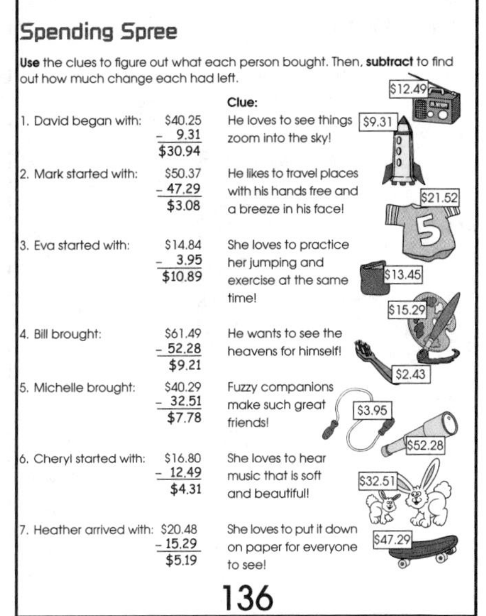

Spending Spree

Use the clues to figure out what each person bought. Then, **subtract** to find out how much change each had left.

		Clue:
1. David began with:	$40.25 - 9.31 = $30.94	He loves to see things zoom into the sky!
2. Mark started with:	$50.37 - 47.29 = $3.08	He likes to travel places with his hands free and a breeze in his face!
3. Eva started with:	$14.84 - 3.95 = $10.89	She loves to practice her jumping and exercise at the same time!
4. Bill brought:	$61.49 - 52.28 = $9.21	He wants to see the heavens for himself!
5. Michelle brought:	$40.29 - 32.51 = $7.78	Fuzzy companions make such great friends!
6. Cheryl started with:	$16.80 - 12.49 = $4.31	She loves to hear music that is soft and beautiful!
7. Heather arrived with:	$20.48 - 15.29 = $5.19	She loves to put it down on paper for everyone to see!

136

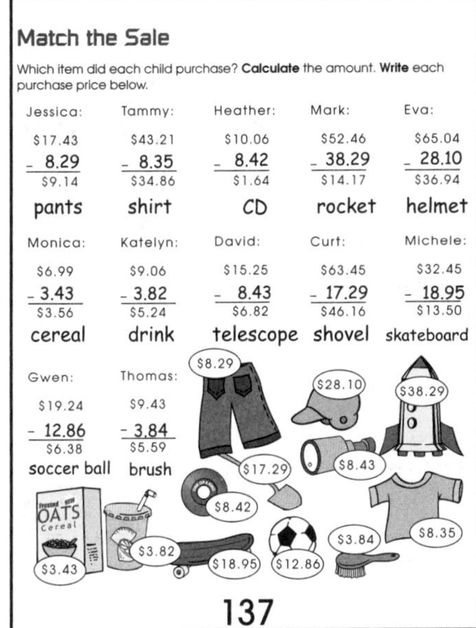

Match the Sale

Which item did each child purchase? **Calculate** the amount. **Write** each purchase price below.

Jessica:	Tammy:	Heather:	Mark:	Eva:
$17.43 - 8.29 = $9.14	$43.21 - 8.35 = $34.86	$10.06 - 8.42 = $1.64	$52.46 - 38.29 = $14.17	$65.04 - 28.10 = $36.94
pants	shirt	CD	rocket	helmet

Monica:	Katelyn:	David:	Curt:	Michele:
$6.99 - 3.43 = $3.56	$9.06 - 3.82 = $5.24	$15.25 - 8.43 = $6.82	$63.45 - 17.29 = $46.16	$32.45 - 18.95 = $13.50
cereal	drink	telescope	shovel	skateboard

Gwen:	Thomas:
$19.24 - 12.86 = $6.38	$9.43 - 3.84 = $5.59
soccer ball	brush

137

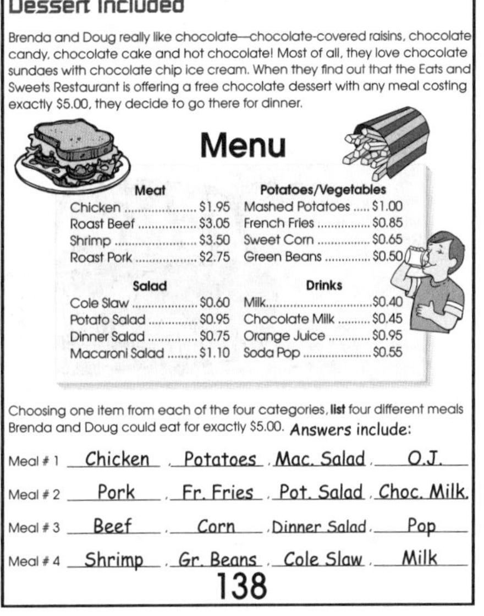

Dessert Included

Brenda and Doug really like chocolate—chocolate-covered raisins, chocolate candy, chocolate cake and hot chocolate! Most of all, they love chocolate sundaes with chocolate chip ice cream. When they find out that the Eats and Sweets Restaurant is offering a free chocolate dessert with any meal costing exactly $5.00, they decide to go there for dinner.

Menu

Meat		Potatoes/Vegetables	
Chicken	$1.95	Mashed Potatoes	$1.00
Roast Beef	$3.05	French Fries	$0.85
Shrimp	$3.50	Sweet Corn	$0.65
Roast Pork	$2.75	Green Beans	$0.50
Salad		**Drinks**	
Cole Slaw	$0.60	Milk	$0.40
Potato Salad	$0.95	Chocolate Milk	$0.45
Dinner Salad	$0.75	Orange Juice	$0.95
Macaroni Salad	$1.10	Soda Pop	$0.55

Choosing one item from each of the four categories, **list** four different meals Brenda and Doug could eat for exactly $5.00. Answers include:

Meal # 1 Chicken, Potatoes, Mac. Salad, O.J.

Meal # 2 Pork, Fr. Fries, Pot. Salad, Choc. Milk

Meal # 3 Beef, Corn, Dinner Salad, Pop

Meal # 4 Shrimp, Gr. Beans, Cole Slaw, Milk

138

Multiplying Money

Money is multiplied in the same way other numbers are. The only difference is a dollar sign and a decimal point are added to the final product.

Steps:

1. Multiply by ones.
   1. 4 x 8 = 32 (Carry the 3.)
   2. 4 x 2 = 8 + 3 = 11 (Carry the 1.)
   3. 4 x 4 = 16 + 1 = 17

$$\begin{array}{r} \scriptstyle 1\,3 \\ \$4.28 \\ \times\ 34 \\ \hline 1712 \end{array}$$

2. 1. Cross out the carried digits.
   2. Add the zero.

$$\begin{array}{r} \times\times \\ \$4.28 \\ \times\ 34 \\ \hline 1712 \\ 0 \end{array}$$

3. Multiply by tens.
   1. 3 x 8 = 24 (Carry the 2.)
   2. 3 x 2 = 6 + 2 = 8
   3. 3 x 4 = 12

$$\begin{array}{r} \scriptstyle 2 \\ \$4.28 \\ \times\ 34 \\ \hline 1712 \\ 12840 \end{array}$$

4. Add.
   1,712 + 12,840 = 14,552

$$\begin{array}{r} \$4.28 \\ \times\ 34 \\ \hline 1712 \\ +12840 \\ \hline 14,552 \end{array}$$

5. Add the dollar sign and the decimal point.

$$\begin{array}{r} \$4.28 \\ \times\ 34 \\ \hline 1712 \\ +12840 \\ \hline \$145.52 \end{array}$$

Multiply.

$$\begin{array}{r} \$3.42 \\ \times\ 25 \\ \hline \$85.50 \end{array} \qquad \begin{array}{r} \$5.42 \\ \times\ 61 \\ \hline \$330.62 \end{array}$$

$$\begin{array}{r} \$3.81 \\ \times\ 46 \\ \hline \$175.26 \end{array} \qquad \begin{array}{r} \$8.20 \\ \times\ 55 \\ \hline \$451.00 \end{array}$$

$$\begin{array}{r} \$9.42 \\ \times\ 31 \\ \hline \$292.02 \end{array} \qquad \begin{array}{r} \$4.23 \\ \times\ 96 \\ \hline \$406.08 \end{array}$$

139

Science Trip

The science class is planning a field trip to Chicago to visit the Museum of Science and Industry. There are 18 students in the class and each student needs $40.00 to cover the expenses. The class decided to sell candy to raise money.

Answer the questions using the chart below.

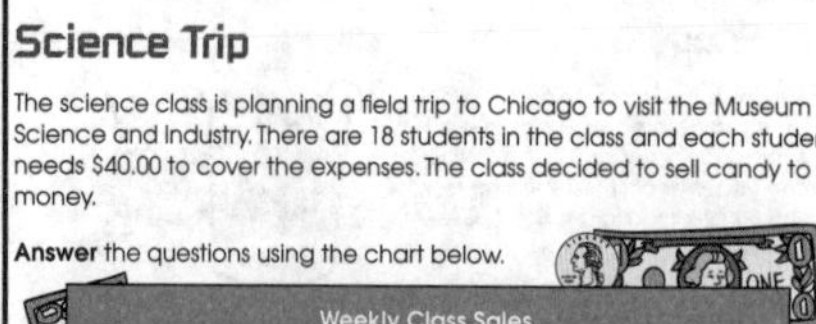

Weekly Class Sales

	Week One	Week Two	Week Three	Week Four
Amount Raised	$282.00	$176.00	$202.00	$150.00

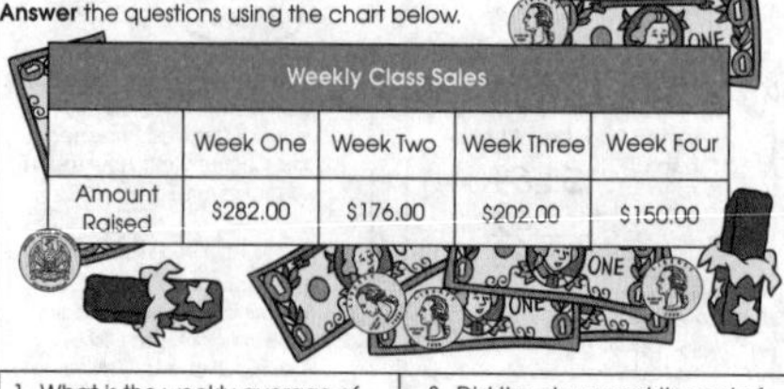

1. What is the weekly average of money raised during 4 weeks of candy sales? **$202.50**
2. What is the average amount of dollars raised per child during 4 weeks of candy sales? **$45.00**
3. Did the class meet its goal of $40.00 per child? **Yes**
4. How much above or beneath their goal per child did the class earn? **$5.00**

140

Perplexing Problems

Solve these problems.

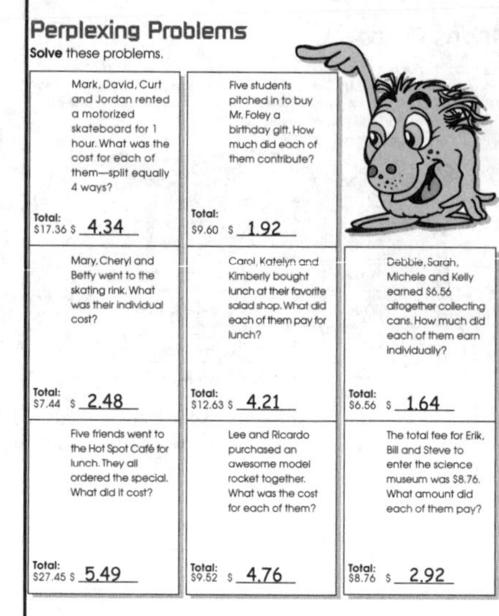

Mark, David, Curt and Jordan rented a motorized skateboard for 1 hour. What was the cost for each of them—split equally 4 ways?
Total: $17.36 $ 4.34

Five students pitched in to buy Mr. Foley a birthday gift. How much did each of them contribute?
Total: $9.60 $ 1.92

Mary, Cheryl and Betty went to the skating rink. What was their individual cost?
Total: $7.44 $ 2.48

Carol, Katelyn and Kimberly bought lunch at their favorite salad shop. What did each of them pay for lunch?
Total: $12.63 $ 4.21

Debbie, Sarah, Michele and Kelly earned $6.56 altogether collecting cans. How much did each of them earn individually?
Total: $6.56 $ 1.64

Five friends went to the Hot Spot Café for lunch. They all ordered the special. What did it cost?
Total: $27.45 $ 5.49

Lee and Ricardo purchased an awesome model rocket together. What was the cost for each of them?
Total: $9.52 $ 4.76

The total fee for Erik, Bill and Steve to enter the science museum was $8.76. What amount did each of them pay?
Total: $8.76 $ 2.92

141

Let's Take a Trip!

You will plan a car trip to calculate approximately how much the trip will cost. You will calculate distances between locations and the amount of gasoline needed based upon miles per gallon of the car. Then, you will estimate the cost of the gasoline, hotel, food and entertainment.

Directions: Using graph paper, plot out your trip starting and ending at "point A." The trip should have five points of travel, including point A. Each square on the graph paper represents 10 miles. Calculate the mileage between points.

Use a copy of the **Expense Chart** on page 143 to keep track of your calculations. Use newspapers, travel brochures and menus to help you estimate the cost of food, gas, hotels, entertainment, etc. You will also want to use a calculator. When you have completed the **Expense Chart**, answer the questions below.

Sample answers given.

1. If two people go on this trip, how will the cost change? it will increase
2. If a family of four goes on the trip, how will the cost change? up to 4 x amoun
3. Would the cost of gas change? No
   Why or why not? going in one car, same distance
4. What else could change the cost of the trip? car repairs
5. Why is this just an estimate? must take actual trip to find exact cost

142

Expense Chart Sample answers given.

Distance to travel
Miles from Point A to Point B: 100
Miles from Point B to Point C: 65
Miles from Point C to Point D: 50
Miles from Point D to Point E: 75
Miles from Point E to Point A: 190
Total miles to travel: 480

Your car gets 22 miles per gallon of gas.
Total gas needed: 22 gal.
Gas costs $1.19 per gallon.
Total amount needed for gas: $26.18

You will stay at a hotel/motel for four nights at $79.00 per night.
Total cost for four nights: $316

Estimated food cost per day (5 days)
breakfast—$2.50
lunch—$4.75
dinner—$9.25
Total per day: $16.50
Total for 5 days: $82.50

Estimated entertainment expenses
Admission to movies: $25
Admission to museums: $40
Admission to theme parks: $100
Admission to sports events: $125

Add all the entries to get a total estimate for the cost of the trip.
Total estimated cost of the trip: $714.68

143